# Dostoevsky's Hamlet in Nineteenth-Century Russia

## GLOBAL SHAKESPEARE INVERTED

Global Shakespeare Inverted challenges any tendency to view Global Shakespeare from the perspective of 'centre' versus 'periphery'. Although the series may locate its critical starting point geographically, it calls into question the geographical bias that lurks within the very notion of the 'global'. It provides a timely, constructive criticism of the present state of the field and establishes new and alternative methodologies that invert the relation of Shakespeare to the supposed 'other'.

**Recent titles**

*Global King Lear: Crisis, Performance, Adaption*
Edited by William R. Rampone, Jr. and Eric S. Mallin

*Recontextualizing Indian Shakespeare Cinema in the West: Familiar Strangers*
Edited by Varsha Panjwani and Koel Chatterjee

*Shakespeare's Others in 21st-century European Performance:* The Merchant of Venice *and* Othello
Edited by Boika Sokolova and Janice Valls-Russell

# Dostoevsky's Hamlet in Nineteenth-Century Russia

## The Paradox of Subjectivity

By Petra Bjelica

THE ARDEN SHAKESPEARE
LONDON • NEW YORK • OXFORD • NEW DELHI • SYDNEY

THE ARDEN SHAKESPEARE
Bloomsbury Publishing Plc
50 Bedford Square, London, WC1B 3DP, UK
1385 Broadway, New York, NY 10018, USA
29 Earlsfort Terrace, Dublin 2, Ireland

BLOOMSBURY, THE ARDEN SHAKESPEARE and the Arden Shakespeare logo
are trademarks of Bloomsbury Publishing Plc

First published in Great Britain 2025

Cover design by Maria Rajka
Cover image: An Englishman in Moscow, 1913-1914, Kazimir Malevich (1879-
1935). Universal History Archive/Universal Images Group via Getty Images

A catalogue record for this book is available from the British Library.

A catalog record for this book is available from the Library of Congress.

ISBN: HB: 9781-3504-5092-9
ePDF: 9781-3504-5094-3
eBook: 9781-3504-5093-6

Series: Global Shakespeare Inverted

Typeset by Deanta Global Publishing Services, Chennai, India

To find out more about our authors and books visit www.bloomsbury.com and
sign up for our newsletters.

*The book is dedicated to the loving memory of my grandmother,*
*Radojka Crnčević Bjelica, her love for beauty and craft of storytelling.*

# Contents

# Acknowledgements

This work would not have been possible without the support of many individuals, institutions and research centres.[1] However, my book would not exist in its current form, or any other, without the encouragement and unwavering support of Silvia Bigliazzi, for which I am beyond grateful. I am indebted for the careful, patient readings and valuable feedback from her, Emanuel Stelzer and Cristiano Ragni, to whom I extend my deep and warm appreciation. To this list of acknowledgements, I add my professors from Belgrade, Zorica Bečanović-Nikolić and Dragan Stojanović, alongside Stefano Aloe, Ewan Fernie and other mentors and colleagues, whose dedication, expertise, and talent have been a continuous source of inspiration. I am indebted to Anđelina Mićić for her help with Russian translations and the Arden Team for their patience and support.

My most intimate and strongest gratitude goes to my family, my partner and close friends for being my roots and my strength, embracing me with continued generosity, patience and encouragement.

Lastly, I wish to close the network of credits with a nod to the poem 'If I must die' by Refaat Alareer, a Palestinian author, professor of English Literature and fellow Shakespearian from the Islamic University of Gaza. His final verses, 'If I must die / Let it bring hope / Let it be a tale', uncannily echo Hamlet's and Dostoevsky's 'Let be' projects explored in this book as a struggle to *let beings be as the beings that they are*.

In the belief that authorship is co-authorship in a different guise, I claim all mistakes as entirely my own.

# Note

1   The University of Verona and the INVITE project provided the
    opportunity to conduct my doctoral research, titled 'Let the other be:
    Hamlet-ideologemes in Dostoevsky's *Demons*', for which I received
    funding from the European Union's Horizon 2020 research and innovation
    programme under the Marie Skłodovska-Curie grant agreement No
    754345, under region of Veneto Decree nr. 193 of 13/09/2016 and under
    Università degli Studi di Verona.

# Prologue

*Hamlet! Hamlet! When I think of his moving wild speech, in which resounds the groaning of the whole numbed universe, there breaks from my soul not one reproach, not one sigh.*

(Dostoevsky, 1914: 4)

*I do not know whether Karamazov thought at that moment of 'what lies beyond' or whether a Karamazov could think, in Hamlet fashion, of what lies beyond. No, gentlemen of the jury, they have their Hamlets, but so far we have only Karamazovs!*

(Dostoevsky, *The Brothers Karamazov*, 1992: 716)

One of the greatest Shakespearean themes is the difficulty of distinguishing the difference between fiction and reality – the enigmatic quality of experience itself. *Hamlet* stands at the forefront of the uncanny encounter with otherness in literature that allows one to assume that 'I am not what I am' (*Othello*, 1.1.65): that self might be just a dream, a fantasy, or a delusion. Fyodor Dostoevsky's work stems from the same fascination with the similarity between fiction and reality, profoundly exploring the illusory aspects of subjectivity. Despite, or exactly because of this, Dostoevsky's novels can be explained as an attempt 'to tell the story of a failure to tell a coherent story, a failure that is itself the best index to a world beyond the reach of ordered vision' (Morson, 1994: 9). His chaotic narration is a way to articulate the chaos of reality. The narrator of such a story is 'a man whose disfigured personality reflects the disintegration of Russian society; who writes in order to make sense of his life by arriving, in the process of composition, at a coherent account of it' (1994), nevertheless, without success. How can such a narrative express the entirety of a subject (a genuine auto/biography) or a national identity (an accurate chronicle of their time)?

In nineteenth-century Russia, 'the novel, Russia and Dostoevsky may each be seen as characterised by particularly urgent problems of self-identification, may be said to have a biography' (Holquist, 1977: ix).[1] Interestingly, one of the main components in all three processes of creating these identities was Shakespeare's *Hamlet*, which served as a model for articulating and representing subjectivity and commenting on an oppressive national situation. Due to severe censorship of overt criticism of the ruling regime, the generation of Russian intelligentsia that had been brought up on Shakespeare utilized the figure of Hamlet as a model for identification in two ways. First, they individually identified with the hero that is incapable of action, while, second, compared the rotten state of Denmark to Russian political and social circumstances. How did Shakespeare's most contradictory, protean, ambiguous and melancholic hero, the bearer of doubt, the epitome of tarrying and deferral, become a tool for political and national identification? Or, more precisely, how and why did the tragedy of the Danish Prince serve to constitute Russian Hamletism as the existential model for a person who tries to make sense of the world and himself, as well as the symbol for a collective national identity amidst political and social turmoil in nineteenth-century Russia? Lastly, how did Dostoevsky's understanding of *Hamlet* and Russian Hamletism form his views on subjectivity, nineteenth-century novel and Russian identity?

According to Yury D. Levin, Dostoevsky treated Hamlet as a personification of 'three possible attitudes to the chaos of life [the other two Shakespearean figures he considered were Othello and Falstaff]. Hamlet, in Dostoevsky's eyes, was a tormented, embittered soul, full of rancor both against himself and against the world, full of black despair; a mind that questioned all values; a heart conscious of its total solitude' (1998: 91). This reading is certainly plausible. However, the foundation of this book stems from a sense that the issue warrants comprehensive exploration that will map possible answers to above raised questions, which is why I propose starting from the beginning.

In a letter to his brother Mikhail dated 9 August 1838, the sixteen-year-old Dostoevsky identifies himself with Hamlet's melancholy, idleness and despair, making his first recorded reference to Shakespeare's play. Inspired by *Hamlet* and the discursive prevalence of Russian Hamletism, he foreshadowed the themes that would feature in his oeuvre up to *The Brothers Karamazov* (1880) as 'a persistent Hamletian subtext' (Stepanian, 2014: 53) and a recurring obsession with the Hamletian question 'to be or not to be' (*Hamlet*, 3.1.55):

It is true that I am idle – very idle. But what will become of me, if everlasting idleness is to be my only attitude towards life? I don't know if my gloomy mood will ever leave me. And to think that such a state of mind is allotted to man alone – the atmosphere of his soul seems *compounded of a mixture of the heavenly and the earthly.* What an *unnatural product,* then, is he, since *the law of spiritual nature is in him violated. . . . This earth seems to me a purgatory* for divine spirits who have been assailed by sinful thoughts. I feel that our *world has become one immense Negative,* and that everything noble, beautiful, and divine, has turned itself into a *satire.* If in this picture there occurs an individual who neither in idea nor effect harmonizes with the whole, who is, in a word, an entirely unrelated figure – what must happen to the *picture*? It is destroyed, and can no longer endure. Yet how terrible it is to perceive only the coarse in veil under which the All doth languish! To know that one single effort of the will would suffice to demolish that veil and become one with eternity – to know all this, and still live on like the last and least of creatures. How terrible! How petty is man! *Hamlet! Hamlet!* When I think of his moving wild speech, in which resounds the *groaning of the whole numbed universe,* there breaks from my soul not one reproach, not one sigh. [. . .] That soul is then so utterly oppressed by woe that it fears to grasp the woe entire, lest so it lacerate itself. Pascal once said: *He who protests against philosophy is himself a philosopher. A poor sort of system!* [. . .] *I have a new plan: to go mad. That's the way: for people to lose their heads, and then be cured and brought back to reason!* [. . .] It is terrible to watch a man who has the Incomprehensible within his grasp, does not know what to do with it, and sits playing with a toy called God! (Dostoevsky, 1914: 3–5, my emphasis)

The letter emanates a melancholic Hamletian style and tone, as young Dostoevsky reflects on the spiritual decay of humanity wrought by sin, likening mankind to King Hamlet's ghost trapped in purgatory, implying a sense of hopelessness and paralysis. He laments the pervasive negativity and disharmony of the world while addressing an existential paradox: an awareness of life's futility and his reluctance to give up on it. Despite a profound despair, he expresses contempt for people who continue living in baseness and triviality. Even his own philosophical protest, incited by this despair, is paradoxically rooted in philosophical ruminations. The evocation of Hamlet and his moving wild speech stands at the centre of the letter, echoing the groaning *of the whole numbed universe*. However, Dostoevsky's focus is on the fact that *even* Hamlet's poignant speech cannot motivate one to act beyond despair. On the contrary, his potential interlocutor is in a state of stasis and silence. The letter itself can be read as Dostoevsky's Hamletian pose, impersonating a Russian Hamlet, in order to justify and understand his own *gloomy mood* and make sense of his existential crisis while appropriating the Hamlet-model as a means of self-fashioning. According to Rowe, in Dostoevsky's later work, the Hamletian question is transformed into what comes after death, 'the immortality of the soul and the existence of God' (1976: 90). However, it is already the central theme behind the letter; the question of all questions for Dostoevsky and the main Hamletian question that will be reformulated and readdressed throughout his work is whether God and immortality exist.

The postscriptum is significantly enigmatic and elusive: 'I have a new plan: to go mad. That's the way: for people to lose their heads, and then be cured and brought back to reason!' (U menya est' prozhekt: sdelat'sya sumasshedshim. Pust' lyudi besyatsya, pust' lechat, pust' delayut umnym.).[2] It might be viewed as a strategic means of donning an *antic disposition* (*Hamlet*, 1.5.170) in order to 'set it right' (2.1.187). The first question to arise is about the nature of this madness. What does it mean for people to lose their heads and how would they be brought back to reason? In this hermetic declaration we can distinguish raving madness as opposite to reason and health. Does Dostoevsky have in mind madness as a disease, a moral and spiritual crisis, a disintegration of the subject, or does he understand this state as a particular folly in the tradition of *iurodivost*? *Iurodivost* is a type of holy foolishness specific to Russian Orthodox tradition that implies a willingly performed madness in the form of mimicking Christ and exposing oneself to the scorn of others while the *iurodivi* 'is seen as a guardian of truth and morality' (Hudspith, 2004: 202) whose practice of provocation 'serves to publicly unmask the sinfulness and hypocrisy of their contemporaries in the hopes that they will repent and change their lives' (Grillaert, 2016: 191).

Intriguingly, the same year Dostoevsky will formulate another crucial revelation for his artistic career. He had confessed to his brother the wish to devote his life to 'studying the meaning of man and of life. [. . .] Man is a mystery. One must solve it' (Dostoevsky, cited in Mochulsky, 1973: 17). These prophetic and intuitive anticipations were his lifelong guiding principles which he brought to life in his later work. They are best set out in his 1880 final notebook as the following endeavour: 'with full realism to find the man in man. [. . .] They call me a psychologist: this is not true, I am only a realist in a higher sense. That is, I depict all the depths of the human soul' (PSS, 17:29). These famous and ambiguous lines summarize two central aspects of Dostoevsky's art: first, his *Christian realism* in which *God is alive, the presence of Christ is visible, and the revelation of the Word is manifested* (Zakharov, 2006 cited in Bowers, Doak and Holland, 2018: 137); second, the 'idea that beauty constitutes a riddle' (98). Dostoevsky embarked on an endeavour to craft a narrative that encapsulates the entirety of oneself, of its relationship with others, and of his nation – an accurate chronicle of his time. His strategy in dealing with such ungraspable themes is paradox – 'the quintessence of "Dostoevskyism"' (Morson, 1999: 472). Therefore, it is not surprising that for this project, he found the perfect model in the character of Hamlet – one of the greatest paradoxical subjectivities in the history of literature.

# Notes

1   'At the center of each such biography stands the question "who am I?" Each in its own way strives to answer the question of what it is by finding a story that will somehow explain how it came to be. Thus, while the task is necessarily different in its implications for each, the novel as a genre, Russian historiography, and the man Dostoevsky all appeal to narrative as the royal road to knowledge of what they are' (Holquist, 1977: ix).

2   This is a translation by Ethel Colburn Mayne. Another possible translation that is also sustained by the original is the following: 'I have a project: to go mad. Let people rage, try to cure me, let them try to bring me to reason' (translated by Michael A. Minihan, cited in Mochulsky, 1973: 17). I will analyse the differences of these translations and their consequences for my discussion in the following chapters.

# Introduction

*All the rest moves around him, like a kaleidoscope.*

(Dostoevsky, *The Notebooks for The Possessed*, 1968: 182)

## Dostoevsky and *Hamlet*

Fyodor Dostoevsky (1828–1880), one of the most provocative and influential novelists of world literature, was already during his lifetime compared to Shakespeare both in form of positive veneration and mocking. His complex and often disturbing work still incites deep and ambivalent effects. Given the undisputable charisma around his figure and his writings, alongside the huge popularity of *Hamlet* and Russian Hamletism in Russia, the lack of an established view on Dostoevsky's reading of Shakespeare's *Hamlet* seems surprising. Why has a precise and simple answer to who Dostoevsky's Hamlet is, among numerous Russian Hamlets, been evading articulation? This book will try to untangle some complicated issues pertinent to this question. A closer examination of one hero and one novel that are particularly embedded and ingrained in themes of Russian Hamletism will guide us to answer that question. My starting hypothesis is that Dostoevsky's most original contribution to Russian Hamletism lies in the creation of Stavrogin, the main hero of *Demons*[1] (1871–2), whom I view as the most radical Russian Hamlet of the nineteenth century. Scholarship has traditionally acknowledged Hal from *Henry IV* and Hamlet as some of many prototypes for Stavrogin, based on textual evidence within the novel (Rybchenko, 2006) and its preparatory materials. Literature dedicated exclusively to parallels between Stavrogin and Hamlet is scarce, while a comprehensive study devoted to a comparative analysis of the two characters doesn't exist. Instead, scattered comments and reflections can be found (Rovda, 1965; Rowe, 1976: 198; Levin, 1988, 1998; Jones, 1983: 272; Dryzhakova, 1979; Belknap, 1984: 69; Catteau, 2009: 298). While their assertions hold merit, they scratch the surface of both text (the novel) and subtext (the preparatory materials), especially overlooking the nuances of Dostoevsky's engagement with *Hamlet* and Russian Hamletism.

More precisely, that Stavrogin may be viewed as a Hamletian character can be found in the preparatory materials for *Demons*. Dostoevsky describes Stavrogin as 'a gloomy, passionate, demonic, and disorderly character, without any sense of measure, with a lofty question, all the way to "*to be or not to be*"? To live or to exterminate oneself?' (*Notebooks*, 1968: 266, my emphasis). He puts his hero in the context of Russian Hamletism by directly attributing to Stavrogin the most famous Hamletian dilemma. By analysing Stavrogin and *Demons* from this perspective, the book both comes closer to identifying how Dostoevsky viewed *Hamlet* and adds an outline of yet another, possibly original stance in the rich tradition of Hamlet-criticism. These are the two reasons why *Demons* takes centre stage in this book, alongside other relevant works.

*Demons*, Dostoyevsky's 'most openly Shakespeare-oriented novel' (Kovalevskaya, 2014: 74), is considered one of his most complicated and darkest novels. Essentially, it is an allegory of the state of Russia depicted through a story about roaring madness that had consumed the whole society, driving to crime or death almost all of the characters and bringing destruction on every scale. The novel interweaves two plots. The first one concerns the philosophical, spiritual and existential crisis of the main protagonist, Nikolay Vsevolodovich Stavrogin, a mysterious, charismatic and seductive young man, who returns to his hometown Skvoreshniki, somewhere in Russia. In his younger years, Stavrogin had embraced and cast off a string of ideologies and philosophies, each of which had been adopted by different characters enchanted by his personality. However, while his quest for meaning remained futile, his acquaintance Ivan Pavlovich Shatov, inspired by some of his ideas, has become a Slavophile who believes in the 'God-bearing' Russian people. On the other hand, Alexey Nilych Kirillov develops instead into a philosophical nihilist and atheist while adopting a series of contradictory justifications for suicide that will finally prove man's freedom in being the master of his own destiny, a 'man-god'. Stavrogin's spiritual crisis and quest for an idea under which he could live by is a pretext for the second, political plot of the novel that has earned Dostoyevsky the reputation of a political prophet, foretelling the fate of Russia in the decades to come. The plot revolves around a cell of revolutionary conspirators led by Peter Stepanovich Verkhovensky, who desperately and unsuccessfully tries to turn Stavrogin into their leader. And while the world of the novel descends into an apocalyptic chaos, questions that haunt the narrative are how one is 'to be' in such a world and what are the reasons against choosing 'not to be'.

This crucial philosophical dilemma is the common denominator between *Demons* and *Hamlet* that motivates my analysis, which I set against the backdrop of Dostoevsky's contemplation of Hamletism in general. The book pivots around three main issues. First, it sheds a new light on Dostoevsky's view of nineteenth-century Russian Hamletism, analysing its philosophical, ideological and political assumptions, while introducing new critical terminology that springs out of Dostoevsky's own poetics, orienting the analysis towards an examination of the way in which *Hamlet* functions as Dostoevsky's source. Second, the book provides a critical discussion of Dostoevsky's original dialogue with *Hamlet* by exploring his revision of current receptions into new Hamletian characters and revealing what I will call the Hamlet-ideologeme, a core Hamletian idea behind his work, in order to answer the question 'who Dostoevsky's Hamlet is'. Third, and finally, the book elucidates Dostoevsky's fictionalization of Hamlet's 'to be or not to be' dilemma as a highly original yet overlooked nineteenth-century resolution of that quandary, taking the form of a religious 'let be'.

These aspects collectively demonstrate Dostoevsky's provocative, intense, and paradoxical enquiry into Hamletian themes challenging and inverting predominantly positive biases about Dostoevsky's reception of Shakespeare. His translation of some aspects of Shakespeare's work into a religious dimension of Christian Byzantine Orthodoxy may constitute a significant contribution to Global Shakespeare. He approached the adaptation of Shakespeare's texts and figures with a distinctly original perspective, addressing fundamental poetic, religious, ethical and spiritual concerns in the broader context of the European cultural and intellectual history of the period. This book delves into the complexities surrounding the issue of how he performs a decolonizing practice against the hegemony of Western individualism and rationalism in his critique of Russian Hamletism. Indirectly, he challenged the prevailing concept of Shakespeare's cultural hegemony, destabilizing established notions of Eurocentric and Anglocentric viewpoints. Thus, revising Dostoevsky's works provides an opportunity to reconsider the significance of Hamletism within global cultural discourses, while dealing with Shakespeare through Dostoevsky unveils vibrant implications across political, ethical and spiritual domains. Given Dostoevsky's profound and intense engagement with *Hamlet* and Russian Hamletism, this book attempts to rediscover the nuances of a dialogue that shaped one of the most vital literary experiences in the novelist's life. By doing so, it also offers a gateway to examining Dostoevsky's novels through an innovative Hamletian lens, bringing us closer to construe what or who Hamlet was for him. Dostoevsky's oeuvre is yet another substantial evidence of the potential of Shakespeare's *Hamlet* to generate ever new narratives and fictional worlds.

Dostoevsky's engagement with *Hamlet* frames his life (Givens, 2016: 767). As the already-mentioned 1838 letter shows, the play immediately left a strong impact on him creating impressions that were typically Romantic and youthful exaltations in line with Coleridge's and Goethe's views on Hamlet as an idealistic and sensitive soul that is unfit and powerless to respond to worldly injustices. The letter builds on Nikolay Polevoy's adaptation that was published in 1837 (as we shall see later). As a mature writer, he had a much more critical, cynical and comical understanding of Hamlet-related issues, generally influenced by the shift from Romanticism to Realism in Russian literature and opinions of Russian critics who saw Hamlet as an egoistic figure entrapped in his thoughts and empty words. Dostoevsky's thinking about *Hamlet* and Russian Hamletism branched out of these sources into a myriad of directions, becoming increasingly profound and intricate which is supported by various references found in his works, personal letters, novels and articles. In his novels, *The Village of Stepanchikovo and Its Inhabitants* (1859), *The Humiliated and Insulted* (1861), *Notes from Underground* (1864), *Crime and Punishment* (1866), *The Idiot* (1868–9), *Demons* (1871–2), *An Accidental Family* (1875) and *The Brothers Karamazov* (1879–80), the presence of *Hamlet* is manifold. Dostoevsky incorporated diverse and contradictory aspects of Russian Hamletism, narrating about the Hamletian dilemma rather than simply referring to Shakespeare's play and interpolating Hamletian allusions mostly when writing about despair, madness, scepticism, the paradoxicality of reason, suicide and the existence of an afterlife, sometimes even in a tragicomic style. Lastly, there is a crucial resonance between the figure of Hamlet and certain characters in his work. He utilized Hamlet's qualities to create some of his most charismatic and enigmatic figures, such as Stavrogin or Ivan Karamazov, but there are others that might be labelled Hamletian: Mr. Golyadkin, the man from the underground, Raskolnikov, Ippolit, Nastasya Filippovna, Kirillov, Versilov, Arkady Dolgoruky, Dmitry Karamazov and even a totalitarian ideologue as Shigalyov. And while critics connected most of these characters with Hamlet before (Levin, 1974, 1975, 1988, 1995, 1998; Rowe, 1976; Dryzhakova, 1979; Stepanian, 2014; Zakharov, 2015), I offer a fresh view on them while analysing Nastasya Filippovna as a Hamletian figure for the first time.

## Shakespeare and Dostoevsky

Shakespeare's impact on Dostoevsky has been extensively documented and reflected upon (Alekseev, 1965; Cox, 1969; Rowe, 1976; Levin,

1975, 1988, 1995, 1998; Catteau, 1989; Lantz, 2004: 392–5; Givens, 2014, 2016; Zakharov, 2015; Stepanian, 2016). However, as Nikolay Zakharov notably observed in 2006, there was no monograph or doctoral dissertation exclusively dedicated to studying the relationship between Shakespeare and Dostoevsky (Zaharov, 2006).[2] Yuri D. Levin's contribution remains the most detailed and comprehensive study of Shakespeare's impact on Dostoevsky, encompassing numerous references and echoes, alongside a detailed account of Dostoevsky's reading and interpretation of Shakespeare. Levin is a prominent authority and the most relevant source of information, laying the ground for further exploration in this respect. Karen Stepanian is another relevant source, especially with his book *Shakespeare, Bakhtin, and Dostoevsky: Heroes and Authors in 'Great Time'* (2016) (Shekspir, Bakhtin i Dostoevskij: geroi i avtory v bol'shom vremeni) that stands out as a significant contribution in this regard. Stepanian's innovative study thoroughly highlights the textual and intertextual connections between Shakespeare, Dostoevsky and Bakhtin. Supporting Levin's assertions, Stepanian emphasizes the importance of *Hamlet* for Dostoevsky, being among the first authors to support the claim that Hamlet serves as a subtextual figure for Stavrogin in *Demons*, drawing attention to the preparatory materials that signal this connection (2014: 60). However, as mentioned above, I suggest that while it is necessary to initiate the research of Shakespeare's and Dostoevsky's relationship in the manner of textual comparison, contemporary scholarship may offer new ways of tackling Dostoevsky's 'Hamlet' that will help me bring its understanding a step further.

Nevertheless, the critical discourse surrounding Shakespeare's relevance for Dostoevsky's work and, in turn, Dostoevsky's own relevance to the history of Shakespearean receptions in Russia is surprisingly limited, considering the immense significance of both authors in world literature and cultures. Furthermore, the existing studies have often chosen not to engage with contemporary critical theory, with only few exceptions such as Movsesian (2020). Within Russian criticism two key concepts, Shakespearization and Shakespearianism, have been highly instrumental in evaluating the dissemination, engagement, adaptation and appropriation of Shakespeare's work in the Russian context. Shakespearianism represents the cultural appropriation and naturalization of Shakespeare's heritage,[3] while Shakespearization refers to the influence of Shakespearean works on Russian arts in general.[4] Dostoevsky is recognized as one of the most innovative contributors to Shakespearianism, as his original interpretations are often subversive and counter-discursive, diverging from more conventional appropriations of Shakespeare during his age. As Lukov and Zakharov demonstrated, 'Dostoyevsky appropriated Shakespeare's artistic innovations and his anthropological beliefs. Dostoyevsky's characters carry a mark of his artistic interpretation of Shakespeare's characters. Othello, Hamlet, Prince Harry, and especially vicious Falstaff attracted him more than others.'[5] But, as we can perceive in these examples, scholarship in this area primarily focuses on thematic and formal connections, often examining how aspects of Shakespeare's poetics manifested in Dostoevsky's work. The predominant critical emphasis remains on the exploration of Shakespeare's influence, author-oriented intertextuality, implicitly or explicitly assuming authorial agency. Consequently, much of the research seeks to elucidate how Dostoevsky's characters, motifs, themes and psychological traits reflect or are influenced by Shakespeare (Rovda, 1965; Rowe, 1976; Belknap, 1984; Catteau, [1989], 2009 Kovalevskaya 2014: 74; Zakharov, 2015; Stepanian, 2016). 'Shakespeare was the yardstick against which Dostoevskii measured his own heroes' (Levin, 1995: 62). This approach, however, tends to perpetuate the view of an inherently superior position of Shakespeare and the old pattern of cultural domination while Dostoevsky's work gains legitimacy through its association with him.

In the field of Shakespeare studies, particularly within the context of Global Shakespeare scholarship, in recent decades there appears to be a notable absence in acknowledging Dostoevsky's role. Moreover, insufficient attention has been directed towards the intricate network of philosophical and literary references that Dostoevsky consciously weaves into his engagement with *Hamlet*. Lastly, another gap in scholarly investigations, which this book undertakes to address, concerns the acknowledgement and exploration of Dostoevsky's contradictory, and unconventional engagement with Russian Hamletism. Although scholars such as Levin acknowledge this aspect (1988), its implications for interpreting Dostoevsky's novels remain largely unexplored, with limited analysis of how Hamletian references contribute to the significance of his work at large. Additionally, a more nuanced distinction between Shakespeare's text and the phenomenon of Russian Hamletism is seldom articulated or considered even in otherwise very relevant books. For example, Eleanor Rowe's *Hamlet: A Window on Russia* (1976) remains one of the most detailed studies of Hamletism and *Hamlet*'s impact on Russian culture without thoroughly taking into consideration the above-mentioned distinction. Rowe devotes a whole chapter to Dostoevsky's interpretation of *Hamlet*, straightforwardly elucidating the aspects of Hamlet's figure that he incorporated in his novels. Hamlet, depicted as 'the embodiment of mental anguish, despair, noble suffering' (Rowe, 1976: 84), prompted Dostoevsky to relate 'the "Hamlet Question" not only with suicide but with concerns about what happens after death – including the most important question of all for Dostoevsky – the immortality of the soul and the existence of God' (90). Dryzhakova (1979) observes how Dostoevsky's Hamlet evolves throughout his works, while Zakharov posits that 'Dostoevsky used Hamlet's qualities to create literary characters of his own' (2015: 379). Givens (2016) argues that 'Hamlet is an important subtext in *The Idiot* (1869), where the famous line "To be or not to be" – quoted in the novel – summarises the *existential quandary at the centre of the novel*', highlighting that this 'theme only strengthens in intensity in *Demons* (1871-2), whose hero, Nikolai Stavrogin, grew directly out of the Hamlet theme' (767–8, my emphasis). And although all these claims are more than plausible, I argue that they fall short of addressing the complexity of Dostoevsky's work and revealing potentially innovative ways of its engagement with *Hamlet*.

Shakespeare's *Hamlet*, and his oeuvre in general, are not obvious sources insofar as they lack developed and overt thematic or structural parallels within Dostoevsky's novels. A complex web of intermediaries connects Shakespeare's texts and Dostoevsky's utilization of them, allowing for stratified relationships. Alongside nineteenth-century interpretations of *Hamlet*, these strata encompass Dostoevsky's own fluid interpretations, since there is no extensive evidence of his reading of *Hamlet*. On the other hand, as Chris Thurman has recently argued, it is important to have in mind the inaccuracies of 'inserting' quotes of Shakespeare's *Hamlet* in Dostoevsky's work in translation. He brings to attention that such insertion of original quotations may contribute to contrived, inappropriate and misdirected comparisons by English-speaking readers more accustomed to Shakespeare's work (Thurman, 2020: 99–100). In other words, if an Anglophone reader while reading Dostoevsky in English, unfamiliar with Dostoevsky's poetics or the history of Hamlet-translations, encounters original quotes from *Hamlet* rather than translations from the versions Dostoevsky had read, they may misunderstand the function and meaning of Hamletian references in the novels. As Thurman rightly reminds us, Dostoevsky did not read the original text. He first became acquainted with Nikolay Polevoy's 1837 seminal translation, 'which was fairly free in its use of "modernised" Russian' (101).[6] Later, he read the translation by Kroneberg (1844), Ketcher's prose translations and *Shakespeare's Complete Dramatic Works in Translations by Russian Writers* (4 vols., St Petersburg, 1865–8, as cited in Levin, 1995: 41–2). As we shall see in more detail later, Polevoy's translation was not a faithful reproduction of the original and occasionally altered its meaning. Because of all this, I argue that direct comparative readings of Shakespeare's *Hamlet* alongside Dostoevsky's novels should be approached cautiously. While such readings may provide inspiring insights, they will not necessarily serve as a solid basis for analysis. Hamletian presence in Dostoevsky's work has more to do with the fact that Russian Hamletism was a dominant phenomenon in his generation, and it had been ingrained in many, if not all, important topics of Russian literature, than with the novelist's conscious and deliberate quoting of Shakespeare's play itself. Thus, even when Dostoevsky was not directly inspired by *Hamlet*, the questions surrounding the play and its reception have been tangential to many central themes of his writings.

For example, the connections between *Hamlet* and *Demons* are rather inspired by the history of the reception of Shakespeare and his play in Russia until the 1870s, as well as the corpus of texts dealing with a Hamletian hero in other Russian works (by Pushkin, Turgenev, Belinsky, Herzen, Lermontov, Chernyshevsky, Pisarev, Dobrolybov, Grigoryev, among others) than Shakespeare's text. However, on a textual level, Dostoevsky employs strategies typical of contemporary Russian literature: characters are compared to Shakespeare's heroes, they read his works or talk about Shakespeare's value. For instance, in *Demons* Liza Tushina recalls that she was told the story of Hamlet and teases her mother about reading *Othello*; the protagonist Stavrogin is compared to Hamlet and Prince Hal from *Henry IV*; Shakespeare is mentioned as a symbol of the highest values of civilization. However, neither claim should be taken at its face value because of the complex relations between the following phenomena: the complexity of Shakespeare's play receptions, translations and circulations in nineteenth-century Russia, the nature of Russian Hamletism as a specific philosophy of life based on the appropriation of the figure of Hamlet until the late 1870s, the corpus of Russian texts dealing with a Hamletian hero, the circumstances of Russian culture in the second half of the nineteenth century, and lastly, the specificity of Dostoevsky's engagement with both the play and its Russian interpretations in his literary and non-literary works. Namely, Dostoevsky uses misleading hints in echoing Hamlet, leaving the reader to reconstruct these links. Lastly, the discourse around the phenomenon of Russian Hamletism itself includes a dialogue with nineteenth-century Western European ideological, political and religious stances such as nihilism, atheism, individualism and rationalism, combined with native traditions and Orthodox Christianity.

In the following pages I will examine this eclectic dialogue with *Hamlet*, tracing it from Dostoevsky's initial encounter with the play, as recorded in the 1838 letter by the sixteen-year-old author, to the development of a complex network of Hamletian references, allusions and figures, culminating in *The Brothers Karamazov* (1880) and 'Pushkin Speech' (1880).

## Dostoevsky's 'Hamlet'

*Hamlet*, Hamlet (the character) and Russian 'Hamlets' generate a rich tapestry of semiotic stratifications. These phenomena can be analysed through various conceptual lenses which pin down each of the three categories in turn. Hamlet can be viewed as an *eternal image* (Val. A. Lukov, Vl. A. Lukov),[7] a 'conceptual persona' (Cutrofello, 2014: 1), a symbol, a 'free-floating signifier' (Foakes, 1993: 15), a cultural figure, a cultural icon, a 'nomad figure' (cited in Rippl, 2016: 229). While each perspective, being plausible and valuable, may shed light on some aspects of Dostoevsky's transformation of Russian Hamletism and his portraying original Hamletian figures, they fall short of fully grasping the relevant dimensions of this complex phenomenon. And, more importantly, the above-mentioned approaches can be problematic because of potentially projecting interpretations of Shakespeare's *Hamlet* onto Dostoevsky's work (Thurman, 2020: 99–100). This book explores the role of this mutable and unstable multi-layered network of Hamletian references, which coalesce into diverse Hamletian figures in Dostoevsky's novels. This issue is intricate, and I contend that currently there exists no suitable methodology for approaching Dostoevsky's work from a Hamletian perspective free from assumptions about what he might have thought or from interpretations of his works conditioned by a desire to locate them under a Shakespearean aegis. For the purpose of disentangling this network of relations a new approach is necessary, which, first, takes into consideration the complex history of reception and dissemination of *Hamlet* in the nineteenth-century Russia, but also springs from and is based on the principles of Dostoevsky's own poetics, that counts on an active role of the reader in co-creation of the meaning of a text.

Thus, I first lay out the terminology I will use for treating *Hamlet* as a source. I concur with Alexei Semenenko's view of '*Hamlet* as a multimodal text, i.e. existing in different semiotic systems/modes' (2007: 12) in the Russian context. Once attained a canonical status, the play ended up being reduced to a sign, 'represented in modes other than the written' (145), which can be identified as a symbol, icon and index. I rely on Semenenko's distinction between these modes: 'as a conventional sign/symbol ("Hamletism"),[8] as an index (the line "To be or not to be"), and as an iconic sign (Hamlet with the skull)', while marking the distinction 'between Hamlet the character, Hamlet the text, and the complex semiotic entity [Hamlet]' (144), which in his view, encompasses these three different iconic, symbolic and indexical signs (145). However, Thomas Grob underlines the difficulty of establishing a 'conceptual framework for the diverse, yet compact *network of Hamlet-related texts*', arguing that 'the Russian Hamlet emerges as *a complex semiotic stratification* in which certain moments become stabilised [. . .] while other are actualized in ever new combinations' (2016: 224, my emphasis).[9] In this case, the framework that will allow some themes to emerge and others to lose relevance is the context of Dostoevsky's work. Margaret Litvin has usefully introduced the idea of 'global kaleidoscope' to define how authors and 'audiences came to know Shakespeare through a kaleidoscopic array of performances, texts, and criticism from many directions' (2011: 3). She aptly notes how 'the would-be appropriator [Dostoevsky in this case] typically receives a text through a historically determined *kaleidoscope of indirect experiences* [. . .] distinct and even conflicting interpretations from which the receiver must synthesize or choose' (6, my emphasis).[10] Once we adopt the kaleidoscopic metaphor to engage with the fluid dynamics of *Hamlet*'s reception, circulation, and reinterpretations, we may realize its relevance to Dostoevsky's writings. Not only that he received *Hamlet* and combinations of 'performances, conversations, articles, abridgments, translations, and other materials that happen to be available, along with or before the text itself [. . .] from multiple cultural traditions' such as the French or German tradition of *Hamlet* receptions and translations, but also the 'assortment and relative significance' of Russian Hamletism highly depended on 'the society's current circumstances: international alignments, social tensions, cultural fashions' (26). Thus, Shakespeare's *Hamlet* is just one of many texts and discourses that should be regarded as his source. However, this kaleidoscopic approach may be further extended to encompass my interpretation of Dostoevsky's method of generating meaning within his prose. What does this approach entail? The kaleidoscope is 'an optical instrument, consisting of from two to four reflecting surfaces placed in a tube, at one end of which is a small compartment containing pieces of coloured glass: on looking through the tube, numerous reflections of these are seen, producing brightly-coloured symmetrical figures, which may be constantly altered by rotation of the instrument' (*OED* n. a). In this context, the metaphor of a kaleidoscopic instrument may provide a specific viewpoint, serving as a tool for focusing on Hamletian references and motifs. If so, various layers of significations (Shakespeare's text, its translations, Russian Hamletism, Dostoevsky's novels, etc.) may function as reflecting surfaces, enabling a kaleidoscopic 'Hamlet' to emerge. By looking through this model, numerous different reflections of a certain Hamlet-figure can be seen, or sometimes even just fragments of these Hamlet-figures. And while they are symmetrical, they can constantly be altered depending on what layers are connected or converged. Each juncture becomes a new point of dispersion of the flux of meaning, implying that it is an ever-changeable, shifting, unfinalized and open structure, arising from the interplay of different layers of signification. All these fragments are in dynamic relations of contradiction, parallelism, supplementation, explanation, criticism, banalization, parody and so on. Thus, the result of such a mobile and composite view refers to the figurative meaning of the word kaleidoscope: 'a constantly changing group of bright colours or coloured objects; anything which exhibits a succession of shifting phases' (*OED*, n. b.). This approach aims at displacing Shakespeare's *Hamlet* from the centre of attention in the interpretative practice, by emphasizing the impossibility of retaining a unified reading of *Hamlet* in any of Dostoevsky's reworking. The accent is put on the traces of the process of adaptation as recreation and the product of adaptation rather than the presence of the source. Katya Tolstaya's claims may prove relevant to the choice of the adjective kaleidoscopic as fitting for describing Dostoevsky's poetical practice and the role of the reader in his open and dialogical works. She explains that:

> Just as all the glass fragments in the kaleidoscope are connected, so everything in the novel is connected on the textual level (symbolism, detail etc.) and on the subject level, and precisely this connection goes beyond the details, but in such a way that it is necessary to consider the concrete details, because the pattern of the glass fragments changes at each turn for each character. And, as in a kaleidoscope, the possibilities of the combinations are unlimited: the dialogue is in perpetual motion. The dialogical model of Dostoevsky's novels allows perspectives to be kept open and prevents any claim to a univocal perspective on the part of the reader. (Tolstaya, 2013: 31–2)

The structure and the connections are stable, but the interplay of their relations has a vast variety of possibilities. To emphasize her claims and the aptness of this approach for this particular study, it may be recalled that Dostoevsky describes Stavrogin in his preparatory materials for *Demons* 'as terribly fascinated by something – *Hamlet* for instance' (*Notebooks*, 1968: 57) and that 'All the rest moves around him, like a kaleidoscope' (182). Dostoevsky writes that 'N.B. Everything is contained in Stavrogin's character' (296), revealing the hero's position at the centre of both the narrative and the story. All other characters are focused on interpreting and understanding Stavrogin; he is the source of ideas that are disseminated and appropriated by the others, and his actions are the main motivators of the plot. There is always a certain dark spot, a secret, an enigma, something alluring that evades readers while inspiring them – something terribly fascinating. Most importantly, this approach gives the reader a privileged place in the process of meaning-making, which is in harmony with Dostoevsky's polyphonic poetics. Apart from Bakhtin's famous position on

polyphony and dialogism in Dostoevsky,[11] Rowan Williams aptly
explained the importance and the role of the reader when describing
the religious, Christian quality of Dostoevsky's work. He elaborated on
Dostoevsky's ethics of authorship which depends on a participation
of a reader who is not an abstract concept, but a singular being with
a unique voice, presence, language and history (Williams, 2008: 141).
Additionally, the 'silence' or 'surrendering' of the author to the reader
as an aesthetic principle gives readers the freedom to participate in
meaning-making according to their particular consciousness, which
entails the responsibility of co-authorship (189). As the book unfolds,
it will become clearer in which way the topics of interpretation, choice,
freedom and responsibility are deeply ingrained in Dostoevsky's
involvement with Hamletian themes and his ethics of adaptation and
writing.

Apart from the text of Shakespeare's *Hamlet*, Russian Hamletism,
the semiotic stratification [Hamlet] and Hamlet the figure as seen in
Russia in the nineteenth century, that all belong to the sphere of *Hamlet*-
reception, I argue that there are three more aspects of Dostoevsky's
kaleidoscopic engagement with these sources that deserve attention:
what I will call the Hamlet-ideologeme, the Hamlet-isotopy network
across the four layers of signification and 'Hamlet'. First, by Hamlet-
ideologeme I refer to the core theme that will be revealed in Dostoevsky's
work starting from his 1838 letter, that is, a sign of a Hamletian ideology,
a constant Hamletian proto-narrative offering readers and critics alike a
stable signifying structure with an array of potential meanings awaiting
to be actualized differently in various contexts. Second, I will identify a
Hamletian isotopy[12] (the semantic network made of units of meaning
across Dostoevsky's writings that are connected to Hamlet/*Hamlet*
and Russian Hamletism), tracing a recurrence of certain themes,
motifs or lexical items that imply a cohesion between Dostoevsky's
1838 letter and his other novels. This network will uncover implicit
connections between deeper layers of meaning across a four-layer
model of signification. I drew this model to include textual, paratextual,
subtextual and intertextual/interdiscursive layers in order to grasp

the interplay of different references to *Hamlet* or Russian Hamletism. The textual layer includes Dostoevsky's fictional works, while the paratextual one includes textual portions around the text, such as epigrams, prefaces, chapter titles and the title itself. The text of *Demons* is a very complex thread of references itself. It has been described as an 'allegorical palimpsest' (Valentino, 1997: 47) with a lacuna at its centre, meaning that the main motivational device, Stavrogin, is enigmatic. First, the reader should systematize motifs and references to follow the hints to *Hamlet* and Shakespeare intentionally left by Dostoevsky. For example, the reader should examine what character is mentioning Shakespeare in the novel or who is comparing Stavrogin to Hamlet or Prince Hal. Second, in order to understand scattered hints to Hamlet or Russian Hamletism one should turn to the paratext, 'a threshold [. . .], an "undefined zone" between the inside and the outside, a zone without any hard and fast boundary" (Genette 1997: 2). Paratext contains an authoritative perspective, an ideological programme that colours the narrative and guides the reader through a meander of possible narrative routes. For example, the title of the second chapter of *Demons's* part one, 'Prince Harry. Matchmaking' (Princ Garri. Svatovstvo), is a place from which Shakespeare's *Henry IV* enters the novel with a metatextual function. Third, the subtextual layer encompasses all the preparatory materials and sources preliminary to the creation of the novel. The analysis of the subtext, in the case just mentioned, can be helpful in discovering the contested relationship between *Hamlet* and *Henry IV* in characterising Stavrogin. The subtext (in the form of preparatory materials for the novels) contains references to Shakespeare and *Hamlet* which illuminate some less evident motifs and details that will resonate with Dostoevsky's Hamlet-ideologeme once we encounter it. In Robert Miola's words, the subtext 'removes the source from above (influence) and from behind (background) to locate it below the text, changing the metaphorical field of reference to the earth or garden. The student of sources, then, does not trace lines of transmission or perceived spatial or temporal relations, but searches for underground pools and dig up roots' (1998: 323). Different relations between the text of the novel and the subtext of the preparatory materials will be part of the discussion proposed in the following chapters. Fourth, the intertextual layer includes references to Shakespeare's *Hamlet,* to other literary texts that bear traces in Dostoevsky's work or include figures of Russian Hamlets, alongside non-literary texts that were relevant for Dostoevsky's Hamlets. Russian Hamletism can be seen as a database of both textual variants and interpretations (intertextuality), reaching a broader intercultural field (interdiscursivity). The interdiscursive layer primarily incorporates Russian Hamletism as a cultural phenomenon adjacent to different ideas that migrated from textual into discursive spheres and had a vivid historical impact on the ideology of the period, including nihilistic and sceptical positions. In this case, references to Shakespeare and *Hamlet* connect Dostoevsky's novels with other Russian literary and non-literary works related to world literature works and phenomena, and cultural contexts in which *Hamlet* was appropriated and naturalized (such as in the example of the Byronism phenomenon and its reception in Russia as will be mentioned later). This four-layer model serves as a tool for identifying and classifying both Dostoevsky's own references to *Hamlet* and Shakespeare and those that the reader/critic may identify. The reader is stimulated to connect and reconnect Dostoevsky's allusions to *Hamlet* and Shakespeare, reconstructing their relations and creating new ones in order to (re) textualize the relevance of *Hamlet* for *Demons* as well as other novels by Dostoevsky. The combination of these layers, which are separate only in theory, enables us to draw a very complex network of literary and discursive references grounding Dostoevsky's engagement with *Hamlet*/Hamlet in a highly connoted ideological and historical context. Lastly, the third term I introduce is 'Hamlet' to encompass the above-mentioned approach to analyse a specific novel, for example *Demons.* If we perceive previous classifications (the Hamlet-ideologeme and the Hamlet-isotopy network) as schemes to analyse Dostoevsky's own dialogue with *Hamlet*/Hamlet and Russian Hamletism, 'Hamlet' will stand for a specific result of these interpretations, producing a (re)textualization / (re)narratization of his reworking of *Hamlet* in a particular text.

The main object of my analysis is not to identify a particular intertextual relation between Dostoevsky's and Shakespeare's text. Rather, the book will explore Dostoevsky's creative revision of contemporary receptions of *Hamlet*/Hamlet into new Hamletian characters with the aim not to define a single Dostoevskian Hamlet but to disclose and explore the Hamlet-ideologeme at the core of Dostoevsky's novels, so as to suggest ways in which readers are invited to co-create ever-shifting 'Hamlets' through Dostoevsky's work. In order to do so, the first chapter will provide a historical and ideological background of Russian Hamletism in nineteenth-century Russia, aiming to contextualize how this discursive formation was rethought by Dostoevsky. The second chapter is devoted to exploring the Hamlet-ideologeme by analysing Dostoevsky's 1838 letter and dealing with *The Double*, *The Village of Stepanchikovo and Its Inhabitants*, *The Humiliated and Insulted*, *Notes from Underground*, and *Crime and Punishment*. Dostoevsky's Hamlet-ideologeme is his response to Russian Hamletism, and it will guide us to understand Dostoevsky's Hamletian subjectivities. In the third chapter I'll examine Dostoevsky's Hamletian heroes in his three major novels: *The Idiot*, *An Accidental Family* and *The Brothers Karamazov*. Finally, the last two chapters will explore 'Hamlets' that can be reconstructed from *Demons*, providing answers to why Stavrogin is the most Hamletian of all his heroes, ultimately showcasing the position of Dostoevsky 'adapted' Shakespeare within the context of Global Shakespeare adaptations in the epilogue.

# Notes

1  The title of Dostoevsky's *Besy* (Бесы) has been translated in various ways (*Demons*, *The Devils*, *The Possessed*). I concur with the choice of *Demons* by Larissa Volkhonsky and Richard Pevear. I consequently rely on their

explanation of this choice, since Pevear argues that 'the Russian title *Besy* refers not to possessed but to possessors' (2006: xiii).

2  Roger L. Cox's monograph *Between Earth and Heaven: Shakespeare, Dostoevsky and the Christian Tragedy* (1969) examines Shakespeare's and Dostoevsky's relationship to Christian tragedy, focusing on their distinct engagements with the texts of the *New Testament* rather than exploring the interconnections between their works. Furthermore, although it includes three chapters on Dostoevsky's novels, *Crime and Punishment*, *The Idiot* and *The Brothers Karamazov*, Cox's book does not address *Demons*.

3  '[Shakespearianism is] an ideological and aesthetic trend characterized by dialogue between Russian and European cultures, based on Russian studies and cultural appropriation of William Shakespeare's heritage. As a term, *Shakespearianism* was first introduced into Russian criticism in the mid-nineteenth century by Pavel Annenkov [. . .] Under the term "Shakespearianism" in research on Pushkin and some other Russian writers (first of all, Fyodor Dostoyevsky) is understood a set of artistic and aesthetic ideas, which characterize Shakespeare's vision and understandings of history and contemporaneity, past and future (strictly, this is what Pushkin named "Shakespeare's view").' SHAKESPEARIANISM | The World of Shakespeare: An Electronic Encyclopaedia (world-shake.ru)

4  '[. . .] Shakespearisation [. . .] [is] a special public interest in William Shakespeare's literary heritage (intensively developed in the second half of the 18th century), on the other hand, the strong influence of the playwright's creative work on the subsequent development of literature, music, visual arts, theater and cinema.' SHAKESPEARISATION | The World of Shakespeare: An Electronic Encyclopaedia (world-shake.ru)

5  The CULT of SHAKESPEARE | The World of Shakespeare: An Electronic Encyclopaedia (world-shake.ru)

6  Thurman focuses only on *Notes from the Underground* and its interpretation through a Hamletian perspective. However, I argue that his remarks are highly relevant in regard to all other works and writings by Dostoevsky. As Thurman discusses: 'Shakespearean allusions thus enrich a particular reading of the Notes – that is, a reading based on *Hamlet*. But they also introduce a potential pitfall. The problem with presenting the Underground Man as a Hamlet-figure in this way is that it can become

the sole lens through which English readers familiar with Shakespeare's plays interpret *Notes from the Underground*. We may no longer be attuned to other literary and philosophical influences; indeed, worse, we may no longer be able to read Dostoevsky without hunting for such influences. A single-minded focus on Hamlet as antecedent of the Underground Man can also lead to overblown claims, clumsy literary criticism or – a particular risk for Shakespeare scholars – an emphasis on textual fragments removed from their dramatic or theatrical context' (2020: 106–7).

7  'Eternal images – literary term used to refer to images traveling from one work to another, and thus building a storage of invariants for literary discourse. Features of eternal images (found collectively, for the most part): depth of meaning and infinite potential for interpretation; high artistic and spiritual value; capacity for cross-cultural and cross-temporal migration, or universality and lasting importance; polyvalency – capability of fitting various stories and uniting with other sets of images and backgrounds without losing unique identity; translatability into other arts, into the languages of philosophy, science, etc.; broad sphere of use.' (Val. A. Lukov, Vl. A. Lukov, ETERNAL IMAGES | The World of Shakespeare: An Electronic Encyclopaedia (world-shake.ru))

8  Hamletism became 'the interpretation of the assumed "mystery" of Hamlet's character and the controversy of his actions' (Semenenko, 2007: 139), having an invariant structure consisting in, first, a possibility to equate an 'X' with Hamlet, 'X being "me", "the nation", "the generation"' (140). An individual 'finds himself in a position of choice, whether he is put there by the circumstances or by himself, and there are different assumptions as to the difficulty of this choice' (2007).

9  According to Grob, reoccurring themes in Russian Hamlet are the following: 'the figural reflection of poets and the intelligentsia; the image of the irreconcilable contradictions between the individual and his or her environment; the themes of creativity and mental overload, reflection and action, as well as the tension between responsibility and powerlessness refracted through a recognition of the rights of noble birth [. . .] Nothing is lost in this stratification: the reflection of the Romantic poet does not cancel out the political; the political does not negate the intimate, nor the poetic the social, nor the appropriation the foreign origins' (2016:

224). However, I contend that Grob's approach still remains a static linear model that inadequately captures the materiality of Russian Hamletism's cultural, semiotic, textual and discursive web-like circulations. By treating the 'multiple and changeable, but ultimately consistent and coherent topological space in which the Russian Hamlet moves – a space that allows for changing attributions of meaning and the assumption of new roles in different cultural environments within a persistent structural framework', Grob somewhat overlooks the complexity brought by the foreign cultural artefact into this 'iridescent interplay' (2016) and the network of relations that transcend the linearity of semiotic stratification. Moreover, Grob's methodology is confined to analyzing Hamlet solely as a literary figure.

10  Litvin writes about the reception of *Hamlet* in Arab countries: 'Arab writers do not first encounter *Hamlet* just by sitting down and reading it. In general, the reception of a prestigious foreign literary work rarely entails a tabula rasa, a direct unmediated experience of an authoritative original. Instead, the wouldbe appropriator typically receives a text through a historically determined kaleidoscope of indirect experiences: some combination of the films, performances, conversations, articles, abridgments, translations, and other materials that happen to be available, along with or before the text itself. These materials come from multiple cultural traditions (not just the "original" source culture) and arrive in various languages. Their assortment and relative significance depends on the society's current circumstances: international alignments, social tensions, cultural fashions, and so forth. They offer distinct and even conflicting interpretations from which the receiver must synthesize or choose' (2011: 26).

11  Polyphony means that Dostoevsky 'surrenders to his characters and allows them to speak in ways other than his own. Heroes are no longer diminished to the dominating consciousness of the author; secondary characters are no longer encompassed by and diminished to their usefulness to heroes – or to the author. Characters are, in short, respected as full subjects, shown as "consciousnesses" that can never be fully defined or exhausted, rather than as objects fully known' (Booth, 1999: xxiii).

12  Umberto Eco develops initial Greimas's definition of isotopy (a
    repetition of one unit of meaning) as follows: 'In other words, the topic
    is a pragmatic device, while the isotopy is a level of possible semantic
    actualization of the text [. . .] isotopy refers almost always to constancy
    in going in a direction that a text exhibits when submitted to rules of
    interpretive coherence' (Eco, 1980: 145; 153).

# 1

# Russian Hamletism and Dostoevsky

*An archetypical 'Russian Hamlet', inwardly torn by the dissonances of Russian life and culture but nonetheless 'a man directly – and even in many ways unconsciously – rooted in the soil, clinging to the pith of his country' (20: 135–136).*

(Dostoevsky, cited in Frank, 1986: 354, my emphasis)

*He loves his fantasy; indeed, he himself is a fantasy.*

(*Pushkin Speech*, Dostoevsky, cited in Bowers, K., Doak, C. and Holland, K. 2018: 473)

The development of Russian national literature in the eighteenth century intertwines with the assimilation and naturalization of Shakespeare, whose importance was firmly 'established in the nineteenth century' (Givens, 2016: 761). This age marked the construction of Russian culture and national identity in contrast to Europe, during which Russian literature modelled itself on its Western counterpart. The relation between Russia and Western Europe during the nineteenth century was often marred by 'ignorance and prejudices' (Đermanović, 2023: 13, my translation), stereotypes, projections and introjections. To this list, one could add mechanisms of othering sometimes accompanied by radical demonization and chauvinism present in contemporary discourse. The ultimate antinomy that underlined the articulation of Russian identity in the nineteenth century and beyond was the polarity between the ideologies of Slavophiles and Westernizers. Westernizers viewed Western Europe as the origin of culture, while Slavophiles saw it as the epitome of civilizational decline. Both treated European values as *others* in comparison to Russian culture. However, this otherness was inherently intertwined with the Russian cultural and literary tradition.[1] While Slavophiles 'reacted against borrowing from Europe and sought to find what was good in Russia's heritage', Westernizers 'maintained that Russia must continue and enhance its development along European lines' (Lantz, 2004: 461). Westernizers were turned towards European 'ideals of open and humane society, democracy, freedom of association, the rights of the individual' (2004). Inspired by the French Revolution, socialism and Enlightenment, German Idealism and materialism, Russian liberals were their main representatives. However, as Offord notes, they are not to be misperceived as 'too closely identified with the ideology implied by the term in the nineteenth century in relation to Western European countries in general and to Victorian England in particular' (1999: 74) but rather 'associated with nobility and officialdom' (1999). Liberalism indicated an aspiration to introduce elements of what was regarded as the superior civilization of Western Europe into Russia. However, the younger generation brought up on 'English philosophical radicals and German materialists' (Lantz, 2004: 461) saw the liberals 'with effete posturing, empty rhetoric, and hypocritical advocacy of high-sounding ideals they are allegedly not prepared fully to translate into practice' (Offord, 1999: 74). One of the radical derivatives of the 1860s were nihilists who consisted mostly of young students. Their nihilism was essentially a part of 'the socialist rebellion against the established values of "liberalism"' (81). On the other hand, Slavophiles saw Western 'societies founded on violence and so needed legal regulation to govern relations among people', while 'fragmentation of the Western spirit showed itself in social conflict between hostile classes and the pursuit of self-interest' (Lantz, 2004: 379). They professed returning to Russian traditional values and Orthodoxy that relied on the moral ideal of brotherhood, and utilized the concepts of *sobornost* and *tsel'nost* as solutions to the importation of Western problems into Russian culture and society. *Sobornost* or conciliarism, in the work of Russian Slavophile author Khomiakov, was described as 'a free and loving association of believers in common spiritual values, inspired by the Holy Spirit – as the essence of Orthodoxy', and it meant 'unity in multiplicity (2004). *Tsel'nost* refers to 'an inner wholeness of being in which reason, sensuality, ethics and spirituality functioned harmoniously' (2004). The antinomy between Slavophiles and Westernizers underpins Dostoevsky's work. He sought to achieve a synthesis and reconciliation in the doctrine of *pochvennichestvo* to which he significantly contributed. *Pocva* means native soil or roots, and the movement represented a way of uniting certain principles from both Slavophilism and Westernism by encouraging the intelligentsia to 'return to their native soil' given their Westernization and alienation from their national tradition and people (324). Dostoevsky's idea was that it was necessary 'to reconcile the educated classes with the peasantry and unite them; the educated classes, however, were not to renounce the principles they derived from their education, nor were the people to renounce their principles derived from our native soil' (Strakhov as cited in Lantz, 2004: 324–5). For Dostoevsky, the central idea of *pochvennichestvo* is brotherhood (*sobornost*), expanded into 'great, general, universal union of fellowship in the name of Christ' (PSS, 27:18-19).

Differences between Westernizers and Slavophiles were strikingly evident in their interpretations of Shakespeare and the cultural capital of his work. Levin identifies three main phases in Shakespeare's reception during the nineteenth century (1998: 79–95). The Romantic phase (1820–30) saw Pushkin appropriate Shakespeare and assimilate his work 'in the interests of its own (Russian) needs and problems' (79). This tendency is particularly evident in Pushkin's ambition to develop a national literature based on imitating Shakespeare's historical dramas in *Boris Godunov*. However, Levin aptly identifies the split between intellectual engagement and concrete political or ethical action, emerging concurrently with a mode of self-identification through Shakespeare. By the late 1840s, Shakespeare became 'widely known' (85). In the second phase (1840s–60s) Shakespeare became central to political and aesthetic debates between Westernizers and Slavophiles. It was one of the most vibrant phases in the reception of his work in which major literary and critical figures (Belinsky, Turgenev, Chernyshevsky, Grigoryev, Lermontov, Pisarev and Tolstoy) read, interpreted and engaged with Shakespeare. Additionally, the range and the importance of the cultural and political debate surrounding Shakespeare's value in the 1860s had become a uniquely Russian phenomenon so much so that he 'became an integral part of Russian culture and has been in its bloodstream ever since' (Kizima, 2021: 186). This organic metaphor casting Shakespeare as 'an integral part' of Russian culture aptly encapsulates the process of his adoption and internalization, wherein Shakespeare's foreignness was transcended by being made *their own*. In an 1861 article titled 'Love of Books and Literacy', Dostoevsky proclaimed that Shakespeare had 'become part of the *flesh and blood of Russian society* [. . .] We were *brought up on him*, he is *one of us*, and in many respects he has been *reflected in our development*' (PSS, 19: 17; cited in Levin, 1995: 43, my emphasis). In commemorating Shakespeare's tercentenary in 1864, Turgenev also declared: 'For Shakespeare is for us not only a famous and brilliant name to which we pay homage occasionally and from a distance; he has become part of our heritage, *our own flesh and blood*' (cited in Levin, 1998: 95, my emphasis). This naturalization became a common perspective. However, as will be seen later, Dostoevsky exhibited an ambivalent stance towards Shakespeare's texts, taking place in between the generation that adored Shakespeare and the following one that was his vocal critic. By the 1860s, Shakespeare's importance began to wane and 'to lose his significance as an active factor in the literary process' (92), particularly under the scrutiny of Nikolay Chernishevsky, a radical democratic thinker and author, who claimed that Shakespeare should be regarded 'without blind veneration' as his plays were 'incapable of giving aesthetic pleasure in our day' (cited in Levin, 1998: 93). Russian realism and social criticism found Shakespeare inadequate to deal with contemporary pressing matters (89–93). Zaitsev and Pisarev, adamant proponents of utilitarian aesthetics, famously argued that commodities like boots, petroleum or cigarettes held more value than Shakespeare's work. In the last phase, Shakespeare's significance and actuality began to diminish. Finally, Leo Tolstoy, with his 'anti-Shakespearean revolt' (92), put a definite end to 'uncritical adulation of Shakespeare' and what he called an 'epidemic hypnosis' (94) surrounding Shakespeare's cult. In his renowned 1906 essay 'On Shakespeare and Drama', Tolstoy argued, in his typically provocative and exaggerated style, that Shakespeare shouldn't even be considered as an average author and criticized *King Lear* for lack of dramatic tension, psychological motivation and for pretentious Shakespearean language (93). While these claims are evidently biased and problematic, if not completely wrong, they echoed strongly given Tolstoy's reputation.

## *Hamlet* and Russian Hamletism in nineteenth-century Russia

'Shakespeare's *Hamlet* effectively marked the birth of Russian theatre' (Grob, 2016: 193) in Sumarokov's 1748 adaptation, which freely rewrote the original with a happy ending, thereby paving the way for future creative appropriations of Shakespeare's work. This meant that from the very beginning *Hamlet* has been perceived as a text suitable for adaptations in accordance with Russian needs and expectations. The establishment of Shakespeare as a canonical playwright in Russian theatres came along with Nikolay Polevoy's (1796–1846) translation[2] of *Hamlet* in 1837. The same year it premiered in Moscow with Pavel Mochalov in the lead role, and in Saint Petersburg, with Vasiliy Karatygin. These performances helped shape the phenomenon that represented a 'philosophy' of life by the 1840s although Polevoy's rewriting was not a particularly original reading of the play. Mochalov's Moscow performance, which was most probably seen by young Dostoevsky (Levin, 1995: 41), echoed strongly in Belinsky's 1838 essay 'Hamlet, A drama by Shakespeare. Mochalov acting the part of Hamlet' on this specific interpretation (Kizima, 2021: 183–5). Kizima highlights that this essay contributed to establishing

Shakespeare on the Russian stage, due in part to Belinsky's awareness of the relevance of *Hamlet* in the repressive era of Nicolas I's reign. Belinsky's realization that Russia 'had found a national narrative' (Givens, 2016: 765) underscored the inception of what was quickly to become a widespread phenomenon fundamental in the shaping of Russian identity, so much so that an Englishman once remarked that 'Hamlet should have been a Russian not a Dane' (Morris cited in Rowe, 1976: xv). Grob demonstrates and evaluates the specificity of this cultural migration:

> There appear to be cases of imported characters that, while not denying their foreign origins, become established as entirely Russian figures, which may represent a specifically Russian phenomenon. Shakespeare's *Hamlet* is arguably the most important and enduring representative of these acculturated 'immigrants' to Russian culture. (2016: 192)

The phenomenon of Russian Hamletism extended beyond individual introspection to encompass broader social and national concerns, becoming one of the main discursive formations of the ruling episteme. The figure of Hamlet served as a model for the national identity and for the Russian intellectuals to achieve self-knowledge. But also, the emergence of Russian Hamletism intertwined with the occurrence of the spiritual type of the superfluous man, a group of so-called alienated figures who had lost their place and role in Russian society. They belonged to a 'tiny minority of educated and morally sensitive men, who, unable to find a place in his native land, and driven in upon himself, is liable to escape either into fantasies or illusions, or into cynicism or despair, ending, more often than not, in self-destruction or surrender' (Berlin cited in Holland, 1999: 23). For the Russian intelligentsia, Hamlet was the Western model of a thinking man who sought to make sense of the world, the self and national identity, yet failed to act. Various interpretations of the enigma of Hamlet's character spurred the development of Russian Hamletism (Levin, 1998: 88).

Polevoy adapted *Hamlet* to a contemporary Russian language and contextualized the hero within the social and political landscape of his generation. His version of Hamlet, that strongly echoes in Dostoevsky 1838 letter and can be regarded as a basis for Dostoevsky's further modifications, 'was somewhat distorted, his state of spiritual loss, his frustration, his despair over man's wretchedness were intensified and stressed' (86). Notably, in Polevoy's version, 'Hamlet is transfigured into a progressive-minded Russian intellectual, helpless against political oppression and mentally tormented by the awareness of his inadequate response', which changed the tone of the play to 'romantic melodrama' (87). This translation and adaptation bears traces from Goethe's portrayal of Hamlet in the Bildungsroman *Wilhelm Meister's Apprenticeship*, 'carrying its implications to their extreme' (Rowe, 1976: 43), as the focus was placed on the hero's inability to act and his weakness of will. However, aside from a feeble will, Polevoy's Hamlet is characterized by self-humiliation and continual lamentation about his own failure when confronted with duty. As Rowe notes, 'when Hamlet calls himself "a rogue and peasant slave", Polevoy has: "an insignificant creature"' (1976). This choice of words implies an even stronger need for self-flagellation and reduces the image of oneself to less than a human. She further notices that some additional lines are included which do not align with Shakespeare's text but rather underscore Hamlet's self-abasement, such as 'Oh Hamlet, Hamlet! Disgrace and shame on you!' (1976). Also, 'Polevoy changes those elements of the plot which show Hamlet as resolute and fearless; for example, the account of his adventures at sea' (1976). As highlighted by Peter Holland, his clear intention to demonstrate 'an individual's powerlessness in the confrontation with a strong but inert state machine [. . .] was in itself a political emphasis perfectly appropriate for the Russia of the early nineteenth century' (1999: 320). Drawing from the Romantic tradition of German idealism, Hamlet was extrapolated from the play, so much so that, eventually, Hamletism represented not only the suffering of the hero, but 'an expression of the intellectual experience of a certain generation, a certain social group, and sometimes even a whole nation undergoing a critical stage in its history' (Levin, 1998: 88). Because of being an imported cultural product associated with higher-class culture, Russian Hamletism was used as space for philosophical and cultural debates. It reflected prevailing power dynamics, entwined with an array of arguments concerning political, ideological and philosophical disparities among different ideological positions. Furthermore, Hamletism in general reflected a strong disillusionment with the ideals of the Enlightenment and rationalism (Levin, 1988: 159, my translation) which will strongly resonate with Dostoevsky's view of Hamlet. The sense of this collapse is part and parcel of the episteme of the Russian Hamletism which was to become the dominant discursive formation in the post-Pushkin age. It is no surprise that Russian Hamletism gained more cultural significance than Shakespeare's play itself in the Russian context, confirming that 'cultural migrations also reveal a culture's mechanisms of semiotic adaptation and of self-definition through other' (Grob, 2016: 192) – in this case, the other being Western literature and culture. The Russian critique and reception of *Hamlet* thus evolved into a means of self-criticism (Levin, 1998: 88). Holland noticed how Russian authors during the 1840s down to the 1860s were interested in 'the social implications abstracted or derived' from the play (1999: 315), pointing out that '*Hamlet* was embedded into Russian social and political history' (1999), and therefore acquired a specific cultural meaning. Consequently, 'while the history of texts is necessarily historically and geographically defined', he continues,

> there is a performative history to a text's function in a culture. The *Russian construction* of *Hamlet* is *neither Shakespeare's nor our own*; instead the play, as it acquires significance across the history of its appropriation, *performs a particular function in Russia*, a function which is *more social and political* than aesthetic. That function is *fragmentary and referential*, deriving from an accumulative cultural meaning which may have only *tangential links* to the original play, and as much from *assumptions* about the play as from any sustained *reading of it*. (316, my emphasis)

Holland's observation that the 'usefulness of Hamlet lies in the audiences' construction of a difference from and a resistance to being Hamlet' (333) echoes the kaleidoscopic mechanism of *Hamlet*-reception described above and the role of readers or audience in the construction of their own meanings. The function of Russian Hamletism in the 1860s was to justify and intellectualize the intelligentsia's own impotence. They identified with a noble, idealistic cause behind passivity while maintaining the status quo of the state – the ruling class and the Tsar are untouchable, action and rebellion are futile, and personal responsibility, consciousness and agency are not sufficient to bring about change. Russian Hamletism also increased the intelligentsia's inclination to auto-flagellation and self-shaming which contributed to widespread despair and passivity. In a different turn of anti-Hamletism, it became regarded as 'an intellectual justification for a social retreat from responsibility and lethargic dissociation' (322). The ways in which it was interpreted reflect the hegemony of power and of ideological perspective that sees injustice enabled by the fault of individuals due to their paralysis and passivity and not by the unjust system itself. In Levin's view, the basis of the tragedy of Russian Hamlets is that the hero should fight the injustices of the world, yet his powerlessness raises doubts about the meaning of life and sees in suicide the only alternative. However, he makes a more important point ideologically and philosophically when he underlined that Hamletism began to take shape at the end of the eighteenth century when certain social and political upheavals in European countries led to the collapse of the Enlightenment (Levin, 1988: 159, my translation). In his opinion, 'rationalistic thinking of the Enlightenment was foreign to Hamletism, because it was based on the idea that the very awareness of contradiction is suficient to overcome it. However, history has dispelled these illusions, clearly showing that awareness alone is insuficient, something else is needed' (1988, my translation). Levin concludes by raising the very question at the root of Hamletism: 'But what else?' (1988, my translation).

## Rethinking Russian Hamletism with Dostoevsky

This comment brings my discussion of Russian Hamletism to two crucial issues. The first is that an awareness of political, moral and spiritual crises, alongside an understanding of their underlying contradictions, and their possible solutions are not enough to overcome them. This argument implicitly puts in question the nature of subjectivity itself, reverberating a Hamletian theme of the inevitable limits of knowledge. Being aware of a wrong and foul deed, knowing what to do about it, and having the means to be an active participant in power games are not sufficient to take an active and effective stand; in other words, knowing does not entail doing, nor does doing entail changing and rectifying things. The second issue concerns the attitude to Shakespeare's text as a source of adaptation and the function of Russian Hamletism in the period between 1860 and 1880. Since the inception of the phenomenon with Polevoy's rewriting of the play, the function of Russian Hamletism has been in service of modernizing *Hamlet* and Hamletian issues in order to make them relevant for contemporary readers. This fact guides my analysis towards prioritizing adaptation processes and results over the identification of traces of Shakespeare's *Hamlet* in Russian Hamletism. Dostoevsky always thought about Shakespeare and *Hamlet* in these terms.

Dostoevsky's contribution to Russian Hamletism should be read as his answer to these two questions, bringing centre stage issues of choice, agency, power and knowledge. Dostoevsky's reception of *Hamlet* grew out of his own response to contemporary receptions of Shakespeare and his play. As already mentioned, Polevoy's adaptation provided a basis for his view of *Hamlet*. However, Pushkin, Lermontov, Turgenev, Belinsky and Chernyshevsky had a prominent place in guiding his counter-discourse to widespread Hamletism. Consequently, Dostoevsky's references to Shakespeare and *Hamlet* are inevitably related to their literary and non-literary works but also to international cultural phenomena, such as Byronism, that belong to other cultural contexts that also appropriated *Hamlet* and naturalized it as their own.

Let us now turn to Romantic Russian Hamlets and the superfluous man, starting from Alexander Pushkin's take on these. Pushkin (1799–1837) did not express overt admiration for *Hamlet*. However, certain aspects of his reflections, while not directly related to Russian Hamletism, prefigure Dostoevsky's own later approach as part of the tradition of Russian Byronism.[3] In a private letter, Pushkin remarked: 'My head is spinning after reading Shakespeare. It is as if I were looking into abyss' (cited in Rowe, 1976: 30). In *Hamlet*, Pushkin recognized that terror can be expressed through laughter (1976) and described Shakespeare's work as a 'playful treatment of a morbid subject' (31). However, Pushkin is more important for creating characters that link Russian Byronism and Russian Hamletism in ways that will prove influential for Dostoevsky. Also, a connection between Dostoevsky and Pushkin can be traced in the reception of Byronism. Byronism became central in Pushkin's construction of Onegin from *Eugene Onegin*, to name but one famous case, paving the way for the emergence of the category of the superfluous man, which later intersected with the Hamletian model.[4] Dostoevsky further developed these traits by exploiting, in the construction of Stavrogin in *Demons*, similar stylistic and lexical choices to those used by Pushkin to characterize Onegin. He understood Byronism as an expression of the 'disillusionment of Europe after the collapse of the ideals of the Enlightenment and the failure of the French Revolution' (Lantz, 2004: 48). For instance, Stavrogin is a great example of the interconnection of different traditions, from transcultural Byronism to Russian Hamletism and the superfluous hero type. This merging of themes can be viewed as an important intertextual and interdiscursive phenomenon, wherein Stavrogin represents a variant, one of the last examples of a Byronic, but also Hamletian figure in Russian literature. Moreover, Dostoevsky employed a complex overlay of Hamletism and Byronism in *Demons* as a metaphor for Russian intelligentsia.

On the other hand, Mikhail Lermontov (1814–41), one of the most important Russian Romantic novelists, held a profound admiration for both the play and the hero. It can be argued that Pechorin, the protagonist of *A Hero of Our Time* (1840), is a prominent figure of Russian Hamletism and a source for Stavrogin, again participating in the continuum of types that link Russian Hamletism, Byronism and Dostoevsky's protagonists. During his formative years, Lermontov was impressed by the alleged madness of Hamlet. As Rowe recalls,

Lermontov focused on 'Hamlet's attempt to force one of the unwilling courtiers to play the flute' and he assigned to Hamlet the following lines: 'If you cannot draw the appropriate sounds out of this small thing, how can you draw out of me, a creature endowed with a strong will, my secret thoughts?' (IV, 416–18, cited in Rowe, 1976: 39). To him, Hamlet was a proud, ironic and sarcastic figure, superior to others and imbued with a strong will – 'characteristics which were subsequently incorporated into Lermontov's most romantic figures' (Grob, 2016: 196), notably in Pechorin. In him, Lermontov melds Hamletian attributes with a Byronic rebellious and subversive spirit, reflecting his own personal inclinations. Pechorin staunchly resists interpretation: 'I make it a rule never to disclose my own thoughts, and am very glad when others divine them because that leaves me loophole for denying them when necessary' (*A Hero of Our Time*, 1951: 95). Lermontov links these motifs to *Hamlet* when Pechorin exclaims: 'I am not a toy for you to play with!' (136). The link becomes increasingly stronger as Pechorin engages in a Hamletian contemplation on life before a duel. Adopting a radically pessimistic and almost nihilistic stance, he claims: 'I have an inborn urge to *contradict*; my whole life has been *a mere chain* of sad and futile *oppositions to the dictates of either heart or reason*' (90, my emphasis). His awareness of the 'mere chain' of oppositions evokes memories of Hamlet's series of oppositions epitomized in his trivialization of language itself, designified in an empty series of 'Words, words, words' (*Hamlet*, 2.2.189). Both the gist of his argument and its formulation closely resemble Stavrogin's insight that 'One can argue endlessly about everything' (*Demons*, 2006: 676). Pechorin embodies the same kind of awareness that everything is subject to endless debate, lacking stable meaning or definite truth. Addressing his sole friend (a character akin to Horatio), he remarks: '*we know in advance that everything can be argued about endlessly*, and hence do not argue [. . .] *Sad things strike us as funny, funny things as sad*, and generally speaking if you want to know, we are rather *indifferent* to everything except ourselves' (*A Hero of Our Time*, 1951: 93, my emphasis). Their radical scepticism brings Pechorin and Stavrogin to 'redoubled hunger and despair' (145–6), which leads them to futile and paralytic torpor, leaving no possibility for overcoming nihilism. Pechorin describes his generation as follows:

> Whereas we, their wretched descendants; who roam the earth without convictions or pride, without joys or fear other than *the nameless dread that constricts the heart at the thought of the inevitable end*, we are no longer capable of great sacrifices either for the good of mankind or even for our personal happiness since we *know that happiness is impossible*; and we pass *indifferently from one doubt to* another just as our forebears floundered from *one delusion to another, without the hopes* they had and without even that *vague but potent sense of joy* the soul derives from any struggle with man or destiny. [. . .] hence it [life] has become as *boring and repulsive to me as a travesty of a long familiar book* [. . .] having made it a rule never to reject anything categorically and never to believe in anything blindly, I *cast metaphysics aside* and began to watch the ground under my feet. [. . .] *I prefer to doubt everything.* (173, my emphasis)

As explicitly articulated in *Demons*, Stavrogin embodies the subsequent phase of the development of Russian Hamletism, representing the next generation wherein indifference, hopelessness, boredom, disgust and scepticism are radicalized.

> [Stavrogin] would shoot his adversary in a duel, and go against a bear if need be, and fight off a robber in the forest – all as successfully and fearlessly as L–n, yet without any sense of enjoyment, but solely out of unpleasant necessity, listlessly, lazily, even with boredom. Anger, of course, constituted a progress over L–n, even over *Lermontov*. There was perhaps more anger in Nikolai Vsevolodovich than in those two together, but this anger was *cold, calm,* and, if one may put it so, *reasonable*, and therefore the most repulsive and terrible that can be. (*Demons*, 2006: 204–5, my emphasis)

Not only is Stavrogin explicitly related to Lermontov, but elsewhere in the novel he is also compared to Don Juan's characteristics of Pechorin. Lermontov crops up again when his interpretation of Hamlet is appropriated from Pechorin. I allude to the enigmatic nature of the character that defies interpretation and the logic of conspiracy surrounding him. Thus, Pechorin can serve as an intertextual expansion of Stavrogin's character, a more extensive explanation of his psychological motivation given in stark lines in *Demons*, and as an interdiscursive link to the social and cultural concept of superfluous men in Russia. Dostoevsky incorporates pervasive contradiction as a key aspect of Lermontov's Russian Hamletism – a certain scepticism wherein opposites converge, causing the hero's indifference and boredom, as well as an awareness that happiness is unattainable. And while Lermontov's Pechorin bears traces of the Romantic demonism inscribed in Russian Byronism, later Russian Hamletism will take on sceptic and nihilistic overtones thanks to Turgenev's own version of demonism.

Ivan Turgenev (1818–83), one of the greatest novelists of the period, played a pivotal role in shaping Russian Hamletism and was a major influence on Dostoevsky through his description of a Hamlet type in his famous essay 'Hamlet and Don Quixote' (1860) and his Hamletian characters in *Diary of a Superfluous Men* (1850), 'Hamlet in the Schigrovsky District' (1852) and *Rudin* (1857), among others. Bazarov from *Fathers and Sons* (1862) belongs to this group while also being the first portrait of a proto-nihilist in Russian literature. Turgenev is hence the first to intersect the Hamlet-figure with arguments of nihilism. By the time Turgenev wrote 'Hamlet and Don Quixote', Hamlet had already become firmly established as one of the central foreign cultural figures in Russia. But Turgenev's focus is on Hamlet type not only as the representative of an entire generation but also as an eternal model. Hamlet is characterized by 'analysis, scrutiny, egotism and consequently disbelief' (Turgenev, 1965: 95). He is 'a *skeptic*, yet always he is in *a stir about himself*; [. . .] Doubting everything, Hamlet pitilessly includes *his own self in those doubts*; he is too thoughtful, too fair-minded to be contented with what he finds within himself' (1965, my emphasis). Because of the intensity of his self-consciousness, Turgenev underscores that Hamlet is aware of his own weakness and the limitations of his power. Paradoxically, Turgenev interprets his self-consciousness as 'a force; emanating from it is the *irony* that is precisely the antithesis of Don Quixote's enthusiasm' (1965, my emphasis). The list of paradoxes continues:

> Hamlet inveighs against himself readily, magnifies his own short comings, *spies upon himself*, is mindful of his minutest defects, despises himself and at the same time, apparently, he thrives on this disdain. He distrusts himself and yet is deeply solicitous about himself; does not know what he is after, nor why he lives at all, and still firmly adheres to life. (95–6, my emphasis)

This analysis of the psychology of Hamletism is important because it highlights the split that is happening in Hamlet, and, by extension, in the Hamletian subject, caused by consciousness. Self-awareness does not produce agency but undermines it. However, what is most interesting here is Turgenev's analysis of Hamlet's pursuit of truth and negation of God. Being a radical sceptic, Turgenev's Hamlet questions the very notion of truth – a motive that will undergo drastic expansion in Stavrogin, Raskolnikov and Ivan Karamazov, among other Dostoevskian characters. As Turgenev writes, 'I presume even that if truth incarnate were to arise before Hamlet, he would remain skeptical of its authenticity. Who knows but that he would challenge it, saying perhaps that there is no truth, just as there are no giants?' (97). This viewpoint, paradoxically, does not exclude the fight and struggle in the name of truth and for truth. Turgenev explains that Hamlet embodies 'the creed of negation' that he shares with Mephistopheles, yet being his counterpart. In Turgenev's view, it means that Hamlet's negation is not evil, but rather 'aimed against evil' (1965) and that

> Hamlet's *spirit of negation is skeptical of the good*, but it is indubitably certain of the existence of evil, and militates against it constantly. The good he mistrusts, somehow or other; he has misgivings about the genuineness of the truth it contains; and when he assails *the good it is because he surmises it to be camouflage, under whose guise evil and sham his old enemies are concealed.* (1965, my emphasis)

Therefore, despite being sceptical about the attainability of truth, Turgenev's Hamlet 'becomes one of the chief vindicators of a truth which he himself does not fully accept', which gives him a powerful position. Lastly, he sheds light on the paradoxical connection between the negative, demonic force of destruction, and its entanglement in creation, deconstructing scepticism as de-camouflaging good and revealing the intrinsic interconnection between good and evil. According to Turgenev, 'in *the spirit of negation* there is, just as there is in fire, *a destructive force*; and how can one confine this force within given limits, or say where it should halt, *when what it destroys, is so often inextricable from what one would preserve?*' (101–2, my emphasis). He elucidates the amalgam of Hamletian and Faustian motifs, and sees Hamlet in light of a human parallel to Goethean Mephistopheles. This last aspect will prove to be the most significant philosophical consequence of Dostoevsky's reimagining of the figure of Hamlet: more precisely, the fusion of Hamlet, as the representative of a whole generation with nihilism and the demonic. Further on, in Turgenev's *Fathers and Sons*,[5] the nihilist is described as 'a person who doesn't bow down before authorities, doesn't accept even one principle of faith, no matter how much respect surrounds that principle' (Turgenev, 1996: 18). At this stage, I suggest that Dostoevsky's later understanding of nihilism with a Hamletian provenance may be inherited from or inspired by Turgenev's merging of positive Hamletian features, such as striving for truth, and nihilistic ideological positions. In this respect, Peter Holland points to an important inversion of arguments in so far as the so-called 'determinism of fate' allowed Turgenev to provide an excuse for the pro-Hamlet faction (1999: 327). More precisely, Turgenev 'denies *the determinism of tragedy*, seeing in its construction of a necessity only *a means of avoiding social responsibility*. Hamlet, far from being accurate in his understanding of the world as fatalist, is seen as providing himself with *an alibi for his own failure*' (1999, my emphasis). This insight serves as an apt overture for the ethical and social criticism of Russian Hamletism by authors that had an anti-Hamletian stance.

The already-mentioned critic Visarion Belinsky (1811–48) emerged as another very influential interpreter of *Hamlet*, who expanded the concept of Russian Hamletism in a way that held particular importance for Dostoevsky. Initially captivated by Shakespeare's hero and Mochalov's performance, in 1838 Belinsky openly identified *Hamlet* with the national situation and used it as a subversive means of metaphorical criticism of the state of affairs by claiming: 'It [Hamlet] is great and deep: it is human life, it is man, it is you, it is me, it is everyone of us' (ii, 254, cited in Kizima, 2021: 185). In addition to Belinsky's view of Mochalov's acclaimed performance, which garnered widespread success across Russia in 1838, he observed that the actor 'brought additional meaning to the text and seems to have been a factor in the initial emphasis, in Russian Hamletism, on a deep-seated melancholy, an overpowering sorrow, and a suffering that Russians found especially kindred and moving' (Rowe, 1976: 45). However, as the principles of Realistic poetics came to the fore, and concrete social action became needed, his analysis of Hamlet as the epitome of Russian intelligentsia had to align with social, political and ethical imperatives. Notably, in glorifying civic responsibility and social duty, 'Belinskii himself subsequently revised his analysis and lambasted the figure of Hamlet as an example of a man of many words but no action' (Grob, 2016: 203). After Belinsky, Nikolay Chernyshevsky (1828–89) offered a direct critique of socially unacceptable Hamletian traits within the Russian intelligentsia, viewing Hamletism as associated with superfluous men. For Chernyshevsky, the problem lay in the social organization that generated a class of people lacking purpose and exploiting others. Joseph Frank in *The Stir of Liberation* (1986) clearly states that Dostoevsky also 'add[ed] his own voice to the chorus of condemnation: the present social situation, he would then declare, no longer holds any place for the Hamlets of Russian culture. It was time, he told them firmly, to overcome their self-preoccupied egoism and devote themselves to the service of the people' (12).[6] Thus, Russian Hamletism was imbued with criticism of social duty, responsibility and practical utility. However, the most scathing criticism of Shakespeare and Hamlet in nineteenth-century Russia undoubtedly came from Tolstoy's essay *On Shakespeare and On Drama* (1906).

> 'What coarse, immoral, mean, and senseless work Hamlet is. [. . .]
> [Shakespeare] was so occupied with effects that he didn't take the trouble
> to give the main character any character.' The extension of the search for
> the definition of the character of Hamlet becomes, in Tolstoy's demolition
> of the play, a *characterlessness* onto which an unthinking intelligentsia
> had projected its approval. (Holland, 1999: 333, my emphasis)

The concept of characterlessness, as conceived by Tolstoy and commented on by Holland, interestingly reflects the widespread tendency at the time to interpret the intelligentsia's needs, desires and condition through the figure of Hamlet. In the development of Russian Hamletism, the habit of relying on fictional projections and appropriations of this kind could be adjusted to circumstances and even opposite aims. In other words, Russian Hamletism endured completely contradictory projections: from being a hero capable of representing anyone to becoming a completely characterless figure. Exactly because Hamlet was entirely extrapolated from the play, he could be freely appropriated as an empty signifier, without close or even relevant connection to Shakespeare's *Hamlet*. Hamlet could literally stand for anything, and so it was appropriated to designate a Russian national type. Alexander Herzen (1812–70), one of the most influential thinkers of nineteenth-century Russia, Westernizer and a political exile, wrote in a private correspondence:

> Tessie says that I have the nature of a Hamlet and that this is very Slavic.
> Truly, this is an extraordinary vacillation, inability to act from the force
> of thoughts and thoughts carried away by a desire for action prior to
> their termination. *Zögern, sich aufreissen*, ironic laughter, vexation
> with everything, most of all with oneself, a feeling of one's weakness,
> incompleteness, mental diffusion and retour. (Cited in Rowe, 1976: 60)

In this example we witness a complete identification between Hamletian and Slavic/Russian traits, serving as a proof of the widely held notion that Russian Hamletism embodied a distinctly national trait. Herzen's insight into the nature of Hamletian/Russian indecisiveness is particularly interesting. The intensity of thoughts and the desire to act are so strong that they consume themselves before reaching the point of actualization, remaining confined to the realm of thought and potentiality. Alongside these self-conscious reflections, there is a robust self-irony, a paradoxical blend of arrogance (stemming from self-awareness allowing for self-irony) and inferiority (arising from the inability to turn potentiality into action and to break free from this cycle of inability). Apollon Grigoryev (1822–64), a close friend and colleague of Dostoevsky's, also played a big role in defining Russian Hamlets. Dostoevsky regarded him as the epitome of the quintessential Russian character and as a 'real' Hamlet: 'As for Grigoryev, he was remembered as an archetypical "Russian Hamlet", *inwardly torn by the dissonances of Russian life and culture* but nonetheless "a man directly – and even in many ways unconsciously – *rooted in the soil,* clinging to the pith of his country (20: 135–6)"' (Dostoevsky cited in Frank, 1986: 354, my emphasis). As Frank notices, for Dostoevsky, 'Grigoryev was one of those "broad" Russian natures [. . .] who combined the most refined and exalted artistic and spiritual aspirations with sordid and disorderly lives [. . .] Such lives were felt by Dostoevsky to be typically "Russian"' (43). Frank explains why Grigoryev was a perfect example of the Hamletism ingrained in Russian nature:

> But, again like Dostoevsky, he was too much a product of Romanticism and too much a modern to accept either his Christian faith or Orthodoxy without a struggle. 'From wherever I begin', he [Grigoryev] acknowledges, 'I always arrive at the same single point: at this deep and sorrowful need to believe in the ideal and the *Jenseits* [the supernatural].' (47)

## Dostoevsky's Russian Hamletism

Dostoevsky's presentation of Apollon Grigoryev as the truly Russian Hamlet suggests the extent to which his take on Russian Hamletism

centres on the paradoxical situation of Russian intelligentsia, educated
in the Western manner, yet struggling to harmonize it with genuine faith
in Jesus Christ as professed by Orthodox Christianity that was of such
importance to him.[7] As Pavel Annenkov claimed, Shakespeare enabled
a whole generation to perceive themselves as capable of understanding
history and the human condition 'even when this same generation,
in real life, had no social role and no voice even in the most trivial
matters of civic life' (Cited in Lantz, 2004: 392). It is no surprise that
the Shakespearean genius was utilized by a marginalized and voiceless
generation to articulate their identity and sense of unity. However, he aptly
notes the split between intellectual engagement and concrete political or
ethical action emerging concurrently with a mode of self-identification
through Shakespeare. My use of the word identification here refers to
'the completion of the subject's passage into the symbolic order' (Evans,
1996: 83) which, according to Lacan, entails an engagement with the
signifier. In this perspective, the ego formation occurs through a series
of such 'assumptions' of appropriations of an external image, which, in
the case of Russian Hamletism, coincides with the image of Hamlet as
the signifier of a whole ideological system belonging to a large group
of intellectuals in their relation with the Western world. Of course, the
moment of identification is part of fabrication threatening to replace
the ego with its own image or representation, so that the self identifies
itself as a fictional representation in a constant process of substitution.
Hamletism, as a cultural phenomenon based on processes of reception
mediated by cultural and political drives, conveys a proto-narrative of
the process itself of a cultural construct and, with it, of the processes
of identification as defined above of a whole intellectual generation.
It reflects their attempt to find a place in a certain historical moment
as well as to make sense of the world and history. It has the function
of mapping the Real, in Lacanian terms, and, at the same time, to
achieve self-identification. Russian Hamletism thus became part of the
'transindividual unconsciousness' of the generation that was brought
up from 1830 to 1860 (Chiesa, 2007: 43); it was a 'symbolic signifying
structure' (44) that also entered Dostoevsky's own unconscious.

As will be seen, Dostoevsky explicitly linked European nihilism, ontological and epistemological uncertainties, national rootlessness, apathy, inertia, cynicism and hyperconsciousness with superfluous men and, in turn, with figures of Russian Hamlets. We can discern one of the central dichotomies in Dostoevsky's conceptions of Russian Hamlets: the distinction between *to be* and *to do*. According to this viewpoint, the Hamletian subject is not defined solely by its action, or at least, not exclusively so; neither is he free to choose freely what to do and what to be. In his novels, Hamlet as a literary figure is employed to address the pivotal problems in the Russian culture of the second half of the nineteenth century: the debate over the influence of Western culture encompassing various understandings of selfhood, nationhood, culture, literature and, consequently, the meaning and value of life. His opinions on Russia, Western Europe, 'and the relationship of nationality to personality are interrelated and for a key part of the ideological axis on which *The Devils* turns' (Leatherbarrow, 1999: 14) – which is another reason why I argue it to be the most important narrative where Dostoevsky tackled Russian Hamletism. More precisely, the novel's aim in criticizing Western liberalism and socialism is expressed in 'Dostoevsky's analysis of the moral and spiritual failings of the educated class which he believes have brought the country to this [the harsh reality of post-reformed Russia] critical condition' (Offord, 1999: 65). The opposing ideological and political factions in the 1860s, Westernized socialists consisting of radical young nihilists were criticized for their revolutionary, militant actions (student protests, spreading agitation material and setting fires in St. Petersburg) by the conservative Slavophiles that were mainly appreciative of the ancient régime. Thus, implicitly, Dostoevsky was criticizing the prevailing aspects of Russian Hamletism as one of the negative factors of the spiritual decay and the lost contact with the Russian people incited by the older generation of Western liberals. Dostoevsky understood Russian 'nihilists' 'not merely as a historical phenomenon but as a broader moral and psychological condition' (Lantz, 2004: 282), while nihilism represented a belief in nothing, 'one pole in the dramatic ideological struggles that lie at the heart of Dostoevsky's major novels' (281). Dostoevsky's multifaceted approach to theodicy, immoralism and atheism was refracted through his engagement with *Hamlet*. However, his ideas are far from just a straightforward and one-sided criticism of Western nihilism in Russian Hamletism. Rather, Stavrogin 'was designed in part to suggest what Dostoevsky saw as the *tragedy* of the Europeanized Russian, whose loss of nationality translates into loss of all purpose and meaning in his life' (Leatherbarrow, 1999: 14, my emphasis). As such, he is the epitome of Russian Hamletism, in its most radical and tragical form. Dostoevsky infused many opposing and contradictory elements of different interpretations of Russian Hamletism, and more than any other author aforementioned, fictionalized the Hamletian dilemma, rather than referring to Shakespeare's play or simply designating these problems to Russian Hamletism. The main ideological parallelism between Hamlet, Russian Hamletism and *Demons* is thus the question of what should be done by the following generation – how to respond to the heritage that was left for them. Alternatively, in Hamletian terms, how to answer the imperative of the dead father's Ghost and what (national, ethical, political or ideological) responsibility to take on their shoulders. As noted before, this question was pertinent to a historical moment pervaded by disillusionment with ideas of progress, rationalism and individualism distinguishing the Enlightenment.

Levin concludes that Dostoevsky's Hamlets are martyrs to the chaos of life, but they are also a moral egoists who torture and torment others, devoid of ideals, spreading decay, spiritual, material corruption, destruction and death (1988: 190, my translation). This is so far the most negative direct characterization of Dostoevsky's Hamlets. And while it is certainly very relevant, it is also a simplification with a view to setting it against other Shakespearean characters such as Othello (Dostoevsky's most loved character who provided a model for Dmitry Karamazov in *The Brothers Karamazov*)[8] or other Russian Hamlets. From all the aforementioned writers, Dostoevsky inherits a Hamlet-figure that, as already recalled, had been naturalized and transformed into a fictional and cultural mask for a group of intellectuals who justified their passivity on the prestige of Shakespearean grounds. With them, and with the arguments that supported their political and ideological posture, he was to polemicize especially in *Demons*. The type of the superfluous man alongside all that had been incorporated into the ideological constellation of what Russian Hamletism had become by the late nineteenth century, from scepticism, to nihilism, from despair to self-destruction, was part of the dialogical space he was to engage with narratively. Dostoevsky's plan was to deal with all these issues, including the demonic by crafting Hamletian characterless heroes in the way Tolstoy referred to *Hamlet*. Famously, Dostoevsky was a master in taking over and rearticulating ideas of others. However, I suggest that his greatest contribution in this case lies in expanding three mutually related ideological contexts, and making the debate more complex, while offering solutions to the contemporary disillusionment with the Enlightenment. First, he refers to Orthodox spirituality as a system of mystical beliefs rather than as a canonical faith. Second, he compares his Hamletian figures in relation to the Russian people (*narod*) to whom he acknowledges having a profound sense of morality and capacity for love and self-sacrifice, while, at the same time, being capable of extremely self-destructive transgressions, caught by whirlwinds of irrationalism and a deeply seated inclination for suffering. Lastly, his rather paradoxical ideas on nationality and universality are the backdrop against which he treated Russian Hamlets, offering an interesting perspective on the ethics of appropriation. The following quote from the preparatory materials for *Demons* constitutes, in my view, the crucial dilemma of Dostoevsky's version of Russian Hamletism:

> It emerges, consequently, that the whole matter lies in the pressing question: *can one believe, being civilised,* i.e. *a European,* i.e. *believe absolutely in the divinity of the Son of God, Jesus Christ*? (for all faith consists only of this) [. . .] And so, here lies the enigma. (Dostoevsky cited in Mochulsky, 1973: 430, my emphasis)

While this question is referred to Stavrogin, it resonates as pivotal for all Hamletian heroes in Dostoevsky's work, steaming from his own existential and spiritual ordeals. One might even posit it as the fundamental drama underpinning Dostoevsky's oeuvre, given his famous confession: 'that I am a child of this age, a child of unfaith and skepticism, and probably (indeed I know it) shall remain so to the end of my life. How dreadfully has it tormented me (and torments me even now) – this longing for faith, which is all the stronger for the proofs I have against it' (1914: 70–1). Its tacit subtext is a struggle between belief and disbelief and the form it takes is that of an experimental exploration of the potential of the nineteenth-century novel as a non-religious narrative form to deal with spirituality, religion and the sacred.

A possible answer Dostoevsky was to offer will be given in the next chapters. As will be seen, to the constellation of Dostoevsky's versions of Russian Hamlets we may add his assumptions from one of his last pieces: 'Pushkin Speech' contains Dostoevsky's most articulated late variant of Russian Hamletism in his interpretation of Aleko from Pushkin's *Gypsies* (1824) and Onegin from *Eugene Onegin* (1825). He sees Aleko as 'that unhappy wanderer in his native land, that historical, suffering Russian who appeared with such historical inevitability in our educated society after it had broken away from the People' (*Pushkin Speech* as cited in Bowers, Doak, Holland, 2018: 466). Dostoevsky adds:

These homeless Russian wanderers continue their wandering even now and, it seems, are unlikely to disappear for a long time yet. And if in our day they no longer frequent the camps of the gypsies to look for universal ideals in their wild and distinctive way of life and to seek in the bosom of nature some respite from our confused and ridiculous Russian life – the life of educated society – then, still, they go running off to *socialism*, which did not yet exist in Aleko's time; they take their new faith to a different field and work it zealously, believing, as did Aleko, that through their bizzare labors they will achieve their goals and find happiness not only for themselves but for the whole world. For what the Russian wanderer needs is the *happiness of the whole world* in order to find his own peace of mind: he will not setle for less – so long as matters are *confined to theory*, of course. (2018, my emphasis)

Likewise, Pushkin's Onegin mixes characteristics of European demonic Romanticism and Russian Hamletism with the features of Russian people. As Alexandra Smith observes, in 'Pushkin Speech' 'Onegin displays traits of slavish admiration for Western values and a Eurocentric outlook' (2013: 136). I concur with Smith that Dostoevsky's interpretation of Onegin's parodic behaviour could be expanded to encompass 'the semiotic models of behaviour of Russian aristocrats aspiring to imitate ancient notions of nobility and honour' (2013). It is exactly this 'mechanical reproduction of European codes of behaviour' that alienated Dostoevsky's Onegin from respecting his native land (2013). However, the solution for the so-called 'accursed question' about universal happiness Dostoevsky recognized for Onegin was to denounce his individuality – the central notion of Western humanism. Dostoevsky somewhat categorically asserts quoting *Gypsies*: 'in accordance with the People's faith and truth: "Humble thyself, O haughty man; first curb thy pride. Humble thyself, O idle man; first labor on thy native soil". That is the solution in accord with the People's truth and the People's wisdom' (*Pushkin Speech* as cited in Bowers, Doak, Holland, 2018: 468). However, this does not clarify in which way rejecting individualism may bring about collective happiness. In order to unravel this idea, Dostoevsky needs to explain the moral superiority of the Russian people as he sees it in Pushkin's Tatiana.[9] Dostoevsky's Onegin, 'a *man of abstractions*, he is a restless dreamer, and has been so all his life' (470); he is a profound portrayal of Russian Hamlets. Dostoevsky recognized the astute diagnosis of Russian Hamletism in Tatiana's painful question: '*Is he a parody, perchance?*' (cited on 11, my emphasis), suggesting that, actually, '*she has solved the riddle*' (471, my emphasis) of his character. Tatiana's demystification of Onegin, the Byronic hero, as a parodic representation of individuality links Hamletism with nihilism, with the foundational perspective that everything is an illusion and nothing is real. Dostoevsky adeptly concludes:

> She knows very well that in essence *he loves only his new fantasy and not her*, the Tat'iana who is as humble as before! She knows that *he*

> *takes her for something other than what she is*, that it is not even her
> he loves, that, perhaps, he does not love anyone and is incapable of
> loving anyone, despite the fact that he suffers such torment! *He loves
> his fantasy; indeed, he himself is a fantasy.* (473, my emphasis)

Tatiana perceives Onegin's newly expressed love for her not merely
as an enchantment with her elevated social status but rather as a
fundamental characteristic of his personality. Lacking inner stability of
feelings and plagued by ennui, he is attracted to vivid impressions of his
imagination, disregarding moral dimensions of other individuals. She
also comprehends that without such an inner moral foundation and
an intersubjective relationship based on respect for others, his identity
disintegrates into mere fantasy. Christianity serves as the backdrop
for this perspective, where the devil is indirectly evoked as the most
renowned deceiver and master of illusion and where truthfulness of
the soul is upheld as the highest value. Mochulsky's comments aptly
expand this aspect: 'In consciousness there occurs *a substitution of the
aesthetic plane for the ethical plane*. Degradation is a torture, but a "too
clear awareness" of degradation can afford pleasures. Looking into a
mirror, it is possible to forget about *what* is reflected and to lose oneself
in *how* it is reflected' (1973: 249, my emphasis). A possible conclusion
is that Dostoevsky's Russian Hamlets are incapable of reaching ethical
integrity or religious belief and only inhabit the aesthetic dimension.
Here Dostoevsky's view of Russian Hamletism closely aligns with
Kierkegaard's aesthetic stage, which operates solely on the level of
the potential rather than the actuality of being, because the actuality
necessitates a choice or stance that would define one's being in ways
that are alien to the aesthetic stage.

> And so you need only to disgrace, dishonor and torment him and
> build your edifice on the tears of this dishonored old man! Will you
> consent on those terms to be the architect of such an edifice? *That is
> the question* [. . .] Tell me, could Tat'iana, with her noble soul and her
> heart that had suffered so much, have settled the matter in any other
> way? (*Pushkin Speech* as cited in Bowers, Doak, Holland, 2018: 472)

In explaining why Pushkin's Tatiana is the ultimate symbol of Russian people, its wisdom and moral superiority, Dostoevsky defends her choice not to run away with Onegin, reformulating the ultimate Hamletian question *to be or not to be* into *let be*:

> this is how a pure Russian soul settles it: '*Let it be* that I alone have no happiness; *let* my unhappiness be immeasurably greater than the unhappiness of this old man; finally, *let no one*, not even this old man, ever learn of my sacrifice and appreciate it; but *I do not want to be happy after having destroyed another!*'
> This is the tragedy: it unfolds, and the line cannot be crossed; it is already too late, and so Tat'iana sends Onegin away. (2018, my emphasis)

For Dostoevsky, the Hamletian riddle was resolved on both ethical and religious planes by Tatiana. He interprets her behaviour as embodying an ideal that opposes Russian Hamletism, incorporating a feminine principle rooted in people's wisdom and morality, underpinned by Russian Orthodoxy. Russian Eastern Christianity values qualities such as self-sacrifice, self-effacement and an unconditional reverence for the sanctity of all human life. At the conclusion of this chapter, the phrase 'Let be' emerges from Dostoevsky's version of Tatiana's final response to a character embodying all the negative traits of Russian Hamletism, such as egocentrism, individualism, selfishness, immorality and inauthenticity. This serves as a fitting introduction to the next chapter, where I will explore the implication of the transition from 'to be or not to be' to 'let be' in Dostoevsky's creation of Hamletian heroes.

## Notes

1   Since Peter the Great's efforts to Europeanize Russia in the eighteenth century, Russian literature and culture have been framed in comparison to Western tradition. Grob underscored that 'the question of Russia's relationship to European culture – generally hypostatized as a single

entity – has been one of the cornerstones of cultural self-definition'
(2016: 192), while Tolz contended that '"the West" (zapad) had become
arguably the most important ingredient of modern Russian identity'
(2010: 197). However, we must bear in mind that the delineations between
East and West, Europe and Russia, were and are not fixed concepts
but rather 'cultural and political constructs "talked and written into
existence"' (2010). These constructs were often 'evoked in "totalising"
and "essentialising" ways, particularly when they were used to designate
the "Other"' (2010). Yet, as Tolz emphasizes, 'their heterogeneity could
also be acknowledged, since one of their components could be viewed
positively and another negatively' (2010). On the other hand, Western
Europe also held a racist and discriminatory backward perception of
Russia. This bias stemmed from an Eurocentric worldview, which upheld
the 'belief in the superiority of "European civilisation" as manifested in
its cultural achievements and scientific and technological progress' (198).
Consequently, it is unsurprising that in challenging this Eurocentric
standpoint, 'Russian thinkers often applied the techniques of othering
through emphasising the difference between Russia and "the West"
(Western Europe) and attacking various features of "the West"' (2010).

2   By today's standards, Polevoy's reworking of Shakespeare's original would
be considered a rewriting or an adaptation. However, it is still referred
to as a translation by critics such as Levin (1993, 1995, 1998) or Holland
(1999). Levin comments on Polevoy's text: 'Judging from his translation
principles and practice, he belonged to that trend of romantic translation
whose adherents strove for self-expression and the realization of a
subjective ideal conception of the original. [. . .] Faithful reproduction
of the original did not rank very high in Polevoy's order of priorities. He
cut *Hamlet* by a quarter and shortened most of the monologues. For the
sake of easy comprehension he simplified complex imagery, eliminated
references to mythology, and omitted any detail he thought might need
explanation. The translator aimed at producing a natural sounding
colloquial text, which lent itself to performance on the Russian stage and
allowed the actors to portray living people whose ways and motives would
be clear to audience' (1993: 154).

3   Similarly to the way of functioning of Russian Hamletism, the
phenomenon of Russian Byronism developed from a fascination with

the life and work of the English Romantic poet. He became a 'fashionable hero' (Simmons, 1964: 272), adored by the generation of Russian Romantic poets. Pushkin's appropriation of his work and personal characteristics initiated a widespread phenomenon of Russian Byronism.

4    For a detailed analysis of the connection between *Hamlet* and superfluous man, see Akhter, Abdullah, Muhammad, 'Hamlet as a Superfluous Hero' (2015).

5    "'Nihilist,'" said Nikolai Petrovich. "That's from the Latin nihil, nothing, as far as I can tell; therefore, the word signifies a person who . . . acknowledges nothing?"

"Say, rather, who respects nothing", Pavel Petrovich put in, and once again set about spreading his butter.

"Who approaches everything from a critical point of view", observed Arkady.

"Isn't it all the same thing?" asked Pavel Petrovich.

"No, it isn't all the same thing. A nihilist is a person who doesn't bow down before authorities, doesn't accept even one principle on faith, no matter how much respect surrounds that principle.'" (Turgenev, 1996: 18)

6    Frank also reveals that 'Dostoevsky's notebooks for 1861-1862, [. . .] include some entries indicating that he planned to continue sparring with *The Contemporary* on the same issue. Under the title of *Utility and Morality*, he sketched a series of essays elaborating on his objections to the Utilitarian approach to art: "Shakespeare. His uselessness. Shakespeare was a backward person . . . (the opinions of *The Contemporary*)" (PSS, 20: 152). Chernyshevsky had indeed questioned whether Shakespeare had really done anything to improve the life of the society of his time; and his crushing answer had been: "As a poet, he did not give this any thought." Even though these projected essays were never written, Dostoevsky did not forget this particular outrage against the English dramatist he revered. Later, he would place an impassioned defense of Shakespeare in the mouth of his marvelous Stepan Trofimovich Verkhovensky – the embodiment of the gentry-liberal ideals of the 1840s – when he replies in *The Devils* to the jeering, yelling mob shouting the slogans of the 1860s derived from such remarks as Chernyshevsky's' (1986: 94).

7    It is well known that Dostoevsky approached the question of belief in Christ with utter seriousness. His famous confession of faith to Madame

Fonvizina in a letter dated March 1854 (*Letters of Fyodor Mikhailovich Dostoevsky to His Family and Friends*, 1914: 69–73) is very illustrative in this matter. In this letter he wrote about his deep veneration and love of Christ, whom he held as the ultimate perfection, and his struggle with doubt.

8    The model of analysing the figure of Hamlet in Dostoevsky's work in this book could be applied to *Othello*. Both *The Idiot* and *The Brothers Karamazov* have many links to different characters, themes, the plot and an overall inclination of Dostoevsky to create characters enchanted by an ideal – the main characteristic of Othello in his view.

9    Tatiana is the main heroine of *Eugene Onegin*, a young romantic and idealistic girl coming from rural aristocracy that becomes dazzled with and falls in love with Onegin. Once she confides her love, Onegin rejects her under the pretext that he is unsuitable for marriage. Years later, once Tatiana becomes one of the leading beauties of St. Petersburg's high society, Onegin tries to win her back despite her being married. She refused him.

# 2

# Dostoevsky's 'Hamlet'

I have a new plan: to go mad. That's the way: for people to lose their heads, and then be cured and brought back to reason!

(Dostoevsky, 1914: 5)

U menya est' prozhekt: sdelat'sya sumasshedshim. Pust' lyudi besyatsya, pust' lechat, pust' delayut umnym.

(PSS, 28: 51)

This chapter is devoted to identifying and resurfacing the Hamletian proto-narrative in Dostoevsky's novels in the form of the Hamlet-ideologeme. Said in abstract terms, Dostoevsky's Hamlet-ideologeme represents the core ideology behind his reading of *Hamlet* and his intervention to the dominant nineteenth-century version of Russian Hamletism. Ideologeme is a way to represent a particular ideology that, in this case, contains a Hamletian 'attitude to reality' and its construction on the 'axiological level' (Lylo, 2017: 19). Mikhail Bakhtin understood the ideologeme in literature as intuitive anticipations of philosophical and ethical ideas (1978: 17), and as such, Hamlet-ideologeme can be viewed as the core of Dostoevsky's philosophical and ethical approach to Hamlet/*Hamlet* and Russian Hamletism. Julia Kristeva offered an advanced understanding, arguing that 'a passage from the *symbol* to the *sign*' happened during Renaissance and that 'the novel is a narrative structure revealing the ideologeme of the sign' (1986: 63). Kristeva's assumption will prove pertinent because the narrative structure of Dostoevsky's novels may expose Hamlet as a sign rather than a symbolical understanding of the hero. Fredric Jameson popularized the term and expanded its use understanding it as 'the emblem of a "pseudo-idea", which is a "conceptual or belief system, an abstract value, an opinion or prejudice", that takes its place in proto-narrative, "a kind of ultimate class fantasy about the 'collective characters' which are the classes in opposition'" (cited in Marling, 1994: 282). Jameson's definition is particularly fitting to explore the figure of Hamlet as a collective's character fantasy of a specific class of intellectuals revealing the power dynamics in nineteenth-century Russia that was reflected in Dostoevsky's writings. Lately, Malysheva aptly adds to the discussion by labelling ideologeme as 'a certain multi-level concept, in the structure of which (in the nucleus or the periphery) there are ideologically marked conceptual features that embody collective, and often stereotypical or mythological intepretation of power, state, society, political and ideological institutions that exist in the minds of native speakers' (2019: 35). Her definition focuses our attention on how issues of power and state, are dealt with by Dostoevsky through this manifold concept.

My aim is to use the concept of ideologeme to resurface the Hamletian proto-narrative in Dostoevsky's novels. The overall methodological approach belongs to the critical practice of symptomatic reading, which considers texts not primarily per se but as symptoms of something else that is yet to be revealed, that is, Dostoevsky's Hamlet-ideologeme in this case. More precisely, symptomatic reading is an interpretative practice based on a premise that 'what a text means lies in what it does not say, which can then be used to rewrite the text in terms of a master code. By disclosing the absent cause that structures the text's inclusions and exclusions, the critic restores to the surface the deep history that the text represses' (cited in Best and Marcus, 2009: 3). I will explore the hypothesis that the Hamlet-ideologeme can be treated as the master code of Dostoevsky's novels or the absent cause that structures them, restoring to the surface the repressed history of Dostoevsky's interplay with Hamlet/*Hamlet*, beyond overt references to Shakespeare's *Hamlet* or direct engagement with Russian Hamletism.

In order to identify the Hamlet-ideologeme of help will be to first discover the already mentioned Hamlet-isotopy network. I will identify a recurrence of certain themes, motifs or lexical items that imply a cohesion between Dostoevsky's 1838 letter and his other novels following the principles of Dostoevsky's prose. Radosvet Kolarov has designed a critical model and convincingly suggested that the manifold themes and motifs recurring in Dostoevsky's novels in general appear clearly interconnected only once they are set within the 'context of the common, though "dissipated", so to speak, signification. [. . .] And it is only when this network is reconstructed, that is, when all its nodes are discovered, that the connection between the motifs in the two works, can be made clear' (2013: 31). He called this dynamic interpretative model *hermeneutic autotextuality* because it shows how two works may help interpretatively mirror each other.[1] I extend the use of this approach to identify and compare Hamlet-isotopy within the broader corpus of Dostoevsky's novels. Dostoevsky's dialogue with Russian Hamletism is also part of this broad autotextual system and, like other themes and motifs, consists of a dissipated network across Dostoevsky's novels without being foregrounded or obvious – it follows a pattern that needs to be decoded. The Hamlet-ideologeme, or the core of his ideological approach to *Hamlet*/Hamlet and Russian Hamletism, constitutes this pattern yet to be fully discovered.

## The letter

Dostoevsky's famous letter of the 9th of August 1838 provides the starting point in so far as it constitutes his first understanding of Shakespeare's hero, but, more importantly, it introduces a range of crucial topics for his poetics and philosophic perspectives in general that will be entirely realized in *Demons*. The letter to his brother Mikhail, where the sixteen-year-old writer, among other subjects, shares his impressions on *Hamlet*, serves as a foundational text for delineating the proto-narrative behind what will gradually emerge as an ideologeme, connected with both *Hamlet*/Hamlet in Shakespeare and Russian Hamletism (from now on Dostoevsky's Hamlet-ideologeme), and as a benchmark for establishing the Hamlet-isotopy network. The selected semantic isotopes will be compared with analogous motifs, themes and references to *Hamlet* and Russian Hamletism in various works, including the novella *The Double*, and novels such as *The Humiliated and Insulted, Notes from Underground, Crime and Punishment,* and *The Idiot, An Accidental Family, The Brothers Karamazov* and *Diary of a Writer.* The letter can be divided into the following isotopic chain:

1. Crisis – Young Dostoevsky diagnoses the disharmony of the world and disintegration of society according to Russian Hamletism as a radical existential and social crisis, expanding it to ontological, metaphysical and religious levels:

    And to think that such a state of mind is allotted to man alone – the atmosphere of his soul seems compounded of a mixture of the heavenly and the earthly. What an unnatural product, then, is he, since the law of spiritual nature is in him violated [. . .] *This earth seems to me a purgatory* for divine spirits who have been assailed by sinful thoughts. (Dostoevsky, 1914: 3, my emphasis)

2. Negativity – Dostoevsky notices not only a radical crisis but an impending decay of values that will cause melancholy, despair, scepticism and nihilism:

    I feel that our *world has become one immense Negative,* and that everything noble, beautiful, and divine, has turned itself into a *satire.* (1914, my emphasis)

3. Lost ideal – In such a state of affairs, any ideal or utopian concept is irretrievably lost:

    If in this picture there occurs an individual who neither in idea nor effect harmonizes with the whole – who is, in a word, an entirely unrelated figure – what must happen to the *picture*? It is destroyed, and can no longer endure. Yet how terrible it is to perceive only the coarse veil under which the All doth languish! (1914: 3–4, my emphasis)

4. 'To be or not to be' – Dostoevsky's suicidal rumination is an effect of being aware of the state of the world:

> To know that one single effort of the will would suffice to demolish that veil and become one with eternity – to know all this, and still live on like the last and least of creatures. [ . . .] That soul is then so utterly oppressed by woe that it fears to grasp the woe entire, lest so it lacerate itself. (1914: 4)

5. Confession – Dostoevsky's confession mimics a pose of a Russian Hamlet:

> How terrible! How petty is man! *Hamlet! Hamlet!* When I think of his moving wild speech, in which resounds the *groaning of the whole numbed universe*, there breaks from my soul not one reproach, not one sigh. (1914, my emphasis)

6. Paradox – Dostoevsky is aware of his self-criticism without being able to find a solution outside the philosophical system he relies on:

> Pascal once said: *He who protests against philosophy is himself a philosopher. A poor sort of system!* (1914, my emphasis)

7. Let be – Lastly, Dostoevsky professes his own 'antic position' as a strategy to overcome previously stated and described crisis:

> *I have a new plan: to go mad. That's the way: for people to lose their heads, and then be cured and brought back to reason!* [ . . .] It is terrible to watch a man who has the Incomprehensible within his grasp, does not know what to do with it, and sits playing with a toy called God! (1914: 5, my emphasis)[2]

Deduced from these quotations, while having in mind the above-mentioned discussion about Dostoevsky's attitude towards Russian Hamletism, the Hamlet-ideologeme in abstract terms may signify a radical crisis on the levels of language, values, being and the need for setting the subject free from the given order of things and self-contradictions. In the following part, I will reconstruct the dissipated Hamlet-isotopy network by analysing these seven isotopes as posited in the letter and trying to find motifs and themes across Dostoevsky's novels that correspond to them.

## Crisis

The time is out of joint.

(*Hamlet*, 2.1.186)

And to think that such a state of mind is allotted to man alone – the atmosphere of his soul seems compounded of a mixture of the heavenly and the earthly. What an unnatural product, then, is he, since the law of spiritual nature is in him violated . . . This earth seems to me a purgatory for divine spirits who have been assailed by sinful thoughts.

(Dostoevsky, 1914: 3)

The first excerpt of the letter explicitly alludes to *Hamlet* and Hamletian themes, the overall atmosphere and the events unleashed with the murder of King Hamlet, particularly the Ghost scene.[3] Some of the issues here tackled resonate strongly throughout Dostoevsky's major works – a radical crisis spanning epistemology, politics, ontology, and metaphysics. The 'unnatural product' Dostoevsky mentions (the man whose natural spirituality is violated) bears resemblance to the disruption of values brought about by the 'questionable shape' (*Hamlet*, 1.4.56) of the Ghost. The Ghost's tale and his place in Purgatory parallel Dostoevsky's *earth* that he sees as 'a purgatory for divine spirits who have been assailed by sinful thoughts' (Dostoevsky, 1914: 3). Hamlet's contemplation on his own immortal soul ('And for my soul – what can it do to that, / Being a thing immortal as itself?' (*Hamlet*, 1.4.66–7)) underscores a theme of importance for Dostoevsky and provides the ultimate criteria to weigh values across his literary corpus. This parallelism marks the first important aspect of the Hamlet-isotopy network as a general crisis created by the encounter with radical ontological otherness and the unknown[4] that can also be found in *The Double, The Village of Stepanichkovo and Its Inhabitants, The Humiliated and Insulted, Notes from Underground* and *Crime and Punishment*.

*The Double* (1846, 1866) is a novella about the breach of 'the other', the actual double of Mr. Golyadkin that may be understood as a representation of his own split consciousness. This central theme is accompanied by a pervasive sense of conspiracy and paranoia by Mr. Golyadkin: 'I have enemies, Krestyan Ivanovich, I have enemies; I have wicked enemies who have sworn to destroy me [. . .]' (*The Double*, 2007: 28). Mr. Golyadkin manifests a paranoid fear of incessant judgement and surveillance, feeling persecuted by imaginary enemies. As Slobodanka Vladiv-Glover has suggested, his fear of the 'other' shows Lacanian overtones in expressing 'the fear of "substitution": he feels that his "rightful" place and his rightful "claim" to his "place" is threatened by "an other" who is exactly like him and who is taking on (or away!) his (Goliadkin's) "identity". Thus he fears what Lacan has called the process of *aphanisis* – the "fading of the subject under the signifier"' (2012: 22). More importantly, 'he "feels" that he is constructed by the "gaze" of the "Other"', while 'he demonises this "Other" who gives him his "existence"' (2012). The themes of decision-making and agency come to the fore as Mr. Golyadkin torments himself masochistically due to the impossibility of asserting himself as the original 'I' in front of his double. The narrator ironically explains how he 'laid up a certain decision in the depths of his soul, and in the depths of his heart he vowed to fulfil it. In truth, he did not know very well how he would act, that is, better to say, he did not know at all; but never mind, it made no difference!' (*The Double*, 2007: 89). This theme becomes amplified with the impostor motif. As the double usurped Mr. Golyadkin's position, he mentioned Grishka Otrepyev.[5] Mr. Golyadkin laments: 'And one doesn't get ahead in our age by imposture and shamelessness, my dear sir. Imposture and shamelessness, my dear sir, do not lead to any good, but end in the noose. Grishka Otrepyev, alone got ahead by imposture, my good sir, having deceived the blind people, and that not for long' (2007). Mr. Golyadkin's journey is a quest for his own identity and, as Vladiv-Glover underlines, his dread, feeling threatened by an impending abyss, may be related to Lacan's concept of the Real:

> This is a desire for recognition as an identity, as Self. It takes the form of a phantasmic 'rivalry' with a phantasmic 'Other'. The phenomenological 'reality' of this other is never established except that *this other is a kind of 'real'*, in Lacan's sense of a wall, an insuperable obstacle, a solid unrepresentable mass, like the 'damp, murky distance' or the black water of the canal, like a solid object that is not one. It is against this 'real' – which represents *the negativity of unreason* – that *the Subject's unity is broken* into a million smithereens. (2012: 445, my emphasis)

Vladiv-Glover's articulation of *the negativity of unreason* resonates fittingly with Dostoevsky's idea expressed in the postscriptum of the letter that people should lose their minds – potentially breaking the unity of their subjectivities – in order to re-emerge with a renewed 'reason' immune to threats by the Real. Mr. Golyadkin remains paralysed in the abyssal, destructive power of the Real presented in the novella:

> His position at that moment was like the position of a man standing over a frightful precipice, when the earth breaks away under him, is rocking, shifting, sways for the last time, and falls, drawing him into the *abyss*, and meanwhile, the unfortunate man, has neither the strength nor the firmness of spirit to jump back, to take his eyes from the yawning chasm; the abyss draws him and he finally leaps into it himself, himself hastening the moment of his own perdition. (*The Double*, 2007: 58, my emphasis)

The example of Mr. Golyadkin's predicament demonstrates the inevitable confrontation with the abyss in front of Dostoevsky's Hamletian characters, a theme that will reverberate in other Hamletian characters. It describes the consequences of the gaze into the Real which can be seen as a different articulation of the first aspect of the Hamlet-isotopic chain.

*The Village of Stepanchikovo and Its Inhabitants* (1859) offers a farcical rendering of this theme: the portrayal of Foma Fomich Opiskin, a complete buffoon, characterized by exaggerated spitefulness, vanity, delusion and an inflated sense of self-importance. Being a selfish megalomaniac, at the age of fifty he finally gains a powerful position, using it to molest the inhabitants of Stepanchikovo with a repertoire of lofty rhetoric, literary allusions and a penchant for eloquence. But, most importantly, he identifies himself with Hamlet, in a speech that strongly resembles Dostoevsky's letter:

> If you should want to find out the extent of my suffering, ask Shakespeare: he will tell you in his *Hamlet* of the state of my soul. I have became fearsome and distrustfull. In my anxious and irritated state, I saw everything in dark colours, and not the kind of dark colours which they sing about in the famous ballad – you can be sure of that! [. . .] that was why you saw me so irritable recently, and so enraged at the human race. Oh! Who will now reconcile me with mankind? [. . .] With reference to Shakespeare once again, I can say that I saw the future like some *dark, bottomless pit, at the bottom of which lurked a crocodile.* I felt that it was my *duty to forestall disaster,* that I was *created, placed on this earth precisely for that purpose* – with what result? *You failed to understand* the most noble asspirations of my soul, and all I got from you in return for the whole of this time was hatred, ingratitude, mockery and humiliation. . . (*The Village of Stepanchikovo and Its Inhabitants,* 2023: 243, my emphasis)

The consequences of the gaze into the Real are presented in a parodic tone – at the end of a Shakespearean abyss lies a crocodile. Moreover, the farcical, inverted Hamletian theme lies in the fact that Foma Fomich is actually the only character perpetrating injustice in the novella, while his Hamletian pose is a justification of his parasitic behaviour of an emancipated and educated quasi-intellectual who molests simple-hearted and good-willed people around him. He can be regarded as an anticipation of the character of Stepan Trophimovich Verkhovensky from *Demons.*

# Negativity

Heaven and earth, /
   Must I remember?

(Hamlet, 1.2.142-3)

I feel that our world has become one immense Negative, and that
everything noble, beautiful, and divine, has turned itself into a satire.

(Dostoevsky, 1914: 3)

The situation of the first isotopy, radical crisis, propels the young
Dostoevsky to a philosophical inquiry, leading him to scepticism,
melancholy, despair, nihilism and the demonic.[6] A leitmotif in the
Hamlet-isotopy is the deterioration of magnanimity and nobleness,
culminating into satirical and parodic portrayals of Hamletian
characters. Dostoevsky's letter is imbued with the same pervasive sense
of decay and loss, as can be found in Hamlet's famous contemplation of
his own melancholic state:

> I have of late – but wherefore I know not – lost all my mirth, forgone all
> custom of exercises; and indeed, it goes so heavily with my disposition
> that this goodly frame, *the earth, seems to me a sterile promontory*;
> this most excellent *canopy*, the air, look you, this brave o'erhanging
> firmament, this majestical roof fretted with golden fire – why, it
> appeareth no other thing to me than *a foul and pestilent congregation
> of vapours*. What a piece of work is a man! How *noble* in reason! How
> infinite in faculties! In form and moving how express and admirable!
> In action how like an angel! In apprehension how like a god! The
> beauty of the world, the paragon of animals! And yet to me what is this
> quintessence of dust? Man delights not me – no, nor woman neither,
> though by your smiling you seem to say so. (*Hamlet*, 2.2. 261–275, my
> emphasis)

Polevoy's translation served as an inspiration to Dostoevsky's
impression: 'I feel that our world has become one immense Negative,
and that everything noble, beautiful, and divine, has turned itself

into a satire' (Dostoevsky, 1914: 3, my emphasis). Dostoevsky adds the satirical characterization of the world's negative transformation. This intervention can be noticed in Dostoevsky's novels and his big atheist characters that are disappointed by and thus reject the world altogether, such as Ivan Karamazov, and especially Stavrogin. My analysis of the interplay between scepticism, nihilism and faith relies on Wilhelm Weischedel's definition of the terms in *The Problem of God in Scepticism* (Il problema di Dio nel pensiero scettico) (1976, 1979). Weischedel's study defines scepticism as a synonym for radical interrogation (1979: 12, my translation); 'nothing can withstand' (13) the radical doubt of a sceptic. While nihilism in its most radical form 'negates the existence of anything', scepticism's extreme doubt in the existence of everything leaves one undecided about the fact if something exists or not (17, my translation). In radically questioning the existence of reality, scepticism doubts the existence of the self as well, leading to a dreadful sensation of existing in 'a dream without a dreamer' – the most radical form of scepticism (16, my translation). This form of scepticism arises from the absence of certainty that anything really exists. Once the reality of others is reduced to an abstraction, this abstraction loses humanistic value and becomes exchangeable with any other conceivable idea. Epistemological uncertainties morph into a sense of ontological inconsistencies, blurring the line between existence and nonexistence; everything may seem to *be* and *not to be* simultaneously. Dostoevsky's most severe critique of Russian Hamletism, attributes scepticism and nihilism to the demonic. Hence, I suggest that Dostoevsky utilized references to *Hamlet* and Russian Hamletism as potential wellsprings for the demonic. In the subsequent subchapters, I examine how this interplay unfolds across various works, while here I focus on two examples from *The Humiliated and Insulted* and *Crime and Punishment*.

An intriguing early reference to Hamlet emerges in *The Humiliated and Insulted* (1861) in the speech of the morally corrupt, cynical and predatory figure of Prince Valkovsky. It appears twice in the episode where he shares a drunken confession to the narrator and young novelist Ivan Petrovich, in order to make a point about the 'a peculiar gratification to be derived from the sudden tearing-down of a mask, from the cynicism of not even deigning to betray any sense of shame in suddenly exposing oneself to another indecently' (*The Humiliated and Insulted*, 2008: 283). He tells the story of a man who, after the incident of opening his coat under which he is naked to provoke a passerby, would 'stand for about a minute in silence, then cover himself up again and, keeping a straight face and with perfect composure, glide past the thunderstruck observer regally, like the ghost in Hamlet' (284). The references to the Ghost, albeit in an absurd way, is confusing. What is the aim in interlinking a reference to the Ghost of Hamlet's father, an epitome of virtue, strength and heroic composure, with such a vulgar image, apart from sheer provocation? Prince Valkovsky later ridicules Hamletian philosophizing, juxtaposing suicidal tendencies and noble despair with premises of egoistic rationalism[7] pushed to its extremes – a discussion that Dostoevsky later expanded in *Notes from Underground*. Prince Valkovsky explains in his confession:

> '*mon ami* . . . you must agree, this is *all nonsense.*'
>   'What is?'
> 'Everything except one's personality, *one's own self.* All's for the taking, and the world's my oyster. Listen, my friend, I still believe one can have a good time in this world. And that's the best thing to believe in, because otherwise one couldn't even have a bad time – there'd be nothing left but to *poison oneself.* They say one fool did precisely that. He got so carried away in his *philosophizing that he renounced everything*, the lot, even the legitimacy of all normal and natural human obligations, with the end result that he was left with nothing, an *absolute zero*, which is why he declared that the best thing in life was a dose of prussic acid. You will tell me this reeks of *Hamlet, of noble despair, in short – of something sublime that's way beyond us* [. . .] but what can I do if I know for certain that behind every human virtue lurks profound selfishness? And the more virtuous the undertaking, the more selfishness there is in it. Love thy own self – that's one rule I recognize. Life's just a business transaction. [. . .] I don't like death and

it frightens me. Hell knows how one may come to die! But why talk about it! It's that *suicidal philosopher* who's got me going. To hell with philosophy!' (285–8, my emphasis)

From his cynical perspective – which is only a mask for fear of death – Prince Valkovsky comes to the conclusion that the only answer to the Hamletian 'to be or not to be' dilemma may be solved in two ways: either as an absolute glorification of the individual, in which one metaphorically becomes the centre and the only objective of one's life, or, for a more sensitive, noble soul endowed with passion, the only way to be, or in other words, to avoid the desperation of being, is not to be – suicide. This passage invites philosophical discussion around issues of scepticism, cynicism and nihilism to be compared with Prince Valkovsky's egoistic hedonism as an answer to a noble but foolish suicide. Dostoevsky, in particular, connects Hamletian despair with abstract rational thought, viewing hyperconsciousness as its root cause. This link between abstract rationality, hyperconsciousness, nihilism and the demonic is an important aspect of the Hamlet-isotopy network. While Dostoevsky's letter represents a youthful, Romantic view on these themes, they will echo differently and strongly in his last novel, *The Brothers Karamazov.* This novel contains the most precise definition of devilish logic. Ivan Karamazov's encounter with the petty devil reveals a striking overlap in devilish reasoning with the Hamlet-isotopy network. The devil's strategy is as follows: 'I'm *leading you alternately between belief and disbelief,* and I have my own purpose in doing so. A new method, sir' (*The Brothers Karamazov,* 1992: 645, my emphasis). Prince Valkovsky finds a counter-argument in placing the self to be the source, cause and end of all actions. Instead of doubt or nothingness there should be hedonism. On the other hand, Dostoevsky's Hamletian characters, especially Raskolnikov, Stavrogin and Ivan Karamazov, hold the most radical position in dealing with scepticism. In order to receive and find proof of God's existence they are consciously provoking 'Him' in their arrogant transgression of human limits. In the following passage from *Crime and Punishment* we can identify that type of arrogance and cynicism in Raskolnikov's reasoning:

it wasn't a human being I killed, it was a principle! So I killed the principle, but I didn't step over, I stayed on this side. . . .All I managed to do was kill. And I didn't even manage that, as it turns out. . . . A *principle*? [. . .] Eh, *an aesthetic louse* is what I am, and nothing more,' [. . .] Yes, I really am a louse,' he went on, gloatingly seizing upon the thought, rummaging in it, *playing and amusing himself* with it, 'if only because, first, I'm now reasoning about being a louse; second, because I've been troubling all-good *Providence* for a whole month, calling it to witness that I was undertaking it not to satisfy my own flesh and lust, but with a splendid and agreeable goal in mind – ha, ha! Third, because I resolved to observe all possible justice in carrying it out, weight, measure, arithmetic: I chose the most useless louse of all and, having killed her, decided to take from her exactly as much as I needed for the first step, no more and no less (and the rest would thus simply go to the monastery, according to her will – ha, ha!). . . . And ultimately, ultimately I am a louse,' [. . .] 'because I myself am perhaps even more vile and nasty than the louse I killed, and I had anticipated beforehand that I would tell myself so after I killed her.' (*Crime and Punishment*, 2021: 287–8, my emphasis)

This paragraph exemplifies a cynical and introspective dissection akin to Hamlet's contemplation of self. However, Raskolnikov's inner monologue meanders from self-irony and self-debasement to an aesthetic parasite with a very precise method in his madness. Within this novel Dostoevsky strongly criticizes Russian Hamletism, epitomized in Raskolnikov's argumentation about egoism, aesthetics, hypersensitivity and self-obsession. These ideas are amplified and radicalized in the novel, driven to their extreme logical consequences, yet equally condemned. Dostoevsky highlights how the consequence of Raskolnikov's ideas and behaviour is a profound alienation from the materiality of the others' existence. The others are perceived as mere abstractions, aesthetic and rhetorical objects available to be manipulated in one's mind, which only reinforces the perception that reality is no more than a dream, irrevocably alienating Hamletian heroes from people, nation and, consequently, their sense of self.

## The 'ideal'

it goes so heavily with my disposition that this goodly frame, *the earth, seems to me a sterile promontory*; this most excellent *canopy*, the air, look you, this brave o'erhanging firmament, this majestical roof fretted with golden fire – why, it appeareth no other thing to me than *a foul and pestilent congregation of vapours*.

(Hamlet, 2.2.263–9, my emphasis)

If in this *picture* there occurs an individual who neither in idea nor effect *harmonises with the whole*, who is, in a word, an entirely unrelated figure – what must happen to the picture? It is destroyed, and can no longer endure. Yet how terrible it is to perceive only the coarse in veil under which the All doth languish!

(Dostoevsky, 1914: 3–4, my emphasis)

The third excerpt from the letter discusses the portrayal of an isolated, alienated individual in a world that is 'out of joint' (*Hamlet*, 2.1.186). While it does not overtly refer to Shakespeare's play, it reflects Dostoevsky's despair over the destruction of an ideal world. One could perhaps draw a distant parallel between the 'coarse *veil* under which the All doth languish' (Dostoevsky, 1914: 3-4, my emphasis) and Hamlet's contemplation of 'this goodly frame [. . .] this most excellent *canopy*' (*Hamlet*, 2.2.264-5, my emphasis). More importantly, this part foreshadows themes that will be relevant to Dostoevsky's engagement with *Hamlet*/Hamlet. In the passage mentioned above the world is conceived as a representation, an image bound to the subject's individual perception.

Dostoevsky will deal with this question in a context imbued with Hamletian allusions in *The Idiot*. Ippolit is one of the supporting characters in *The Idiot*, a mortally sick youth that decides to kill himself in order to retain his freedom and dignity from the impending death. He sees suicide as a means to win over death by achieving a sense of autonomy; that is, he will freely choose to die instead of being helpless in front of his sickness. While contemplating suicide, he ponders about Hans Holbein's *The Body of the Dead Christ in the Tomb* (1520–2) and

wonders whether 'something that has no image [can] come as an image?'
(*The Idiot*, 2012: 390). The question revolves around the possibility of
representing death and divinity in art, specifically the Dead Christ that
will be resurrected. However, Holbein's sombre and disturbing picture
presents a realistic and detailed depiction of Christ after Crucifixion,
emphasizing his suffering and humanity. The paradoxical question
pertains to the possibility of representing the divine attributes of Christ,
which cannot be accurately depicted, within a realistic portrayal of a
dead and suffering human body. If read as a metatextual comment, it
may be expanded to the question how divinity can be represented in
Dostoevsky's novel. However, Dostoevsky surrounds the question with
irony. It forms part of the confession of the mortally ill teenager, which
was meant to be his last word to the world, but ended up being a farce
patching together several Hamletian motifs. Dostoevsky demonstrates
how any attempt to fully express oneself and one's (philosophical)
system ends in self-contradiction. Like the man from the underground,
Raskolnikov and Shigalyov (as we shall see later), Ippolit has been
obsessed with his philosophical ideas in solitude, longing to finally
test them before other characters from *The Idiot* in order to prove
their worth and veracity. Similarly to the man from the underground,
Raskolnikov and Shigalyov, his contradictory beliefs are shaded by
Hamletian irony, self-debasement, and hyper-rationalism:

> It seems to me that I have just written something terribly stupid, but
> I have no time to correct it, as I said; besides, I give myself my word
> purposely not to correct a single line in this manuscript, even if I
> notice that *I am contradicting myself every five lines*. I precisely want
> to determine tomorrow during the reading whether the *logical course*
> of my thought is correct; whether I notice my own mistakes, and thus
> whether everything I have thought through during these six months in
> this room is true or mere raving. (388, my emphasis)

Dostoevsky's inquiry anticipates his critique of Hamlet's solipsism and
individuality, alongside the absence of ethical responsibility towards
other(s), aligning with his own criticism of Hamletism built upon

Turgenev's criticism of justified inaction because of excessive thinking. It is essentially a criticism of a tragic worldview as a justification and rationalization for ethical irresponsibility. In the latter part of his confession, as he reflects on the painting, Ippolit meditates that even Christ, who overcame death, remains subject to the terribly destructive force of nature, depicted by Holbein in the state of horrendous decay – as a lifeless human body:

> Here the notion involuntarily occurs to you that if death is so terrible and the laws of nature are so powerful, how can they be overcome? How overcome them, if they were not even defeated now, by the one who defeated nature while he lived, whom nature obeyed, who exclaimed: 'Talitha cumi' and the girl arose, 'Lazarus, come forth' and the dead man came out? *Nature* appears to the viewer of this painting in the shape of some *enormous, implacable, and dumb beast*, or, to put it more correctly, much more correctly, strange though it is – in the shape of some *huge machine of the most modern construction*, which has senselessly seized, crushed, and swallowed up, blankly and unfeelingly, a great and priceless being – such a being as by himself was worth the whole of nature and all its laws, the whole earth, which was perhaps created solely for the appearance of this being alone! The painting seems precisely to express this *notion of a dark, insolent, and senselessly eternal power, to which everything is subjected, and it is conveyed to you involuntarily.* (408, my emphasis)

Ippolit's description of nature can be paralleled with the descriptions of reality in *The Double* – the menacing abyss threatening and attacking Mr. Golyadkin that can be interpreted through Lacan's concept of Real. Ipollit calls nature a beast and a huge machine of modern construction, later linked to a *huge and repulsive tarantula*, stating that:

> All this came to me in fragments, perhaps indeed through delirium, sometimes even in images [. . .] *Can something that has no image come as an image?* But it was as if it seemed to me at moments that I could *see that infinite power, that blank, dark, and dumb being, in some strange and impossible form.* I remember it seemed as if someone holding a candle led me by the hand and showed me some *huge and*

> *repulsive tarantula* and started assuring me that this was that dark, blank, and all-powerful being, and laughed at my indignation. (409, my emphasis)

Ippolit's impression that came to him 'in fragments, perhaps indeed through delirium, sometimes even in images' (2012) may remind us how the Real eludes signification, as in *The Double*. Morson suggests that Dostoevsky's metafictional question ('Can something that has no image come as an image?') constitutes the central inquiry of his poetics, which he encapsulates in a paradoxical sentence describing the essence of Dostoevsky's approach: 'What art represents, it misrepresents' (Morson, 1981: 8).[8] In other words, this paradoxical sentence refers to the quality of Dostoevsky's art 'bordering on self-contradiction' (1981). According to this insight, the figure of Hamlet does not serve merely as a model for a realistically portrayed psychological type, as in Turgenev's essay, but rather as a fluid textual construct whose semantic fragments are often distorted throughout Dostoevsky's work, serving as a catalyst for developing and exploring certain themes – or, to paraphrase Morson, the references to *Hamlet* in Dostoevsky's work appear to convey a particular meaning; however, they paradoxically serve to misrepresent that very meaning, signaling to something beyond language and representation.

## The 'to be or not to be' dilemma

> To be, or not to be – that is the question;
>
>                           (Hamlet, 3.1.55)

> To know that one single effort of the will would suffice to demolish that veil and become one with eternity – to know all this, and still live on like the last and least of creatures.
>
>                           (Dostoevsky, 1914: 4)

As Semenenko demonstrated, the 'to be or not to be' soliloquy 'was interpreted as the main part of the play, its quintessence, and –

more importantly – most typical of Hamlet's character' (2007: 53). Commenting on this part of the letter, Rowe remarks that it 'can be seen to anticipate Kirillov's suicide in *The Devils* (also known as *The Possessed*, 1871-2), an effort to transcend man's limitations by the ultimate act of will' (1976: 84). However, in the letter, Dostoevsky expresses his choice to live and prevail despite being aware of the world's negativity and baseness. This love for the world and life will reverberate in some of Dostoevsky's Hamletian characters, remaining one of his trademarks. Ivan Karamazov famously claims: 'I've asked myself many times: is there such despair in the world as could overcome this wild and perhaps indecent thirst for life in me, and have decided that apparently there is not. [. . .] True, it's a feature of the Karamazovs, to some extent, this thirst for life despite all [. . .] I want to live, and I do live, even if it be against logic' (*The Brothers Karamazov*, 1992: 230). However, many Hamletian characters will chose suicide for a myriad of different ideas, as we shall see in further analysis.

We can follow this isotopy in *Crime and Punishment*, *The Double*, *The Brothers Karamazov* and *Notes from Underground*. *Crime and Punishment* is more elaborately related to *Hamlet* than other novels, as shown by Stepanian (2016). Here it is to consider one issue only, that is, how the variations of the 'to be or not to be' question are used to define the identity of characters. Famously, *Crime and Punishment* portrays Raskolnikov's murder of an old woman, which differently from the assassination of the King in *Hamlet* is committed for 'nothing' – for a 'whim' only. Parallels in plot and character can be traced in Raskolnikov's approach to the murder, his pondering the decision, his paranoid internal dialogues and the surveillance and spying. All these themes embody a dynamic fictionalization of the 'to be or not to be' question. In his recent article "The Poetics of Schism: Dostoevsky Translates Hamlet" (2020), Movsesian highlights the parallels between Hamlets' and Raskolnikov's soliloquies. He examines the way Dostoevsky 'translates' the 'to be or not to be' soliloquy into his novel, and claims that 'The question of the nature of truth takes on various forms in *Hamlet* and *Crime and Punishment* and is often expressed through indecisive rhetoric and the conjunction, "or", prevalent in Hamlet's famous "To be or not to be" soliloquy, which Raskolnikov adopts' (2020: 5). Movsesian further elaborates that 'speech as performance has a different flavor in *Hamlet* due to its dramatic structure and genre expectations', while in *Crime and Punishment* 'the "or" monologues continue through narrative commentary, further solidifying Raskolnikov's schism' (2020). He demonstrates this point with the following Dostoeveskian quote:

> 'It was clear that now the time had come, not to languish in passive suffering, arguing that questions were insoluble, but to act, to act now and with speed. He must decide on something *or* other, come what might, or [. . .] '*Or* renounce life altogether!' he exclaimed suddenly in a frenzy – 'submit obediently to destiny, as it is, and stifle everything within oneself, renouncing every right to act, to live, *or* to love!' (PSS, 6:39, cited in Movsesian, 2020: 5, my emphasis)

The most explicit allusion to Hamlet's soliloquy, 'Well now, shall I go or not?' (*Crime and Punishment*, 2021: 184–5), and its connection to a whole array of possible, variously interpretable, reasons behind it, go as follows:

> '*Well now, shall I go or not?*' thought Raskolnikov, stopping in the middle of the street, at an intersection, and looking around as if he were waiting for the final word from someone. But no reply came from anywhere; everything was blank and dead, like the stones he was walking on, dead for him, for him alone. (2021, my emphasis)

The Hamletian isotopy network is reinforced by Raskolnikov's dilemma of whether to go to the police and surrender himself for the crime he committed or not. The 'final word' stands for a final answer, signifying the end to his desperate anguish and sense of isolation. The next example is a subtle variation of the 'to be or not to be' question in which Raskolnikov compares himself to the historical figure of Napoleon, whom he regards as an archetype of an extraordinary man – decisive, powerful, beyond and above moral and legal norms in the pursuit of a greater good. He asks himself: 'would Napoleon *have gone ahead or not?'* (441); whether he would kill the old lady. However, in a typically Dostoevskian manner, the other option for Raskolnikov if he is not being as Napoleon, is on the opposite spectrum of values. He can either be an extraordinary man or be a parasite: 'I wanted to find out then, and find out quickly, *whether I was a louse like all the rest, or a man? Would I be able to step over, or not! Would I dare to reach down and take, or not? Am I a trembling creature, or do I have the right. . .'* (2021, my emphasis). Dostoevsky's criticism engages with ethical and religious considerations – Raskolnikov's demeanour is disrespectful and irresponsible towards others. He does not consider other characters as human beings, in their ethical, emotional and spiritual fullness, but rather thinks of them only as a prolongation of his own consciousness. The more he contemplates, the more he deepens his detachment from other people, leading to their derealization. Here, Dostoevsky's criticism of Russian Hamletism aligns with Belinsky's and Chernyshevsky's critique.

In *The Double*, instead, we encounter a parodic transformation of the 'to be or not to be' dilemma into 'To go or not? Well, to go or not? I'll go . . . Why shouldn't I go?' (2007: 100). Mr Golyadkin faces the ostensibly 'important' decision of whether to go to a party. His internal monologue can be read as a caricatured version of Hamlet's 2.2 soliloquy where he famously accuses himself of cowardice after the player's performance of the Hecuba speech. Besides, the manner in which Mr Golyadkin arrives at the decision to enter the ballroom resembles the abruptness of the 'readiness is all' line (*Hamlet*, 5.2.200), albeit in a farcical register:

> '*To go or not? Well, to go or not?* I'll go [. . .] Why shouldn't I go? The brave man makes his way everywhere!' Having encouraged himself in this way, our hero suddenly and quite unexpectedly retreated behind the screens. 'No', he thought, 'what if somebody comes in? There, somebody has; why was I gaping when nobody was there? I should have upped and penetrated!. . . No, there's no penetrating when man has such a character! What a mean tendency! I got frightened like a chicken. Getting frightened is what we do, so there! Mucking things up is what we always do: don't even ask us about it. So I stand here like a block of wood and that's that.' [. . .] here Mr. Goliadkin forgot

everything that was going on around him and directly, like a bolt from
the blue, appeared in the ballroom [. . .] Having stood in the courtyard
for some time our hero was about to decide on something. But the
decision was not destined to take place, evidently. (*The Double*, 2007:
100, my emphasis)

When read next to the passages from *Crime and Punishment*, not only
that Mr. Golyadkin's dilemma may be read as a parody of Hamletian 'to
be or not to be' dilemma, but also, we may notice a similar mechanism of
deconstructing the idea of a possibility of a free choice in Raskolnikov's
decision to murder the old lady.[9] Their soliloquies seem to paradoxically
strengthen the impression of their impossibility to choose, decide what
to do, while their speech, seen from that perspective, translates as
posturing. In *Notes from Underground* (1864), the fixation on becoming
'someone' or doing 'something' is deconstructed by the man from the
underground when he starts reflecting on how doing defines being,
that is, on how one's identity is dependent on one's actions. Here is an
example:

> Not just wicked, no, I never even managed to become anything: neither
> wicked nor good, neither a scoundrel nor an honest man, neither a
> hero nor an insect. And now I am living out my life in my corner,
> taunting myself with the spiteful and utterly futile consolation that it is
> even impossible for an intelligent man seriously to become anything,
> and only fools become something. Yes, sir, an intelligent man of the
> nineteenth century must be and is morally obliged to be primarily a
> *characterless being*; and a man of character, an active figure – primarily
> a limited being. (*Notes from Underground*, 1993: 7, my emphasis)

The man from the underground's self-awareness and self-irony intersect
with other relevant issues for Russian Hamletism. Considering that the
underground man from *Notes from Underground* was partially composed
as a response to Chernyshevsky's philosophy of rational egoism and
Turgenev's Hamlets, we can also read the novel as deconstruction of
ideas of free will and useful action, as Frank thoroughly explains:

Such thematic resemblances need not be denied; but this pervasive motif in Russian literature of the 1850s and 1860s is given a special twist by Dostoevsky and shown as the unexpected consequence of the doctrines advanced by the very people who had attacked the 'Hamlets' most violently – the radicals of the 1860s themselves. For the pseudo-scientific terms of the underground man's declaration about 'hyperconsciousness' are a parody of Chernishevsky, and the statement is a paraphrase of Chernishevsky's assertion, in *The Anthropological Principle in Philosophy*, that no such thing as free will exists or can exist, since whatever actions man attributes to his own initiative are really a result of the 'laws of nature'. (1986: 318–9)

Thus, the crucial question 'Where are the primary causes on which I can rest, where are my bases?' links Russian Hamletism and the loss of a metaphysical ground in Dostoevsky's Hamletian heroes. The man from the underground contemplates about the interdependence of thinking and doing in the following manner:

For in order to begin to act, one must first be completely at ease, so that no more doubts remain. Well, and how am I, for example, to set myself at ease? *Where are the primary causes on which I can rest, where are my bases?* Where am I going to get them? *I exercise thinking, and, consequently, for me every primary cause immediately drags with it yet another, still more primary one, and so on ad infinitum. Such is precisely the essence of all consciousness and thought.* (*Notes from Underground*, 1993: 17, my emphasis)

In considering 'the essence of all consciousness and thought' (1993) as a continuous confutation of statements, *Notes from Underground* can also be interpreted as an extension of Russian Hamletism. This topic is further developed in Stavrogin's suicide letter, where he claims that 'One can argue endlessly about everything [. . .] I know it will be one more deceit – the last deceit in an endless series of deceits' (*Demons*, 2006: 676). In all characters mentioned here, undecidability appears as the ultimate, paradoxical reason for suicide (being unable to decide turns out to be the reason for deciding 'not to be').

Finally, this isotopy culminates in *The Brothers Karamazov*, in the scene where the devil himself provokes Ivan Karamazov by challenging his inability to decide whether 'to go', emphasizing not only that his free will does not exists but signals to the unconscious reasons why is it so:

> And can you have made up your mind? You've not made up your mind. You'll sit all night deliberating *whether to go or not*. But you will go; you know you'll go. You know that whichever way you decide, *the decision does not depend on you*. You'll go because you won't dare not to go. Why won't you dare? You must guess that for yourself. That's a *riddle* for you! (*The Brothers Karamazov*, 1992: 654, my emphasis)

Already in a disturbed psychological state, Ivan Karamazov complains about this conversation to his brother Alyosha, insisting that he had talked to the devil himself, and not with his own split consciousness is calling him: 'a coward, Alyosha! *Le mot de l'enigme* is that I'm a coward!' (1992). Ivan answers the Hamletian question about his incapability to decide, in a Hamletian manner, by calling himself a coward.

## Confession

> O, what a rogue and peasant slave am I
> Is it not monstrous that this player here,
> But in a fiction, in a dream of passion,
> Could force his soul so to his own conceit
> That from her working all the visage wanned
> – Tears in his eyes, distraction in this aspect,
> A broken voice, and his whole function suiting
> With forms to his conceit and – all for nothing –
> For Hecuba?
>
> (*Hamlet*, 2.2.485–93)

How terrible! How petty is man! Hamlet! Hamlet! When I think of his moving wild speech, in which resounds the groaning of the whole numbed universe, there breaks from my soul not one reproach, not one sigh.

(Dostoevsky, 1914: 4)

The fifth part I selected correlates with the passage from the letter referring to Hamlet's speech, which provokes commentary. Hamlet's speech resonates as an echo of a universe that, paradoxically, groans in anguish while remaining numb. Conversely, Hamlet's speech may also be interpreted as the lament of an hypersensitive and disoriented man. The impact of such a speech on young Dostoevsky is to provoke a paralysed form of empathy, with Hamlet's despair so immense and all-encompassing that it can only be met with silence, an acceptance of his grief, and a world desensitized by the overwhelming amount of suffering. In the following section, I will connect the theme of confession to references to *Hamlet* across a few of the novels.

All the main characters in *The Double, Notes from Underground, Crime and Punishment, An Accidental Family, The Idiot, Demons* and *The Brothers Karamazov*, confess themselves and find releasement of tension through speech. In Dostoevsky's novels, confession becomes either a parody of confession, a ridiculous posture or a testament to the impossibility to know and express the truth about oneself. As Ghidini recently concluded apropos the genre of confession in Dostoevsky, a perfect self-knowledge is only a chimaera of modernity (2023: 120, my translation). In criticism, Stavrogin's confession is clearly characterized as a 'travesty of a confession, an exercise in self-evasion rather than self-revelation' (Leatherbarrow, 2000: 18). In the above-mentioned example, when Prince Valkovsky recalls an episode of a man that uncovered himself completely and exposed his naked body only to 'cover himself up again and, keeping a straight face and with perfect composure, glide past the thunderstruck observer regally, like the ghost in Hamlet' (*The Humiliated and Insulted*, 2008: 283), we can identify the radical ridicule of Dostoevsky's parody, as in the case of the underground man:

Even this would be better here: if I myself believed at least something of all I've just written. For I swear to you, gentlemen, that I do not believe a word, not one little word, of all I've just scribbled! That is, I do believe, perhaps, but at the same time, who knows why, I sense and suspect that I'm lying like a cobbler. (*Notes from Underground*, 1993: 34)

However, this characteristic is also a type of pervasive self-irony, which operates in a way to blur the difference between truth and falsehood. It is deeply entrenched in the literary consciousness of Dostoevsky's Hamletian characters regarding their own dependence on literature: 'I knew I'd been speaking stiffly, affectedly, even bookishly; in short, I couldn't speak any other way than "as if from a book"' (90). The underground man takes pleasure in the self-abasement of humiliating confessions that swiftly transform into a mode of self-irony, as the following example shows: 'But I was putting on a show, as they say, to preserve decency, though the fit was a real one' (104). Dostoevsky's fascination with self-consciousness offered extraordinarily fertile ground for cultivating epistemological, as well as self-referential, paradoxes (Morson, 1999: 484). The subjectivity embedded in Russian Hamletism is a fragmented performative self: when interpreting Hamletism in *Notes from Underground*, Mochulsky claims that consciousness is the main problem of the man from the underground because 'from consciousness comes inertia, from inertia there is boredom. Not acting, not living, man out of boredom begins to "compose life"' (1973: 248). Mochulsky gives an important interpretation: 'The underground existence becomes *fantasy; this is a game in front of a mirror.* The man suffers, rejoices, is angry and, as it were, with complete sincerity. But each sensation is reflected in the mirror of consciousness; in *the actor there sits a spectator who appraises his art*' (1973, my emphasis). The subject is split into seeing oneself as a fantasy, an illusion, in a game in front of a mirror and seeing others watching the same game: this aptly describes the mechanism of Dostoevsky's critique of Russian Hamletism that he fictionalized in his Hamletian characters. For example, a similar hyper self-awareness is evident in Raskolnikov: 'Well done? Natural? Not exaggerated?' (*Crime and Punishment*, 2021: 264), or: 'But what if it only seems so to me? What if it's a mirage, what if I'm completely mistaken, get angry on account of my inexperience, and fail to keep up my vile role? Maybe it's all unintentional? Their words are all ordinary, but there's something in them' (267). The exploration of Hamletian self-performativity illuminates the paradoxical nature of Dostoevskian subjectivity, wherein characters are devised to be irresolvable between yearning 'authenticity' and the artifice they perpetuate. This problematic, with its ethical consequences, is visible in the example of Morson's interpretation of Ivan Karamazov's behaviour as akin to the liar's paradox. He highlights that for Ivan, 'the paradox becomes a way of playing with ideas without committing himself to them [. . .] without ever participating in life', because of that Ivan 'always claims (in a joking voice) to be merely joking, or even, as he later tells Alyosha, to have been merely joking when he said he was joking' (Morson, 1999: 485). We can conclude that the sixth isotopy, referring to an intention and yet an inability of Hamletian figures and characters to confess, includes the liar's paradox and a fictionalization of an idea that the confessional truth is always paradoxical.

## Paradox

There are more things in heaven and earth, Horatio,
Then are dreamt of in your philosophy.

(Hamlet, 1.5.165-6)

Pascal once said: He who protests against philosophy is himself a philosopher. A poor sort of system!

(Dostoevsky, 1914: 4)

Dostoevsky's writings are replete with paradoxes that may be regarded as one his main devices to bring readers to question their views, expose false truths and open the path towards deeper insights (Salmon, 2023: 19, my translation). The sixth isotopy might serve as a direct continuation of the previous discussion, because the paradox of Pascal's philosophical system likewise calls into question the distinctions between truth and falsity, as his comment implies. Daria Farafonova has convincingly showed in a recent article on Pascal and Dostoevsky that 'Pascal's conceptual horizon, which can be individuated in some of the crucial points of Dostoevsky's prose, especially those pertaining to the criticism of reason based on revealing its abyssal contradictory nature' (2022: 42). The parallels between Dostoevsky's and Pascal's thought are striking. The framework of Pascalian logic, particularly its *abyssal nature*, is a crucial component of the first Hamlet-isotopy as demonstrated. Farafonova cites Pascal in order to assert that 'judgement can be fully applied to the dynamics determining Dostoevsky's artistic thought' (45): 'the "dialectic rhythm of a thought that passes through overturnings from *pro* into *against*, where the truth is never affirmed without taking into account the opposite, where the reason keeps in check the reason"' (10). She remarks that in his 1838 letter, Dostoevsky aligns himself with Pascal's paradoxical criticism of rationality and one of his crucial ideas about 'the urgency to show man his multiplicitous and contradictory nature, the irreducible coexistence of the contrasts in him, and the lacerating condition of being caught between nothingness and the Absolute' (45). Howe contends that Pascal's paradoxical dialectic employs 'a procedure of double negation aiming at the destruction of all worldly values and certainties' (1973: 120) and further remarks that in Pascal's dialectic 'both pure affirmation and pure negation possess some epistemological value, implying at least the recognized existence of a true and a false' (1973). As Howe explains, 'paradox, as the statement of a contradiction whose two terms are equally valid, reveals the possibility of an infinite number of separate and contrary truths. For Pascal, *true knowledge becomes an absolute, a totality which can only exist by embracing contradiction itself*' (1973, my emphasis).

All Hamletian characters in Dostoevsky's narratives are embroiled in a dialectical struggle between *pro* and *contra* arguments for various reasons, but Stavrogin stands out as the most radical example because he embodies the most extreme opposites simultaneously. Stavrogin may be regarded as Dostoevsky's most radical portrayals of man's contradictory nature. In Kirillov's opinion (the supporting character that under the influence of Stavrogin becomes an avid nihilist), he is enchanted in a paradox and 'eaten by an idea' (*Demons*, 2006: 526); but Kirillov also aporetically concludes: 'No, I myself guessed it: if Stavrogin believes, he does not believe that he believes. And if he does not believe, he does not believe that he does not believe' (2006). While this contradictory and complicated statement will be analysed later, here it is important briefly to linger on its logic of double negation. What are the consequences of such a logical stance? Nikolay Stavrogin is capable neither of believing nor of not believing. When applying these hypotheses to Stavrogin's questions of belief and disbelief, we recognize the existence of both states and the boundary that separates them, as in Kirillov's reasoning. Stavrogin's portrayal exemplifies a hero struggling and failing to embrace the radical contradictions about belief within himself. Thus, the sixth isotopy pertains to a paradoxical philosophical system wrapped up in its own logical contradictions and Dostoevsky's realization of the paradoxical nature of truth. It is important to note that many characters remain stuck in these paradoxes without transcending them by embracing contradiction. Dostoevsky's project of 'letting be' is a means to overcome the logical dead end of contradictions by embracing madness, love for life and irrationality as we shall see below.

## Madness

To put an antic disposition on –

(*Hamlet*, 1.5.170)

I have a new plan: to go mad. That's the way: for people to lose their heads, and then be cured and brought back to reason! (Dostoevsky, 1914: 5)

From the analysis of the previous portions of the 1838 letter we can gather that the Hamlet-isotopy network is set against the background of death and faith, that is, life after death. How can one live in such an unjust, immoral and farcical world if there is nothing after death; live and not lose one's reason? This last part summarizes Dostoevsky's concluding response to the Hamletian or the Pascalian problem of dealing with paradoxes. Going mad may signify the embrace of contradictions. Madness as an enthusiastic state may be a counter-stance to scepticism and nihilism, these two philosophical perspectives that deal with the origin of the Absolute. I propose that Dostoevsky's 'Let be' project as formulated in his letter provides his own response to the 'to be or not to be' dilemma, evolving into the acceptance of the paradox of 'to be *and* not to be' simultaneously. This viewpoint allows both 'to be' and 'not to be' to exist at the same time in the mystery of belief. As such, this argument transcends the Hamletian problems of radical scepticism and nihilism.

## 'I have a project: To go mad'

I will focus on the hermetic ending of the letter because it may be interpreted as Dostoevsky's own appropriation and revision of Hamlet's worldview and an answer to the dilemma between to be and not to be. Here is the passage in Russian: "U menya est' prozhekt: sdelat'sya sumasshedshim. Pust' lyudi besyatsya, pust' lechat, pust' delayut umnym." (PSS, 28: 51). The text at this point may be interpreted in different ways, first as 'I have a project: to make myself mad. Let people rage, let them heal me, let them make me wise' (my translation), second as 'I have a project: to go mad. Let people rage, try to cure me, let them try to bring me to reason' (translated by Michael A. Minihan, cited in Mochulsky, 1973: 17) which reads Dostoevsky as the subject of 'becoming mad', inciting rage in people who would eventually heal *him* and make *him* wiser or reasonable. Madness may be understood as a path to reason or wisdom.

However, the passage may also be interpreted as follows: 'I have a new plan: to go mad. That's the way: for people to lose their heads, and then be cured and brought back to reason!' (Dostoevsky, 1914: 5). In this case, society (everyone) is the subject of this transformation from madness to reason/wisdom. His strategy to go mad has the aim of maddening and then curing the people, as a sort of feigned sacrifice of his reason for *their* betterment. In both cases, Dostoevsky's madness is voluntary and controllable, implying that it is not a disease or a wild reaction but a premeditated strategy. Also, the means (his project of madness) and the way (letting go of rage and going mad in order to reach sanity, serenity and wisdom) are the same. However, in the first case, the object of analysis and intervention is an individual, in the second one, the entire society. At this stage, it is important to have this dichotomy in mind, since it is the main axis around which the Hamletian 'to be or not to be' dilemma in Dostoevsky's work revolves: to be or not to be for oneself/ to be or not to be for others. In both cases, Dostoevsky's interpretation of *Hamlet* may be read as the following paradox: 'let one/the society go mad in order to be cleansed and become reasonable', which brings us to the next question. What did Dostoevsky mean by reason? It may be understood better when read in the context of his comments in another letter to his brother written in the same year:

> What do you mean precisely by the word *know*? Nature, the soul, love, and God, one recognizes through the heart, and not through the reason. [. . .] But we are earth-born beings, and can only guess at the Idea – not grasp it by all sides at once. The guide for our intelligences through the temporary illusion into the innermost centre of the soul is called *Reason*. Now, Reason is a material capacity, while the soul or spirit lives on the thoughts which are whispered by the heart. Thought is born in the soul. Reason is a tool, a machine, which is driven by the spiritual fire. When human reason (which would demand a chapter for itself) penetrates into the domain of knowledge, it works independently of the *feeling*, and consequently of the *heart*. But when our aim is the understanding of love or of nature, we march towards the very citadel of the heart. (6–7)

Young Dostoevsky was influenced by German Romantic views of art, spirit and nature. According to these ideas, aesthetics is regarded as the bearer of truth rather than reason. As Marcus Levitt explains, he adopted 'the tradition of German "organic" aesthetics which culminated with Schelling', that prioritized artistic intuition over philosopher's 'fully conscious logic as the primary, and only integral, way to truth' (2018: 132). Thus, according to the letter of the young Dostoevsky, an idea in its entirety can only be intuited and revealed gradually. In this process of comprehension, reason serves as the guiding tool of logical apprehension, navigating between the realms of intelligence and the soul to acquire knowledge. However, it cannot aid in delving into the mysteries of nature or God. Levitt aptly notes that 'only in the works of an inspired poet-artist, who combines an intuitive vision of the world with his conscious reason, can one fully penetrate the essence of reality', bringing to attention that, in his later work, Dostoevsky 'adapted the "organic" view of aesthetic cognition into a specifically "Orthodox" frame of reference' (132-3). As we can see in the above-mentioned letter, young Dostoevsky understands reason as a tool for gaining knowledge and poetry as a divine enlightenment. Moreover, he concludes that 'philosophy cannot be regarded as a mere equation where nature is the unknown quantity. I remark that the poet, in the moment of inspiration, comprehends God, and consequently does the philosopher's work' (Dostoevsky, 1914: 7). This difference between reason as intellect or knowledge and reason as so-called wisdom is in accord with the postulates of Russian Orthodoxy: 'Eighteenth Century Russian language distinguished мудрость (wisdom) from знание (knowledge). Wisdom was a gift of God; the wise one grasped eternal values, whereas knowledge was cognition of both the eternal and the commonplace, [. . .] those who bore wisdom were all bearers of the true divine enlightenment [. . .] and the pursuit of knowledge was equal to moral and religious searching' (Artemyeva, 2014: 23-4). By applying the difference between reason and wisdom in deciphering of the cryptic post scriptum of the Hamlet-inspired letter, it seems that the sentence makes more sense if the madness brings the speaker along with others to wisdom, as a divinely inspired cleansed state, rather than reason as pursuit of new knowledge. Thus, I suggest the following translation: 'I have a project: to make myself mad. Let people rage, let them heal, let them be wise.'

## Hamlet's 'Let be' (5.2.201–2)

This 'project' from the letter anticipates, in my view, Dostoevsky's answer to the Hamletian dilemma in ways that appear coherent with a famous passage from *Hamlet*. I will turn to Shakespeare's text and its commentary in order to find similarities and differences with Dostoevskian 'let be' project:

> Not a whit, we defy augury; there's a special providence in the fall of a sparrow. If it be now, 'tis not to come; if it be not to come, it will be now; if it be not now, yet it will come: the readiness is all. Since no man knows aught of what he leaves, what is't to leave betimes? Let be. (*Hamlet*, 5. 2. 197–202)

In the second scene of the fifth act Hamlet is invited to enter the hall and fight Laertes, when Horatio warns him, 'If your mind dislike anything, obey it' (5.2.195), worried for Hamlet's performance in duel. However, Hamlet, as the previous quote demonstrates, defies not only what may come to his mind as Horatio suggests, but also any superstition and accepts whatever may come, and whenever: 'Let be' (5.2.201–2). Harold Jenkins reads Hamlet's concluding 'let be' as a simple breaking off the dialogue with Horatio to allow the action to continue (1993: 407). However, the whole passage is clearly imbued with a Christian perspective, pivoting on human submission to God's will and providence. Thus, even if we follow Jenkins 'let be', he suggests that language, whether within a soliloquy or a dialogue, is no longer required as a means to defer action or resolve Hamlet's dilemma – the stage is now set for action. The editors of the last revised Arden edition of *Hamlet*, Ann Thompson and Neil Taylor, interpret the line

*Let be* as 'leave it alone; say no more' (2017: 478). If we follow their explanation, Hamlet trusts the divine providence and events upon which he cannot act and change, opening himself to any event that may arise in the future and accepting the epistemological limits of man. What is the cause of such an abrupt change in Hamlet in comparison to previous indecisiveness? Benson notes that 'It is one of the great gaps in English literature, an enigma within the mystery of this most elusive play. For one thing, it takes place offstage, in the interim between the two scenes. Moreover, it happens within Hamlet, but he does not soliloquize the change – we only see its aftermath as 5.2 opens' (2017: 161). But what do these lines actually mean? How to understand this special providence? Recent studies discuss the issue of religiosity in Shakespeare's work, approaching it both from a historicist perspective, for instance by analysing the background of Catholic-Protestant conflicts, and from postmodern philosophical, theological and ethical readings of his plays. Albeit from different positions, most critics, nevertheless, reach similar conclusions: 'The lines between secular and sacred, transcendent and immanent blur so continuously that we begin to doubt our own vocabulary and historical paradigms in our attempts to describe the strange otherness of Shakespeare's religion, the way in which he can, again, deliberately and systematically strip away the layers of religion until nothing is left – nothing except the desire for something more or better that cannot be fully disentangled from religion' (Jackson and Marotti, 2011: 9); 'religious and secular issues creatively intersect' (Lowenstein and Witmore, 2015: 8); 'notably open-ended and flexible in his religious thinking as he worked creatively in a multifaceted Protestant culture that not only destroyed but assimilated vestiges of its Catholic past' (12), and so on. In *Heterodox Shakespeare* (2017), Sean Benson explained why Shakespeare's religious examination is vast enough to include Orthodoxy, radical unorthodoxy and heterodoxy at the same time: 'To argue that any theological (or, alternatively, secular) understanding of Shakespeare's plays is mistaken is unnecessarily dismissive and reductive of the plays' rich complexities' (9). In addition, he makes two important points: that secular readings are perfectly plausible and that 'the religious is always reflected through the aestheticism of his art' (20). In the introduction to *Spiritual Shakespeares* (2005) Ewan Fernie explains Shakespeare's spirituality as a 'distinctive, inalienable and challenging dimension of the plays, one that might be illuminated by, but remains irreducible to, any established theory or theology' (2). He claims that his plays render the struggle between possible absolutes and resistance to them.

Before dying, Hamlet firmly establishes this acceptance in action and not only words. 'As this fell sergeant death / in strict in his arrest, oh I could tell you – / But let *it* be' (*Hamlet*, 5.2.331, my emphasis). The rest is silence, silence that frames the discourse, changes, covers and swallows it. After letting it be, Hamlet accepts *it* – the concrete materiality and restrictions of history and his existence in it – alongside the silence. Yet, 'the justice of the last act remains finally undecidable' (Fernie, 2005: 207). Shakespeare's irony can be seen in the fact that letting go/be is a dramatic device precisely like Hamlet's hesitance and his deferral of 'action' – it allows the last act to unfold to an end, without a true revolution or resolution happening. We have no assurance that Hamlet's dying voice given to Fortinbras will set the joint right and that it will not continue the circle of violence.

Nevertheless, I highlight Fernie's claim that 'No one [. . .] has placed Hamlet's crucial transition from "To be, or not to be" (3.1.58) to "Let be" in the context of rich history of indifference and letting-be in the history of ideas in the Western tradition' (204).[10] One of Martin Heidegger's most important concepts – *Gelassenheit* or letting be/ letting go of will – has been understood to derive from Hamlet's *Let be* from Act 5:[11]

> Freedom for what is opened up in an open region lets beings be the beings they are. Freedom now reveals itself as letting beings be [. . .] Ordinarily we speak of letting be [. . .] in the negative sense of leaving something alone, of renouncing it, of indifference and even neglect [. . .] However, the phrase required now – *to let beings be* – does not refer to neglect and indifference but rather the opposite. *To let be is*

*to engage oneself with beings* [Sein-lassen ist das Sicheinlassen auf das Seiende] [. . .] To let be – that is, *to let beings be as the beings that they are* – means *to engage oneself with the Open and its openness into which every being comes to stand,* bringing that openness, as it were, along with itself. (GA9:188/144, cited in Davis, 2007: xxvii, my emphasis)

From a Heideggerian perspective two crucial lines that point to a resolution of the dilemma are *readiness is all* and *let be.* The first line may refer to an openness to *engage oneself with beings,* looking forward, expecting and waiting for a Heideggerian *being* to come and accepting it for whatever it is. 'Let be' signals the dynamic of praising opposites and their coexistence as an all-encompassing principle of existence – *to let beings be as the beings that they are* – which is in accordance with opinions of some critics. As Russell M. Hillier writes in 'Hamlet the rough-hewer: moral agency and the consolations of Reformation thought', 'Hamlet's affecting "Let be" (5.2.220) is a creative, not a defeatist, utterance, a fiat akin to the divine fiat of Genesis 1, where Creator and creature are reconciled to one another and cooperate in the unfurling of a providential plan' (2014: 181). Also, for example, James Calderwood claims how '"To be *and* not to be" is the basic logical form of Hamlet's assertions' (Cutrofello, 2014: 10) and Graham Priest concludes that 'the dialetheic[12] moral of the play is to be *and* not to be' (11). Thus, if we read 'Let be' as an answer to 'to be or not to be', we should not take it only as its resolution, but maybe as a synthesis as well – it may contain both being and non-being.

This ending echoes the ambivalence of Dostoevsky's project. My aim is not to suggest a plausible or coherent reading of Shakespeare's text but to explore the relevance of that particular line to Dostoevsky's own narrative project. What may be underlined at this stage is that Hamlet's resolution of the 'to be or not to be' dilemma in Dostoevsky's engagement through Providential faith gains new overtones in the context of Eastern Christianity. The main difference between Western and Eastern Christianity as understood by many Eastern Orthodox believers and shared by Dostoevsky is in the fact that 'Western

Christianity's cultivation of reason, beginning with the Scholasticism of the Middle Ages and continuing through the Renaissance and the Reformation, resulted in a religion that rationalizes faith and grows aloof from its spiritual side; Eastern Christianity, on the other hand, treasures the mystical experience of faith. Dostoevsky not only shared this view, he condemned Western Christianity, and especially Roman Catholicism, for having betrayed its essence by allying itself with the state' (Grillaert, 2016: 187). Looked at from this perspective, as a mystical experience of divine enlightenment rather than rationalization of faith (comprehension of faith), Dostoevsky's 'Let be' project can be seen as an Eastern Orthodox kenotic practice. Kenosis is an ascetic practice of 'self-emptying for the sake of the Other' (Lathouvers, 2014: 376), as the Greek Orthodox archbishop and theologian John Zizioulas explained in *Communion and Otherness* (2006). In the process of depriving oneself, the believer mimics Christ's self-emptying. This can be understood as a horizontal mystical relationship with Christ, but kenotic spirituality is also, according to Zizioulas, 'realized through the communion of love, through obedience and self-emptying for the sake of love for the other' (2014). Letting go of oneself to something irrational and mystical, divinely inspired, could be understood as surrendering and emptying oneself to achieve a communion in *sobornost*. The perspective of Eastern Orthodoxy and especially kenotic spirituality offers a foundational framework for Dostoevsky's own idiosyncratic resolution of the same problem. But let us now turn to Dostoevsky's work, starting with *Demons* and returning to the letter and its main topics, to explore if these hypotheses stand and how are they connected with Hamlet-isotopy.

## Dostoevsky's 'Let be project'

Dostoevsky's paradoxical 'project' of going mad to reach wisdom is equivalent to the epigraph of *Demons* from *The Gospel of Luke* (8.32-6) which recounts the episode about the Gadarene swine, symbolically summarizing the plot of the novel. The episode from the Gospel tells about Jesus releasing demons from a possessed man into a herd of swine that, in possessed madness, jumped from a cliff into the sea. That was the way Jesus healed a possessed man. The first parallel may be drawn between the possessed swine and the society possessed by nihilistic, and overall Western, ideas. Second, as the swine are driven to destruction, the plot of the novel is full of violent chaos, involving multiple murders, rape, arson, terroristic conspiracies by people driven mad. Third, similarly to the possessed man ultimately healed by Jesus, despite the gruesome events the novel offers a path of healing. The presence of a similar, though less developed, attitude in the Hamlet-inspired letter signifies the maturation of one of the central themes in Dostoevsky's novels. As mentioned, the Hamletian *antic disposition* may be juxtaposed with the Russian Orthodox tradition of the holy fool (*iurodivy*) – defined as 'foolishness for Christ's sake' – mimicking Christ through self-humiliation, self-asceticism and madness (Murav, 1992: 1). The project from the letter thus mimics Hamlet in order to perform what Christ performs in the Gospel in the epigraph for *Demons*. *Iurodivy*, or the so-called 'fools from birth', were seen as God's people who unconsciously prophesied God's will and were manifestations of his special favour (3) but they were also considered to be close to demonic possession. *Iurodivost* can also be connected to another paradoxical principle of Dostoevsky's work, *philosophia cordis*:

> In Dostoevsky's novels, we find such genuine philosophia cordis, sensitive to the harmonies and discords of life; a philosophy which willingly appreciates, listens, and responds to the primal 'songs of the heart'. Unprecedented *openness to the abyss of life*, where no question is answered once and for all, and where '*all contradictions live together*', is Dostoevsky's *golden signature*. The human heart is one of the most enigmatic of these contradictions and Dostoevsky invites his readers to join him in artistic exploration of this enigma. (Cherkasova, 2009: 11, my emphasis)

Dostoevsky's 'Let be' project epitomizes a *philosophia cordis*. Towards the end of *Crime and Punishment*, on the path of Raskolnikov's atonement, the narrator claims: 'besides, he would have been unable to *resolve* anything consciously just then; he could only *feel*. Instead of *dialectics*, there was *life*, and something completely different had to work itself out in his consciousness' (2021: 579, my emphasis). As especially seen in the examples from *Notes from Underground*, Dostoevsky's overt and covert reuses and allusions to *Hamlet* / Hamlet(s) point to the absurdity of rational, abstract logic, which signifies stagnation and death in his own poetics.

Dostoevsky's 'Let be project' is an anticipation of his later writings and dismantling of the binary opposition inherent in the 'to be or not to be' dilemma. Various aspects of the Hamlet-isotopy as defined above reflect this same problem in different ways. Dostoevsky is confronted with a radical ontological, epistemological and political crisis. A certain resistance to the unjust historical and ideological circumstances and an obsessive pursuit of truth pervades all of his Hamletian characters, while Dostoevsky explores different ways to embrace the ultimate uncertainty. The hermetic conclusion of his letter suggests that scepticism and nihilism, resulting in chaotic destruction and terrorism, could be transcended only by a leap beyond logic in favour of faith.

The aim of this chapter was to resurface the Hamlet-ideologeme as the underlying structure of Dostoevsky's engagement with *Hamlet/* Hamlet and Russian Hamletism, by exploring the seven isotopes of the Hamlet-isotopy network. This proto-narrative, representing hypotheses derived from the letter and subsequent developments of these themes in later writings, can be reconstructed as follows: first, young Dostoevsky identifies the disharmony of the world and disintegration of society according to Russian Hamletism as a radical existential and social crisis, extending his concerns to ontological, metaphysical and religious dimensions. The analysis of his later novels exposed a specific enchantment with the gaze into the abyss of existence, directly into the above-mentioned crisis. Second, he observes this profound crisis and notes an impending decay of values leading to melancholy, despair, scepticism, and nihilism. His characters consequently undergo profound alienation and derealization of others in their consciousness, transgressing into sin. Third, in such circumstances, any ideal or utopian concept is irretrievably lost in reality, yet remains vivid in yearning and imagination. In Dostoevsky's novels, Hamletian characters yearn for their lost ideals as well, and no matter how much they are desecrated and destroyed, the ideals preserve their value at least in their imagination. Fourth, Dostoevsky's suicidal rumination reflect his awareness of the world's condition, mirroring the existential dilemma of 'to be or not to be'. However, as we have seen in examining the Hamlet-isotopy, characters struggle to decide for themselves, while the freedom of their choices in the framework of scepticism and rationalism, often remains an illusion. Fifth, his confession mimics the posture of a Russian Hamlet, acknowledging his self-criticism without finding a solution outside the philosophical framework he depends on, as the sixth isotopy shows. This appropriation of a Hamletian posture demonstrates an obsession with expressing truth only to come to a realization that truth cannot be directly conveyed – it is paradoxical and in communication often comes out either as a parody of a confession or as a failure, a lie. Lastly and seventhly, he adopts an 'antic position' as a strategy to navigate and potentially overcome the crises he described. I suggest that his resolution implies a leap beyond logic into madness and a kenotic stance by embracing contradictions, while mimicking *iurodivost* in order to bring to healing and cleansing of the demonic. Thus, by going through the Hamlet-isotopy network throughout his novels, the following answer emerges: the Hamlet-ideologeme stands for a hero's indecision regarding his identity; his/hers incapability to decide whether 'to be or not to be'. As such, the Hamlet-ideologeme represents a destabilized identity and a subject in crisis on a quest for meaning, incapable of deciding between what to be and what to do. Who is one if not the sum of one's actions? And if one cannot exert control over one's own being by choosing one's own actions – if one cannot be the author of one's identity – how can one be free? Can one truly provide a resolution to the Hamletian dilemma between 'to be or not to be' by means of *letting be*?

# Notes

1   To illustrate his point, Kolarov gives an example from *The Meek Girl* and *The Idiot*: 'These may look like rather tentative hypotheses about the relationship between the two characters. One particular detail in *The Meek Girl*, however, lends them certainty since it is a quotation that comes directly from *The Idiot*. As in the longer novel, it refers to the heroine's death and constitutes the "spoonful of blood" motif. The narrator of *The Meek Girl* arrives at the scene of the tragedy only minutes after his wife has thrown herself from the window. This is what he says as he goes back to that moment: 'I only remember that workman. He kept shouting to me that, "Only a trickle of blood (literally a handful of blood: *s gortsky krovi*) came from her mouth, a trickle, a trickle!" and he pointed to the blood on a stone' (MG, II, 3). A little later the same detail again finds a place in the narrator's frantically rushing thoughts: 'And, you know, when she fell, nothing was crushed, nothing was broken! Nothing but that "trickle of blood". A dessertspoonful, that is. From internal injury' (MG, II, 4). Compare this to the similar detail in *The Idiot* from the passage where Rogozhin tells Prince Myshkin how he killed Nastasia Filippovna: [. . .] 'and . . . and this is what is such a marvel to me, the knife only went in a couple of inches at most, just under her left breast, and there wasn't more than half a tablespoonful of blood altogether, not more [. . .] (Idiot, IV, 11).' (2013: 29)

2   Translated by Ethel Colburn Mayne. Another possible translation that is also sustained by the original is the following: 'I have a project: to go mad. Let people rage, try to cure me, let them try to bring me to reason' (translated by Michael A. Minihan, cited in Mochulsky, 1973: 17)

3   It is interesting to draw a parallel signalling that in 1866 at the village of Lyublino at his sisters' place Dostoevsky 'played the role of the king's ghost in a parody on Hamlet' (Mochulsky, 1973: 277).

4   The sense of dread evoked by this encounter resonates within various
    iterations of Russian Hamletism. Some authors, such as Pushkin, showed
    a higher sensitivity for *Hamlet*'s atmosphere of 'looking into the abyss'
    (cited in Rowe, 1976: 30), while Lermontov interpreted the sense of
    dread with less metaphysical emphasis – his Pechorin is not fascinated by
    metaphysical otherness. Conversely, Polevoy and Belinsky scrutinize the
    Hamletian crisis in political and ethical terms, whereas Grigoryev aligns
    more closely with Dostoevsky's identification with Hamletian despair, the
    presence of the supernatural and existential questioning of life after death.

5   Grigory ('Grishka') Otrepev, known as 'the False Dmitri', was a defrocked
    monk who claimed the Russian throne by pretending to be the lawful heir,
    the prince Dmitri, murdered in childhood through the intrigues of Boris
    Godunov (1551-1605), who thus made himself tsar. In 1605, by order
    of the patriarch Job, the impostor Grigory Otrepev was anathematized
    and cursed 'in this age and the age to come' in all the churches of Russia'
    (Pevear, 2006: 621). As known, Stavrogin will be called the same way by
    his wife: 'Grishka Otrepev, anathema!' (*Demons*, 2006: 250).

6   A more precise meaning of demonic in Dostoevsky's work, being a very
    complex and multilayered concept itself, will be presented and discussed
    in detail later. At this stage, it stands as a traditional quality of the devil
    against the background of Christian tradition. The *OED* defines demonic
    as 'of relating to demons or a demon; of the nature of a demon', but also,
    a synonym for the demonic since 1853 is '*demonic possession*, n. the state
    or condition of a person (supposedly) being inhabited and controlled by a
    demon'.

7   Rational egoism was a philosophical concept created by Nikolay
    Chernishevsky in his novel *What Is to Be Done?* (1863). He claimed that
    individuals act out of self-interest and that by pursuing their own good
    in rational terms they will contribute to collective well-being. It was a
    scientific and materialistic approach to morality that rejected self-sacrifice
    as counterproductive. Dostoevsky deeply and fervently disagreed with
    such a rationalistic view of peoples' will and desires.

8   Morson explains that: 'As Dostoevsky was well aware, his novels were
    likely to appear shapeless to most readers [. . .] and he therefore outlined
    a theory of realistic art to justify, and to aid in the development of, his
    aesthetic practice. Like the novels themselves, which have had such

great influence on twentieth-century European literature, this theory
seems remarkably modern. Briefly put, Dostoevsky increasingly came
to view the concept of "realistic art" as bordering on self-contradiction.
For art, he reasoned, strives for coherence and order, but reality, as the
principal narrator of *The House of the Dead* observes, "strives toward
fragmentation." What art represents, it misrepresents. Moreover, by the
mid-1870s Dostoevsky had come to believe that social "disintegration,"
"fragmentation," and "dissociation" – terms frequently used and discussed
in the Diary – were, in all probability, literally apocalyptic in extent and,
therefore, that the divergence between art and reality was particularly
extreme, perhaps absolute. Can there be art at Armageddon? Or as
Ippolit Terentiev (in *The Idiot*) poses the central question of Dostoevsky's
aesthetic thought: "Is it possible to perceive as an image that which has no
image?" (1981: 8)

9   Morson illuminates the complex paradox behind Raskolnikov's 'choice' to
    commit murder: 'In *Crime and Punishment*, Raskolnikov declares that he
    will never forgive the old woman he has killed – certainly, a thrilling line,
    since she had no intention whatever of dying at his hand or of haunting
    his dreams. But the line and the dreams express Raskolnikov's feeling
    that he was led into the crime. I suffered these deeds more than I acted
    them, says Oedipus at Colonus, and that is how Raskolnikov feels, as if
    transgression somehow happened to him. In a purely psychological sense
    that is almost true, since he never actually chooses to commit murder.
    Rather, he holds the possibility open as long as possible until to do so
    he must be at her apartment with his axe, still not having decided. Then
    the sheer momentum of his condition leads him to kill the old lady as
    if a purely mechanical process were going on. One reason Raskolnikov
    afterwards cannot decide what his motive was for choosing murder is that
    he never chose it, he only entertained the possibility of choosing it and
    refused to give up that possibility. Could it be that most crimes happen
    that way?' (1999: 473)

10  The line 'Let be.' (5.1.201–2) can be found in the Second Quarto of
    *Hamlet*, while the First Quarto and the First Folio lack it. I rely on the
    latest Arden Shakespeare revised edition, reprinted in 2017 and edited
    by Ann Thompson and Neil Taylor. This edition of *Hamlet* contains three
    separate and modernized versions based on Q1, Q2 and F. (*Hamlet*, 2017:

90). Guided by the rule that 'F is a likelier authority than Q2 for emending Q1, F is a likelier authority than Q1 for emending Q2, and Q2 is a likelier authority than Q1 to emending F' (2017: 549) they include the line 'Let be.' (5.1.201–2) in their edition.

11  See Cutrofello (2014: 82) and Fernie (2005: 205).

12  Dialetheism is a doctrine that statements may both be true and false, thus, some contradictions might be true, for example, that to be or not to be mean also to be and not to be.

# 3

# 'Hamlet' in Dostoevsky's major novels (*The Idiot, An Accidental Family, The Brothers Karamazov*)

*...but if you only knew, Prince, what a theme we've got going. Remember in Hamlet: 'To be or not to be'? A modern theme, sir, modern! Questions and answers. . . . Come closer, Prince, and decide! Everybody's been waiting for you, everybody's only been waiting for your happy wit [. . .]*

(*The Idiot*, 2012: 368, my emphasis)

*She [Nastasya Filippovna] promised Afanasy Ivanovich and me that this evening at her place she will say the final word: whether it's to be or not to be! So now you know.*

(*The Idiot*, 2012: 30, my emphasis)

*Here's a fine man and he's committed suicide – Kraft has shot himself, for an idea, for Hecuba [. . .] Besides, what's Hecuba to you?*

(*An Accidental Family*, 1994: 165, my emphasis)

*Sad, I feel sad, Pyotr Ilyich. Do you remember Hamlet? 'I am sad, so sad, Horatio . . . Ach, poor Yorick!' It is I, perhaps, who am Yorick. Yorick now, that is, and later – the skull.*

(*The Brothers Karamazov*, 1992: 406, my emphasis)

*Is there a God, or not?*

(*The Brothers Karamazov*, 1992: 642)

Nikolay Zakharov states that 'Fyodor Dostoevsky used Hamlet's qualities to create literary characters of his own: Ivan Karamazov (in *The Karamazov Brothers*), Nikolay Stavrogin (in *The Possessed*), Ippolit (in *The Idiot*), Versilov (in *A Raw Youth*), and Aleksey Ivanovich (in *The Gambler*)' (2016: 184). The already mentioned existing scholarship on the topic explores the hypothesis of Hamlet being a model for Dostoevsky's characters, which I argue needs further exploration, as the book demonstrated so far. I will take a different approach than most academic discussions by identifying the Hamlet-isotopy and concentrating on the analysis of how Dostoevsky engaged with Hamlet/*Hamlet* and Russian Hamletism. This will involve continuing to trace the Hamlet-isotopy as established in the previous chapter while considering Dostoevsky's reworking of Russian Hamletism and his Hamlet-ideologeme in order to outline the framework for different 'Hamlets'.

As we proceed with this exploration, we come closer to the realization that the main characters as well as the main themes of Dostoevsky's novels are refracted through a Hamletian kaleidoscopic lens, meaning that the problems related to Russian Hamletism found its fictional realization in Dostoevsky's prose. The following characters battle with Hamletian dilemmas: Prince Valkovsky (*The Humiliated and Insulted*), the man from the underground (*Notes from Underground*), Raskolnikov (*Crime and Punishment*), Ippolit, Nastasya Filippovna, and Prince Myshkin (*The Idiot*), Kirillov, Stavrogin and Stepan Vekhovenski (*Demons*), Versilov and Arkady Dolgoruky (*An Accidental Family*), Alyosha, Ivan and Dmitry Karamazov (*The Brothers Karamazov*). In the subsequent part, we shall delve in more detail into how these heroes are represented in three major novels: *The Idiot, An Accidental Family* and *The Brothers Karamazov*.[1]

## *The Idiot* (1868–9)

Dostoevsky's *The Idiot* (Идиот) is famous for the writer's attempt to create a perfect, Christ-like hero, as close as possible to an ideal man. However, Prince Lev Nikolayevich Myshkin is an epileptic, deeply affected by a specific condition that grants him the ability to 'see through' people in a prophetic way but also limits his capacity for relations or communication. The novel is plotted around his release from a sanatorium in Switzerland and arrival to St. Petersburg, only to be immediately drawn into scandals and conspiracies of the aristocratic world, where the centripetal force is a *femme fatale*, Nastasya Fillipovna. The rest of the novel concerns the question of who she is going to marry leading to her murder, and, on the other side, Prince Myshkin's mental decline and abandonment of life in high society.

As already noticed, the Hamletian theme emerges in *The Idiot* in connection to Prince Myshkin (Stepanian, 2014: 58). One supporting character clearly mentions *Hamlet* and asks Prince Myshkin to decide:

> but if you only knew, Prince, what a theme we've got going. Remember in Hamlet: '*To be or not to be*'? A *modern theme, sir, modern*! Questions and answers . . . [. . .] Come closer, Prince, and decide! Everybody's been waiting for you, everybody's only been waiting for your happy wit. (*The Idiot*, 2012: 368, my emphasis)

Prince Myshkin is expected to 'set it right' (*Hamlet*, 2.1.187) by everyone. A victim of projections and desires of others, he demonstrates the opposing end of the spectrum compared to all other Hamletian characters. Yet, the catastrophic outcome awaits. In Prince Myshkin, we can identify the constant reluctance to decisively act, interpret others, or take up a specific role and position in society. Moreover, there is more of a tendency *to be no one*, to renounce or erase his own identity. This tendency to have no identity or a character can be a subversive way out from the given Symbolic order. The Hamletian obsession with being someone or doing something falls into the trap deconstructed by the man from the underground. The idea that an act determines one's identity is the crucial dichotomy that is foregrounded in the 'to be or not to be' question, appropriated in Russian Hamletism and deconstructed in Dostoevsky's work. Lastly, this theme of identity reverberates in Myshkin, making him an equally suspicious character as other openly malicious manipulators: 'You're a terrible skeptic, Prince, [. . .] I've noticed that since a certain time you've become an extreme skeptic; you're beginning not to believe anything and to suppose everything' (*The Idiot*, 2012: 312–3). If we have in mind the present 'Othellian' subtext, and Dostoevsky's abandoned idea to mould Myshkin after Iago (Stepanian, 2014: 58), the famous line – *I am not who I am* (*Othello*, 1.1.65) – comes to mind. In the preparatory materials for the novel we find: 'PLAN FOR IAGO. IAGO WITH THE CHARACTER OF THE IDIOT. But he ends in piety' (PSS, 9:161, as cited in Stepanian, 2014: 58). Like many of Dostoevsky's comments, this one may be equally confusing; however, I would rather focus on the obvious parallelism of characterlessness and paradoxical thinking. Moreover, in a recent article, 'Doing Things with Paradoxes: Shakespearean Impersonations', Silvia Bigliazzi offers an important conclusion about Iago's use of paradox that may correspond to the prince's scepticism from the previous quote. Namely, 'Iago's final tautology tells us that knowledge is not achievable; it is not an awareness of not knowing, in a Socratic sense, but is identical with not-knowing. This is his final word which eventually inverts the negative diaphora into a tautology. It suggests meaning while finally eroding all possible sense' (Bigliazzi, 2022: 72). This sensation of senselessness looms over all Hamletian characters, even the good-hearted Prince Myshkin.

However, a character that unexpectedly fits into Hamletian heroes emerges in a connection rooted in the famous quote, 'to be or not to be'. I am referring to Nastasya Filippovna from *The Idiot*: 'She promised Afanasy Ivanovich and me that this evening at her place she will say the final word: whether it's *to be or not to be*! So now you know' (*The Idiot*, 2012: 30, my emphasis). It may seem somewhat surprising to associate a female character with Hamlet in this manner, although I contend that her character resonates with many themes from the Hamlet-isotopy network. For Nastasya Filippovna, one of the pivotal questions of subjectification revolves around marriage and the male gaze. She rebels against the specific Symbolic order and a traditional female role within it. Moreover, her defiance towards being objectified and construed as an object of male gaze and desire echoes elements of the Hamlet-isotopy network. This assertion can be strengthened in exposing her resemblance to other Hamletian characters.

Nastasya Filippovna is a character obsessed with self-consciousness, guilt and performativity. The narrative portrays her akin to Stavrogin's representation. Described as possessing demonical beauty like Stavrogin – she is also a centripetal force within the novel that allures, seduces and ultimately destroys other characters and herself. As Stavrogin, she is an enigmatic and deeply fascinating figure, with her character gradually unfolding through the narrative of gossip and others' impressions. Supremely intelligent and proud to the level of arrogance, she demonstrates her power over others by provocations and irrational acts that mask her wounded heart. Moreover, the development of her destiny in the novel depends on the logic of rumours. She demonstrates some Hamletian traits that are obvious in the following description of her character:

> a being who was completely *out of the ordinary*, that this was precisely the sort of being who would not merely threaten, but would certainly act, and above all would decidedly stop at nothing, the more so *as she valued decidedly nothing in the world*, so that it was even impossible to tempt her. Here, obviously, was something else, implying some heartful and soulful swill – like some sort of *romantic indignation*, God knows against whom or why, some *insatiable feeling of contempt* that *leaps completely beyond measure* – in short, something *highly ridiculous and inadmissible in decent society*, something that was a sheer punishment from God for any decent man to encounter. [. . .] *Valuing nothing, and least of all herself* (it took great intelligence and perception to guess at that moment that she had long *ceased to value herself and, skeptic and society cynic* that he was, to believe in the seriousness of that feeling), Nastasya Filippovna *was capable of ruining herself*, irrevocably and outrageously, facing Siberia and hard labor, if only she could wreak havoc on the man for whom she felt such inhuman loathing. (43–4, my emphasis)

I emphasize one direct link to the Hamletian feature of Stavrogin to prove my claim. As already mentioned in the book, the preparatory materials for *Demons* characterize Stavrogin as 'a gloomy, passionate, demonic, and disorderly character, *without any sense of measure*, with a lofty question, all the way to "to be or not to be"? To live or to exterminate oneself?' (Dostoevsky, 1968: 266, my emphasis). Thus, analogously to Stavrogin, Nastasya Filippovna is a character whose contempt *leaps completely beyond measure* and is connected with the 'to be or not to be' dilemma.

The portrayal of Nastasya Filippovna, as demonstrated by the description of her painting that fascinates several characters in the novel, is deeply intertwined with perceptions, projections and desires of others in which she mirrors herself. This mirroring functions in a similar vein as the mirror game of the underground man, a Hamletian spectacle in front of the mirror for the audience. Her confessions often veer towards mock-confessions rather than genuine expressions. However, her reliance on others spans from economic dependency to social and eventually, existential, since she will be murdered by Rogozhin. Her self-perception is made by projections of others, leading to her inherited guilt complex and an idea of being stained. However, while gaining power over others by establishing herself in the gaze of the other, for Nastasya it is simultaneously a torment because, much like it is for Gertrude, according to Armstrong: 'the glass gives back to the woman not herself, but the superegoic patriarchal figure, the assimilation of which implies her guilty submission to the gaze' (1996: 235). Her scepticism and cynicism spring from these roots, deliberately provoking and then punishing others for their desires projected on her. However, while being a victim of femicide at the end of the novel, she is a defiant victim, who provokes her own punishment to assert her power over the perpetrator. The assertion of power comes from her ability to emasculate men by remaining detached while Rogozin, who is obsessively and pathologically in love with her, remains frustrated and deprived.

She emerges as a tragic figure because she is seen by others kaleidoscopically (their projections are governed by their desires), yet she is both unable to live in the desire of the other (both male's and female's), and unable to live in accordance with her own desire, because it is interrelated with desires of others, trapped in the Hamletian spectacle game in front of the spectatorship. Her case exemplifies a feminine iteration of the Hamlet-ideologeme. Yet, at the core of her struggle is the need for salvation from despair, a fruitless yearning for faith. Her need for belief can be noticed in another significant marker that she shares with Stavrogin: her interest in reading the Apocalypse. A minor character claims how he calmed her down by 'reading the Apocalypse. A lady with a restless imagination, heh, heh! And, besides, I've come to the conclusion that she's much inclined towards serious topics, even unrelated ones. She likes them, likes them, and even takes it as a sign of special respect for her' (*The Idiot*, 2012: 201). This signal to Apocalypse is just one of the threads in the Hamlet-isotopy network in Dostoevsky's novels which usually stands for the end of history, time and all desires. This isotopy ensures Nastasya Filippovna's place among nihilistic, Hamletian heroes, defined by despair.

## An Accidental Family (1875)

*An Accidental Family*[2] (Подросток) is constructed as a novel in pursuit of sense in a world of meaningless relations and values. It depicts a story about a nineteen-year-old named Arkady Makarovitch Dolgorukov on a path of self-discovery and societal positioning, navigating between the influences of his estranged father, the aristocrat Versilov, his family and his own ideals of becoming a powerful individual. The novel is clearly foregrounded and connected to *Hamlet*, so much so Mochulsky assumed that the phrase 'The time is out of joint' could serve as an epigraph to *The Adolescent* (Stepanian, 2014: 44). The crucial links between *An Accidental Family* and *Hamlet* are most elaborately covered by Karen Stepanian (2014); however, I aim to elucidate a few other aspects connected to the Hamlet-isotopey network, such as issues related to isotopes of crisis, suicide, confession and the lost ideal. As Stepanian also noted, preparatory materials begin with Dostoevsky's note: 'A

Christian Hamlet' (*The Notebooks for a Raw Youth*, 1969: 24). The editor of *The Notebooks for a Raw Youth*, Edward Wasiolek, comments that it is 'probably a first reference to the future Versilov. Versilov will have an overdeveloped sense of analysis, which paralyzes his capacity for action. This corresponds to Turgenev's depiction of Hamlet [. . .]' (1969) However, Stepanian discusses differently:

> Did Dostoevsky want to create in his *Life of a Great Sinner* [Zhitie velikogo greshnika] (*The Adolescent* being part of that master plan) the image of Hamlet the Christian as something of a counterweight to Shakespeare's Hamlet? Because that novel's plot is, after all, closer than any other to a Shakespearean tragedy: the protagonist's mother leaves her lawful husband (Makar Dolgorukov) and enters into an illicit cohabitation with Versilov (who is here the protagonist's actual father, against whom the Adolescent long seeks to 'avenge himself,' in a parallel first pointed out by Rimma Iakubova). It must also be remembered that Dostoevsky originally intended 'the great sinner' to be 'terribly enamored' of Hamlet. (PSS, 9:129, cited in 2014: 63)

Recently, Boborykina argued that *Hamlet* permeates the whole novel in form of quotations and as a model for the main hero; moreover, the Hamletian theme is spread as a thin thread, sometimes at the level of a deep subtext or rising to the surface, while other times in the form of hints, towards a complex inner development of thoughts and their associative functioning (2021: 114, my translation). She suggested that the laconic note ('A Christian Hamlet') might be 'interpreted as some transcendental goal to which the author is leading his hero from the very first line of the novel's plan' (89, my translation).

While I propose that 'A Christian Hamlet' may be a counterweight to the politicized Russian Hamlets in an Orthodox attire rather than to Shakespeare's Hamlet who can also be understood within a Christian framework, I contend there is more to be elucidated by exploring the Hamlet-isotopy. First, I agree that the reference to *Hamlet* should be regarded as referring to Arkady and not Versilov because Versilov represents the epitome of Russian Hamletism. As Stepanian remarks,

Arkady is the main protagonist and the true Hamletian figure. Dostoevsky emphasizes: 'THE PROTAGONIST is not HE but THE BOY!' (PSS, 16: 24; see further 28, 121, 127, 175, cited in 2014: 63).

Arkady Makarovitch Dolgorukov is in pursuit of his identity and the main core of values in the disintegrated society, having a youthful, often radically idealistic wish to 'set it right'. As the narrator of the novel, he is in the position of writing his autobiography – a sequence of Hamletian dilemmas – or one big Hamletian soliloquy that re-enacts the split between the 'I' of the utterance and its statements, that is the Arkady that wishes to present himself in a certain way and the Arkady that emerges from the text. The novel begins with his confession:

> I CANNOT contain myself. I have sat down to write this story of my first steps in life when I could very well not have done so. I know one thing for sure: I'll never again sit down to write my autobiography, even if I live to be a hundred. One's got to be too grossly in love with oneself in order to write about oneself; without shame. I only excuse myself with the thought that I'm not writing for the reason others write, which is to receive the reader's praise. (*An Accidental Family*, 1994: 5)

Remarkably similar to Ippolit, Arkady is obsessed with himself yet unable to forge a coherent identity or maintain a unified perspective on events. He becomes untangled in a world of gossip, preoccupied with the scrutiny of others and driven to mask his feelings and his complex of inferiority with lofty ideas and grandiose behaviour. 'Because I was so full of other people's ideas, where could I get any of my own from when decisions had to be made? I had no one to guide me' (314). Lacking a desire of his own, Arkady mimics his father's attraction to the same woman. Furthermore, when his friend commits suicide, another facet of the Hamlet-isotopic network becomes evident in Arkady's comment, directly referencing Hamlet's soliloquy about Hecuba: 'Here's a fine man and he's committed suicide – Kraft has shot himself, *for an idea, for Hecuba* [. . .] Besides, *what's Hecuba to you?* Life here is nothing but your intrigues, messing about with all your lies and deceits and plots – Just shut up!' (165, my emphasis). However, we might interpret that this particular suicide was *for nothing*, for a youthful fictitious idea and a projection, thus having little to do with the truth. On the other hand, his father Versilov is not to be taken literally for his words because he confesses that 'it's better not to elaborate. In any case, it's my way of doing things – talking without elaborating. And that's the truth. And it's a strange thing, you know, but if I begin elaborating on an idea in which I believe it almost always ends up with my ceasing to believe in what I am saying' (234). In a way that is identified in the *confession* isotopy, Versilov pours out his thoughts, heart and soul, only to later renounce these expressions as inauthentic to him. In a world of such fluid and paradoxical subjectivities, everything may get caught in a game of abstractions because, as Arkady laments, words do not suffice. 'Anyhow, do words matter now? Isn't all this beyond mere words? Versilov once said that Othello didn't kill Desdemona and then himself because he was jealous, but because he had been deprived of his ideal!' (273). In this instance, we also observe an interconnection between Shakespeare's *Othello* and the theme of the *ideal*, which can be linked to the Hamlet-isotopy. Arkady, who is entangled in a love triangle with his father Versilov, confesses to him about the events that followed his declaration of love. This confessions echoes Hamlet's discourse, particularly the 'to be, or not to be' line: 'Listen, do you think I should go to her right now to *find out the truth, or not*?' (292, my emphasis). However, while Arkady holds a Hamletian position in the plot, I argue that Versilov is one of the most important characters of Russian Hamletism in Dostoevsky's novels. He tries to explain himself: 'It was the nostalgia only felt by the Russian nobleman – true, I can't put it better than that! A nobility nostalgia and nothing else' (490). However, he is even a stranger amalgam of class contradictions present in Russian Hamletism. Versilov is described as:

> He is a nobleman of ancient lineage, and at the same time a Parisian communard. He is a true poet and loves Russia, yet denies her absolutely. He is without any sort of religion, but yet almost ready to die for something indefinite, to which he cannot give a name, but in which

he fervently believes, like a number of Russian adherents of European civilisation of the Petersburg period of Russian history. (595–6)

Being such a complex and contradictory character, he foreshadows many arguments that Dostoevsky expresses in his 'Pushkin Speech' (see Epilogue). His lofty and dramatic rhetoric, usually mocked by Dostoevsky in other registers or writings, here receives a tragic undertone that would reverberate in Ivan Karamazov. Nevertheless, he shares the same dream about the Golden Age with Stavrogin:

> I dreamed a dream that was a complete surprise to me, for I had never had any dreams of the sort before. In the gallery at Dresden there is a picture by Claude Lorraine, called in the catalogue 'Acis and Galatea,' but I used to call it 'The Golden Age,' [. . .] I dreamed of this picture, but not as a picture, but, as it were, a reality. [. . .] It seemed a memory of the cradle of Europe, and that thought seemed to fill my soul, too, with a love as of kinship. Here was the earthly paradise of man [. . .]

> Marvellous dream, lofty error of mankind! The Golden Age is the most unlikely of all the dreams that have been, but for it men have given up their life and all their strength, for the sake of it prophets have died and been slain, *without it the peoples will not live and cannot die*, and the feeling of all this I lived through, as it were, in that dream; [. . .] it was *the love of all humanity*. (491–2)

Versilov's dream could be read as the ultimate lost ideal that cannot even be depicted in the novel except as repressed in subconsciousness and manifested through a dream. I will analyse the dream later in the chapter about Stavrogin. At this stage, however, I note that Versilov's dream represents the ideal in the form of a painting that is part of Western civilization. Opposing Versilov's inner ideal, Makar Dolgorukov, the pilgrim and official caretaker of Arkady, offers a different ideological and spiritual horizon. He makes a profound diagnosis of the state of Russian people that I interpret as Dostoevsky's criticism of Russian Hamletism, deconstructing them as *worldly men of vanity*, representing Russian intelligentsia and their bourgeois subjectivities.

There's no knowing what sort they are – large, small, silly, clever, even simple, working people – but it's all vanity. They spend their whole lives reading and thinking, sating themselves with book-learning, but they themselves remain just as bewildered as ever and cannot solve a thing. Some have gone this way and that and lost sight of themselves. Others have become hard as stone, though they still have dreams in their hearts. Others have no feelings, no thoughts at all and are just content to snigger. Yet others have merely chosen what they think are pretty posies from books, but are themselves vain and indecisive. I repeat – they all have a great boredom. The small men of this world are in sore need, they have no bread, cannot feed their children, sleep rough, yet their hearts are joyous and light. They swear and sin, and yet their hearts are light. But the great of this world eat and drink well and have heaps of gold, but are filled with a great boredom. Some have studied all there is to know, yet still they yearn for more. I always think the greater a man's mind, the greater his boredom. And here's another thing: people have taught things since the beginning of the world, but what good thing have they taught that could make the world the most beautiful, the happiest, the most joyous place in which to live? And I will say this, too: they have no true nobility and do not even want it. They have all come to ruin and yet each one praises his ruined state and gives no thought to the one and only truth of God; and yet to live without God is nothing but torment. And it transpires we curse the one thing that may light the way for us and do not know it. For you must know it is impossible to be a man and not bow down and worship. A man cannot tolerate himself, no man can. And if he rejects God, then he will bow down before an idol – a wooden one or a gold one or one made of ideas. They are become idolaters, not atheists – that's what they should be called. (395–6)

The first serious criticism here is against education and culture that leads to vanity, confusion, an incapacity to root one's being into a decision, and ultimately, to lifelessness and depression. As a representative of people's wisdom, Makar perceives how the wanderers of Russian people, the Russian Hamlets, cannot come to a conclusion about what to be and what to do. He lists different possible outcomes incited by intellectualizing, reading and dealing with science, only to denounce them all for perpetuating fantasy and torment. Lastly, in contrast to 'small men' whose hearts are light and merry, Russian Hamlets cannot bear the burden of themselves and their corrosive self-awareness. Some of the idols, to which the intelligentsia of the 1840s bowed to alongside Claude Lorrain and European art, are *Hamlet* and Shakespeare. In *An Accidental Family*, Dostoevsky demonstrates the ruining consequences of such identifications and appropriations when turned into idolization.

The analysis conducted above enables us to delineate seven isotopes in the novel within the Hamlet-isotopy network. As previously noted, the *crisis* isotopy is represented in the disintegration of values and Arkady's accidental family. While the young protagonist personifies the 'to be or not to be' dilemma, being the bearer of the Hamlet-ideologeme of indecision regarding his identity, Versilov, his father, stands as the representative of the sceptic Russian Hamlet (the second isotopy of *negativity*) who dreams of the Golden Age (the *lost ideal* isotopy). Their confessions articulate their paradoxical subjectivities, reflecting the isotopes of *confession* and *paradox*. Lastly, the *let be* isotopy is exemplified in the figure of Makar Dolgorukov and his teachings which are intended to guide Arkady towards overcoming the demonic rationality and bourgeois individuality of Dostoevsky's Hamletism.

## The Brothers Karamazov (1880)

Dostoevsky's last masterpiece, *The Brothers Karamazov* (Братья Кара мазовы), is built around a Hamletian theme of parricide. It is a story about a generation of young men, three brothers, Dmitry (a former officer), Ivan (intellectual and writer) and Alyosha (monastery novice), and stepbrother Smerdyakov, each representing a certain worldview and attitude that fit into the Hamlet-isotopy network and represent different epitomes of Russian Hamletism. As already mentioned, they are defined as Russian versions distinct from European Hamlets: 'No, gentlemen of the jury, they have their Hamlets, but so far we have only Karamazovs!' (*The Brothers Karamazov*, 1992: 716). The central plot revolves around a conflict between the father Fyodor and Dmitry over inheritance and a love interest, Grushenka. As the story unfolds, Fyodor Karamazov is murdered by his fourth and unrecognized son Smerdyakov, who, inspired by Ivan's philosophical debates on atheism, theodicy and freedom, does the killing. The last part of the novel is devoted to the prosecution of the unjustly accused Dmitry and the transformation of all brothers. Smerdyakov commits suicide; Ivan succumbs to a mental breakdown and a profound spiritual crisis, while Alyosha abandons the monastery. As Lantz notices, 'the motive of the trial – the quest of a just decision brought about after hearing evidence "pro and contra" – runs through the entire novel' (2004: 42). Following the previous analysis, we may connect this motif to the Hamlet-isotopy.

At the very beginning of *The Brothers Karamazov*, an image of Ophelia's suicide by drowning along with the irrational and absurd invention of romantic reasons to kill herself, is evoked by the narrator to explain the caprice behind the relationship between Dmitry's mother and the disgusting Fyodor Karamazov.

> But then, I once knew a young lady still of the last 'romantic' generation who, after several years of enigmatic love for a certain gentleman, whom, by the way, she could have married quite easily at any moment, ended up, after *inventing all sorts of insurmountable obstacles*, by throwing herself on a stormy night into a rather deep and swift river from a high bank somewhat resembling a cliff, and perished there decidedly by her own caprice, only because she wanted to be like *Shakespeare's Ophelia*. Even then, if the cliff, chosen and cherished from long ago, had not been so picturesque, if it had been merely a flat, prosaic bank, the suicide might not have taken place at all. This is a true fact, and one can assume that in our Russian life of the past two or three generations there have been not a few similar facts. In the same way, the action of Adelaida Ivanovna Miusov was doubtless *an echo of foreign influences*, the *chafings of a mind imprisoned*. (*The Brothers Karamazov*, 1992: 7–8, my emphasis)

This first reference to *Hamlet* signals a deeper link to Shakespeare's play, although here the woman kills herself out of a destructive need for escapism into a fantasy, rather than being actually comparable to Ophelia. Similarly to how the influence of an idol is depicted in *An Accidental Family*, here it is also seen as possessing a detrimental influence, encouraging a detachment from reality and fabrication of unreal circumstances, when Romantic literature is taken as a model for life. Dostoevsky extends satire considerably, asserting that a woman killed herself solely because 'she wanted to be like Shakespeare's Ophelia' (1992: 7). His critique is broadened to encompass the entirety of Russian society, diagnozing it not merely as afflicted by external influence but also by the anguish of a mind imprisoned and colonized by foreign ideas. This marks the introduction of this theme in *The Brothers Karamazov*, but it will recur in the novel. Also, as we saw and will see in more detail on the example of *Demons*, this colonization of one's imagination is one of the leitmotifs in relation to Shakespeare's *Hamlet*.

Parallels between *The Brothers Karamazovs* and *Hamlet* have been noted and researched (Matlaw, 1957; Rowe, 1976), but as previously discussed, I believe they deserve more analysis. Here is a map of arguments for further investigation leaning on the perspectives enabled by the Hamlet-isotopy network and by identification of the Hamlet-ideologeme. First of all, the Hamletian motives are spread out through the novel, in all major characters and in all major themes. As George Steiner claimed, we can talk about a 'deliberate use of Hamlet [. . .] to control the dynamics' (161: 140) of *The Brothers Karamazov*. We may say that, in his last novel, Dostoevsky offers a range of Russian Hamlets; moreover, as emphatically repeated in the trial for patricide at the end, he constructs Karamazovs as Russian rivals to Hamlets. Second, the ultimate accursed question 'to be or not to be' is transformed into 'Is there a God, or not?' (*The Brothers Karamazov*, 1992: 642) asked by Ivan, but repeated by many characters. Third, at the end of the novel the juxtaposition of Hamlets and Karamazovs is subtly interwoven throughout the whole novel to resonate most strongly in the trial for the murder of the Karamazov father. The prosecutor at the trial for the murder of Fyodor Karamazov seizes the opportunity to criticize Russian society in his speech, accusing the Russian youth in order to raise awareness for their lack of spirituality: 'Look, gentlemen, look at how our young men are shooting themselves – oh, without the least Hamletian question of "what lies beyond"' (694) – a motif that goes back to Ippolit from *The Idiot*. The prosecutor continues:

> There is a good deal of posturing here, of romantic frenzy, of wild Karamazovian unrestraint and sentimentality – yes, and also something else, gentlemen of the jury, something that cries out in the soul, that throbs incessantly in his mind, and poisons his heart unto death; this something is conscience, gentlemen of the jury, the judgment, the terrible pangs of conscience! But the pistol will reconcile everything, the pistol is the only way out, there is no other, and beyond – I do not know whether Karamazov thought at that moment of 'what lies beyond' or whether a Karamazov could think, in Hamlet fashion, of what lies beyond. No, gentlemen of the jury, they have their Hamlets, but so far we have only Karamazovs! (716)

On one hand, the motif of Romantic frenzy and posturing is again linked with destructive behaviour, in this case murdering someone rather than drowning oneself to resemble Ophelia, as Dmitry's mother did. On the other hand, the direct reference to the difference between Karamazovs and Hamlets is, actually, a crucial irony of the text, because the dilemma about what lies beyond death is literally propitiating all the action in the novel and is discussed by all the brothers. Ivan Karamazov explains to his younger brother Alyosha without irony:

> Well, then, what are they going to argue about, seizing this moment in the tavern? About none other than the universal questions: is there a God, is there immortality? And those who do not believe in God, well, they will talk about socialism and anarchism, about transforming the whole of mankind according to a new order, but it's the same damned thing, the questions are all the same, only from the other end. And many, many of the most original Russian boys do nothing but talk about the eternal questions. (234)

Of interest here is the association of a theistic and atheistic position – they both seek for a solution to the same problem – bringing to life a new, just order, or to use Hamletian discourse, 'setting it right'. Ivan insists even that 'all the modern axioms laid down by Russian boys on the subject, which are all absolutely derived from European hypotheses; because what is a hypothesis there immediately becomes an axiom for a Russian boy' (235), elucidating a direct and strong European influence on Russian youth. Thus, the juxtaposition given by the prosecutor is false, used with the intention to appease the courtroom:

> 'And browbeating, did you notice how he kept browbeating us? Remember the troika? "They have their Hamlets, but so far we have only Karamazovs!" That was clever.'
>
> 'Courting liberalism. Afraid.'
>
> 'He's also afraid of the defense attorney.'
>
> 'Yes, what will Mr. Fetyukovich say? Well, whatever he says, he won't get around our peasants.' (724)

As usually in Dostoevsky, some anonymous audience members see through this intention and deconstruct the cliché of Russian Hamletism, hinting at the fact that in this novel Dostoevsky actually offers answers to the accursed Hamletian questions. In any case, the whole novel begins and ends with clear references to *Hamlet*, in which a need to mimic the desire to be lofty and civilized as the 'Europeans' is foregrounded. However, a much deeper connection with *Hamlet* exists.

If we follow the Hamlet-isotopy network established in the second chapter, we can discern all seven introduced isotopes. First, the isotopy of the radical crises of all values are present in the event of patricide and may be reflected in Ivan's famous claim that if God is dead then everything is permitted. Second, the demonic philosophy in the novel takes its most developed form, particularly in Ivan Karamazov's conversation with the devil – or the hallucination of the devil – due to his severe mental breakdown. The third isotopy of the lost ideal is best epitomized in the struggle of faith that Alyosha

Karamazov undergoes once his venerated Father Zosima, the *elder*
who was in charge of his spiritual development in the monastery and
considered by some to be a living saint, dies. The whole community
awaits a miracle and believes that Zosima's exposed dead body will
not succumb to nature, indicating his sainthood. However, once
the body begins to stink, not only that Alyosha's ideal is lost, but
in this example we can recall the discourse of young Ipppolit and
even the image of Holbein's Dead Christ. Further on, the 'to be or
not to be' question is the leitmotif of the novel, albeit in the form
of Ivan's question 'Is there a God, or not?' (642). I draw attention to
the fact that it is Dmitry Karamazov who holds long and passionate
Hamletian logorrheic discourses, representing the fifth and sixth
isotopes of confession and paradox alongside Ivan who is more
frequently compared to Hamlet. More precisely, Dmitry is also
embodying the Hamlet-ideologeme, as being torn between the
ideal of 'Madonna and Sodom'. His most famous speech about the
broadness of human's split subjectivity is imbued with Hamletian
overtones similar to Dostoevsky's 1838 letter:

> I am that very insect, brother, and those words are precisely about
> me. And all of us Karamazovs are like that, and in you, an angel, the
> same insect lives and stirs up storms in your blood. Storms, because
> sensuality is a storm, more than a storm! Beauty is a fearful and terrible
> thing! Fearful because it's undefinable, and it cannot be defined,
> because here God gave us only *riddles*. Here the shores converge, here
> *all contradictions live together*. I'm a very uneducated man, brother,
> but I've thought about it a lot. So terribly many *mysteries*! Too many
> riddles oppress man on earth. Solve them if you can without getting
> your feet wet. Beauty! Besides, I can't bear it that some man, even with
> a lofty heart and the highest mind, should start from t*he ideal of the
> Madonna and end with the ideal of Sodom*. [. . .] No, *man is broad, even
> too broad, I would narrow him down. Devil knows even what to make
> of him, that's the thing!* What's shame for the mind is beauty all over
> for the heart. Can there be beauty in Sodom? [. . .] Here *the Devil is*

*struggling with God, and the battlefield is the human heart.* [. . .] (108, my emphasis)

Dmitry's speech is also a variation of the theme of *philosophia cordis* marking the heart as the central metonymy of a man, an essentially paradoxical creature in whom all contradictions live together – in accordance with Dostoevsky's *let be* project. The indecisiveness of the Hamlet-ideologeme is extended to the religious level, while the demonic tempts through physical beauty and erotic desire. In another episode when talking to Alyosha, Dmitry may be seen as connected to the Hamletian thread by declaring his despair; yet, instead of focusing and clinging onto it, he is turned towards the omnipresent gaze of God and finds solace in the transparency of his heart. And, as Shakespeare's Hamlet, he finds assurance in God's Providence: 'In a miracle of divine Providence. God knows my heart, he sees all my despair. He sees the whole picture. Can he allow horror *to* happen? Alyosha, I believe in a miracle' (121). Later, once Dmitry is falsely accused of killing his father, when, in a ridiculous and melodramatic way, he tries to confess his deepest feelings only to be completely misunderstood and humiliated, he will identify himself with Yorick the fool: 'Sad, I feel sad, Pyotr Ilyich. Do you remember Hamlet? "I am *sad, so sad, Horatio* . . . Ach, poor Yorick!" It is *I, perhaps, who am Yorick.* Yorick now, that is, and later – the skull' (406, my emphasis). Although it is noted that Alyosha could be the 'holy fool' of the novel, I argue that Dmitry might also fit into this group, especially through connecting the motifs of the Hamlet-isotopy network.

In the portrait of the second brother Ivan Karamazov, who shares most Hamletian characteristics as understood in nineteenth-century Russian Hamletism (nihilism, scepticism, atheism or rather antitheism, despair, melancholy, philosophizing), there are other aspects of the Hamlet-isotopy network worth noting. His despair is coupled with irrational love for life, and this vitality characterizing all the Karamazovs is Dostoevsky's typical criticism of lifeless theoretical thinking. Ivan exclaims in a confession to Alyosha:

> True, it's a feature of the Karamazovs, to some extent, this *thirst for life despite all;* it must be sitting in you, too; but why is it base? There is still an awful lot of centripetal force on our planet, Alyosha. I want to live, and I do live, even if it *be against logic.* Though *I do not believe in the order of things,* still the sticky little leaves that come out in the spring are dear to me, the blue sky is dear to me, some people are dear to me, whom one loves sometimes, would you believe it, *without even knowing why;* some human deeds are dear to me, which one has perhaps long ceased believing in, but still honors with one's heart, out of old habit. (230, my emphasis)

This love for life echoes the ideas expressed in the letter of young Dostoevsky: 'To know that one single effort of the will would suffice to demolish that veil and become one with eternity – to know all this, and still live on like the last and least of creatures. How terrible! How petty is man! Hamlet! Hamlet!' (Dostoevsky, 1914: 4). One of the crucial themes that resonates with Dostoevsky's project of madness is this thirst for life against and despite logic, despite dis/belief in the order of the world, despite rational explanations. Moreover, Ivan will profess the same love – a love bordered on absurdity, or, better, a love regardless of its absurdity – towards European culture, despite of calling it a graveyard:

> I want to go to Europe, Alyosha, I'll go straight from here. Of course I know that I will only be going to a *graveyard,* but to the most, *the most precious graveyard,* that's the thing! The precious dead lie there, each stone over them speaks of such ardent past life, of such passionate faith in their deeds, their truth, their struggle, and their science, that I – this I know beforehand – will fall to the ground and kiss those stones and weep over them – being wholeheartedly convinced, at the same time, that it has all long been a graveyard and nothing more. And I will not weep from despair, but simply because I will be happy in my shed tears. I will be drunk with my own tenderness. Sticky spring leaves, the blue sky – I love them, that's all! Such things *you love not with your mind, not with logic, but with your insides, your guts,* you love your first young strength. (*The Brothers Karamazov,* 1992: 230, my emphasis)

Europe serves as a toponym for civilizational values for Ivan, embodying ideals of the French Revolution, socialism, liberalism, fraternity and equality. Yet, in his opinion, these values no longer exist in Europe. Ivan seems to be aware of his deep, instinctual desires, but as the novel unravels, he will not manage to escape rationalization in attempting to come to terms with the existence of God:

> if I cannot understand even that, then it is not for me to understand about God. I humbly confess that I do not have any ability to resolve such questions, I have a Euclidean mind, an earthly mind, and therefore it is not for us to resolve things that are not of this world. [. . .] It's not God that I do not accept, you understand, it is this world of God's, created by God, that I do not accept and cannot agree to accept. With one reservation: I have a childlike conviction that the sufferings will be healed and smoothed over, that the whole *offensive comedy of human contradictions* will disappear like a pitiful mirage, a vile concoction of man's Euclidean mind, feeble and puny as an atom, and that ultimately, at the world's finale, in the moment of eternal harmony, there will occur and be revealed something so precious that it will suffice for all hearts, to allay all indignation, to redeem all human villainy, all bloodshed; it will suffice not only to make forgiveness possible, but also to justify everything that has happened with men – *let* this, *let* all of this come true and be revealed, but I do not accept it and do not want to accept it! [. . .] That is my essence, Alyosha, that is my thesis. (235–6, my emphasis)

Possessing an earthly mind, Ivan is not an atheist but an antitheist because he rejects God and the world he envisions, rather than simply denying God's existence. He is rebelling against God, driven by the offence at the baseness of human disgrace and he refuses to accept the ultimate salvation and forgiveness promised in Christ's Second Coming. The Grand Inquisitor is Ivan's story about Christ's Second Coming who is confronted by a Spanish Inquisitor that 'puts God on trial' (Lantz, 2004: 42), ultimately problematizing questions of responsibility and 'issues that had gripped Dostoevsky all his mature life: how to achieve justice on earth?' (43). Ivan grapples with notions of authorship, being obsessed with conceptual creation. He is capable of

conceiving the silent Christ who offers only a kiss to the inquisitor as his
defence, but does not have the capacity to humiliate his arrogance and
accept that he is not entitled neither to accept nor deny the existence
of the world. Dostoevsky's criticism of Russian Hamletism expressed
in the 'Pushkin Speech' suggest that Russian Hamlets should humble
themselves. However, in Ivan we see the tragic fall of a noble and sharp
mind, painfully yearning for justice but incapable of humbling himself
and truly loving any other being. Another very interesting and subtle
reference to *Hamlet* is inserted at the end of the conversation between
Ivan and Alyosha. Ivan mentions:

> 'I think that if the devil does not exist, and man has therefore created
> him, he has created him in his own image and likeness.'
>
> 'As well as God, then.'
>
> 'You're a remarkably good 'implorator of unholy suits,' as Polonius says
> in Hamlet,' [. . .]
> 'So you caught me, but let it be, I'm glad. A nice God you've got, if man
> created him in his image and likeness.' (*The Brothers Karamazov*, 1992: 239)

By comparing Alyosha to Polonius, Ivan identifies as Hamlet. In this
comparison, the youngest brother Alyosha, who is preparing to be a
monk, is connected with a buffoon, Polonius. Moreover, this turning
one's words against him as a characteristic of men that 'created' Alyosha's
God is a very subtle and subversive hint to the manipulative capacity of
religious rhetoric and the power struggles between the believers and
nonbelievers. If we treat Ivan as a theoretician of Russian Hamletism,
*Hamlet* is a vehicle of coming closer to faith through disbelief as fully
expressed in the devil's long Hamletian speech:

> By some pre-temporal assignment, which I have never been able to
> figure out, I am appointed 'to negate,' whereas I am sincerely kind and
> totally unable to negate. No, they say, go and negate, without negation
> there will be no criticism, and what sort of journal has no 'criticism
> section'? Without criticism, there would be nothing but 'Hosannah.'
> But 'Hosannah' alone is not enough for life, it is necessary that this

'Hosannah' pass through the crucible of doubt, and so on, in the same vein. I don't meddle with any of that, by the way, I didn't create it, and I can't answer for it. So they chose themselves a scapegoat, they made me write for the criticism section, and life came about. We understand this comedy: I, for instance, demand simply and directly that I be destroyed. No, they say, live, because without you there would be nothing. If everything on earth were sensible, nothing would happen. Without you there would be no events, and there must be events. And so I serve grudgingly, for the sake of events, and I do the unreasonable on orders. People take this whole comedy for something serious, despite all their undeniable intelligence. That is their tragedy. (642)

The devil is presented as a farcical and comical figure, paradoxically appointed to be the critic of all things because without his doubt nothing would exist. In his reversal of points of view and spinning of arguments, the devil presents himself as the scapegoat. He is a comedian with the ultimate trick of being taken seriously for the wrong reasons. Devilish rhetoric involves acknowledging an error only to adopt the counter-argument, often supporting the exact position he 'seemingly' seeks to undermine. His rhetoric in *The Brothers Karamazov* is strikingly similar to Stavrogin's insight that 'One can argue about everything' (*Demons*, 2006: 676). Whether he is Ivan's hallucination, a manifestation of a certain aspect of Ivan's own ideas or an actual devil, it is irrelevant to the fact that these ideas have driven Ivan Karamazov to madness. His obsession is evident in his frantic behaviour and in repeating the same question to the devil that he had previously asked Alyosha, a variation of the 'to be, or not to be' phrase:

'So you don't believe in God, then?'

... 'Well, how shall I put it – that is, if you're serious. . .'

'Is there a God, or not?'

[. . .] 'Let's say I'm of one philosophy with you, if you like, that would be correct. *Je pense donc je suis*, I'm quite sure of that, but all the rest around me, all those worlds, God, even Satan himself – for me all that is unproven, whether it exists in itself, or is only my emanation,

> a consistent development of my I, which exists pre-temporally and
> uniquely [. . .] (*The Brothers Karamazov*, 1992: 642)

The absurdity of questioning the devil about his belief in God – and
further, inquiring as if he possesses certain knowledge of God's existence
– serves as a powerful example of Dostoevsky's irony. The irony is
deepened by the devil's response, which echoes a Cartesian perspective.
Both Ivan and the devil are trapped in 'the prison of [modern] self-
consciousness' (Gillespie, 2016: 97). Through this irony, Dostoevsky
deftly subverts the very foundations of Western rationalistic philosophy
that is based on 'the critical spirit that calls everything into question'
(98). Through the invocation of Descartes in this context, Dostoevsky,
while subtly referencing the 'to be or not to be' dilemma, amplifies a
nihilistic interpretation of *Hamlet*.

Lastly, the epitaph of the novel, 'Verily, verily, I say unto you, Except a
corn of wheat fall into the ground and die, it abideth alone: but if it die,
it bringeth forth much fruit' (John 12:24), implies a death of the seed
in order to have rebirth, and while in the middle of the book Zosima
expands on this motif, the devil appropriates it in Ivan's hallucination.
There is a paradoxical proximity between demonic and sanctity and the
difficulties of discerning one from the other are paramount. Zosima
words are different however: '*let* him cast it [the seed of an idea] into
the soul of a simple man, and it will not die, it will live in his soul all
his life, hiding there amidst the darkness, amidst the stench of his sins,
as a bright point, as a great reminder. And there is no need, no need of
much explaining and teaching, he will understand everything simply'
(*The Brothers Karamazov*, 1992: 294, my emphasis). In his words we
can identify the 'Let be' project that is even more precisely described
in Zosima's advice to Madame Khokhlakov, where he explains what
letting go to faith means in practice. He offers the solution to 'European'
Hamletian contradictions and the way against the demonic logic: 'By
the experience of active love. Try to love your neighbors actively and
tirelessly. The more you succeed in loving, the more you'll be convinced
of the existence of God and the immortality of your soul. And if you reach

complete selflessness in the love of your neighbor, then undoubtedly you will believe, and no doubt will even be able to enter your soul' (56). In *The Brothers Karamazov*, we might find a way to endure Ivan's shattering realization of the cruelty of the worldly injustice following Zosima's teachings, based on the epiphanies of his late brother Markel: 'truly each of us is guilty before everyone and for everyone, only people do not know it, and if they knew it, the world would at once become paradise' (298).

## Dostoevsky's Hamletian Heroes

In order to better understand the cryptic messages from *The Brothers Karamazov*, these characters and their links to Hamlet/Hamlet and Russian Hamletism should be considered within the broader context of Dostoevsky's conception of subjectivity within Russian tradition. It is problematic to find a Russian equivalent for the concept of Western 'self', 'soi, or selbst of European cultural traditions' as Yuri Corrigan highlights, since in Russian intellectual history such a word does not have a single equivalent (2017: 11). Different terms may be used, such as 'soul (*dusha*), personality (*lichnost'*), person (*chelovek; litso*), individual (*osoba*), and selfhood in the more negative sense (*samost'*)' (2017). The closest counterpart is the first pronoun, I (*ja*), frequently used by Dostoevsky. But this lexical difference has its root in ideological and even theological traditions. 'As an enemy of individualism, Dostoevsky categorically rejected the concept of a self that was not inherently integrated into other selves. He conceived of the Christian ideal as the overcoming of the "I", the development of an ability "to annihilate this I, to give it wholly to all and everyone, undividedly and selflessly" (PSS, 20: 172), and he persistently criticised the European bourgeois conception of selfhood' (2017). As demonstrated in the chapter on Dostoevsky's take on Russian Hamletism, we may suggest that he saw the figure of Hamlet as a European bourgeois subjectivity, or its amalgam with Russian notions of selfhood emerging in the class of

Russian intelligentsia. Dostoevsky's views on the European bourgeoisie are unconditionally negative, most radically, satirically and sometimes chauvinistically expressed in his polemic text, *Winter Notes on Summer Impressions* (1863).[3] However, in this text he offers a counterpart – an example of the difference between individuality and personality:

> Is salvation to be found in the absence of individuality? My reply is no, on the contrary, not only should one not lose one's individuality, but one should in fact, become an individual to a degree far higher than has occurred in the West. You must understand me: a voluntary, absolutely conscientious and completely unforced sacrifice of oneself for the sake of all is, I consider, a sign of the highest development of individual personality, its highest power, highest self-possession and highest freedom of individual will. (Dostoevsky, 2016: 68)

Here, we find one of his crucial paradoxes of developing personality by sacrificing individuality – or in other terms, of sacrificing the idea of an autonomous and sovereign humanistic liberal self. Moreover, Corrigan brings to attention that Dostoevsky wrote in his notebooks how, according to Christianity, identifying 'where your personality ends and another begins [. . .] is unthinkable' (PSS, 27: 49). Corrigan suggests that Dostoevsky managed to solve the paradox of subjectivity as reflected in the subtitle of this book, or the 'paradox of the self as both individually distinct and open-endedly plural', by 'an innovative and synthetic topography of the personality, a *metaphysical psychology* by means of which he attempted to rescue *spiritual notions of self and soul for a secular age*' (2017: 4, my emphasis). I agree with his conclusion that Dostoevsky was 'searching for a psychological way of conceiving of the social and metaphysical ideals of *sobornost*' (organic collective unity) and *tsel'nost* (wholeness of personality)' (6). And, I add the following: Dostoevsky's Hamletian heroes – as an amalgam with the split Western, bourgeois subjectivities – stand in the way of the historical, personal and cultural path to ideals of *sobornost* and *tsel'nost in* practice.

My conclusion is that Hamletian characters in Dostoevsky's major novels are driven and defined by a desire to be. The desire to be is intricately linked with the desire to be seen and perceived in their particularity and totality. They rely on other characters as their audience, before whom they enact their performances. Thus, they are subjected to the desire and gaze of the other, in which they mirror themselves, internalizing phantasmal projection of others. Hamletian heroes either rebel against being inscribed in the domain of the Other or constantly fail in their attempts to refuse it. Their biggest anxiety revolves around being pinned down or explained by another character, as they might be reduced to a signifier easily appropriated and modified by other's discourse. This is the second crucial statement for the identity of Hamletian heroes that indicates the problem of interpreting them. I argue that this issue constitutes the central theme of their inner struggles, and it is also a structural and formal aspect of Dostoevsky's narrative.

At this stage, we can without hesitation remark that Dostoevsky's criticism of *Hamlet* is profoundly negative, despite being ambiguously rendered in his most compelling characters. Dostoevsky's heroes are often bearers of radical doubt and self-reflection, oscillating between extreme pride alongside self-abasement and self-humiliation, harbouring negative faith and melancholy. These traits cause an ironical ambivalence towards notions of good and evil, leading to nihilism, despair, potential madness, and contemplation of suicide or homicide. Epistemological and metaphysical uncertainties are crucial for their pursuit of self-knowledge, fuelling an obsessive desire for autonomy. Dostoevsky crafts them as performative subjectivities with protean possibilities. Finally, these characters question whether a specific act can define their being, reflecting on the interplay between actuality and potentiality within a self. Hamletian subjectivities embedded in Dostoevskian novels participate in the drama of watching and being watched, confession and performance, in the frame of a religious context. These elements – *being seen, confessing and performing* – serve as evidence of one's existence for sceptical Hamletian heroes. Namely, Hamletian characters entail a sense of being paranoid about the fact that their existence is certain only if they are perceived by others, if they confess their interiority and if they incite a reaction through their 'performance'. The question arises: Is there a divinity that observes and sees all, acting as an omnipotent witness and primary interlocutor? These existential questions torment Dostoevsky's Hamletian heroes, who grapple with the reality of their existence, power dynamics, and truthfulness of confession/expression in language or gestures. They are haunted by the fear that without being seen, they cease to exist. This visual regime lies at the heart of Dostoevsky's novels and his poetics, wherein he integrates the idea of God as a constant witness and judge. In Dostoevsky's Hamletian characters, the ultimate 'Big Other' – a silent, omnipotent, and omnipresent witness and judge – is God. When the existence of this 'Big Other' is called into question, they become undecided, lacking a principle upon which to base their decisions (because if there is no God, "everything is permitted" (*The Brothers Karamazov*, 1992: 263)). Consequently, in their quest to define what to be and determine what to do, they adopt various masks and employ phantasms shaped by the desires of others, hindering their authentic connection with their own desires. Thus, 'Lacan's deconstruction of Cartesian consciousness, a consciousness founded on the illusion of the self "seeing itself as self"' (Wilson, 2007: 121) seems an apt perspective to view Dostoevsky's Hamletian characters whose split selves are in the form of the hallucinated devil from *The Brothers Karamazov*, declaring his Cartesian provenience.

But what constitutes a Hamletian hero in Dostoevsky's opus? In the light of the above and what has been discussed in the previous chapters, his heroes can be said to be interconnected by what I termed the Hamlet-ideologeme – the undecidability about their identities enacting a drama of the desire to be and to have faith, while realizing the inherent impossibility to decide what to do and what to be based on rational, logocentric terms. And, second, these characters possess strong links with the Hamlet-isotopy network as demonstrated. In this chapter, a wide range of different 'Hamlets' emerged. However, I suggest that these readings should be seen only as first steps in identifying traces that could further be explored. Every single isotopy may be a path for further research – in either reconstructing widely the interplay of meaning between these three novels or in analysing the links with *Hamlet*. In the next two chapters, I will demonstrate the full span of my critical model exemplified on *Demons*.

# Notes

1 *Crime and Punishment*, despite being one among the so-called five major novels by Dostoevsky alongside *The Idiot, Demons, An Accidental Family* and *The Brothers Karamazov*, is excluded from the analysis in this chapter for two reasons. First, there is already relevant scholarship about the links between this novel and Shakespeare's play (Stepanian, 2016; Movsesian, 2020), and second, because I examined some aspects of the Hamlet-isotopy in regard to this novel in the previous chapter.

2 The title of the novel is translated by Constance Garnett as *A Raw Youth* (1916) and *The Adolescent* by Richard Pevear and Larissa Volokhonsky (2003), Andrew R. MacAndrew (1971) and Dora O'Brian (2017). In 1994 Richard Freeborn offered a new translation, *An Accidental Family*, for Oxford University Press. Freeborn offers an explanation for his choice with which I agree: 'Dostoevsky's use of the term *podrostok* or "under-ager", "juvenile", "teenager" as a title for his novel poses certain problems for a contemporary English translation. Nowadays a 20-year-old writing about his 19-year-old self could legally regard himself as a young adult writing about his young adulthood, not as a raw youth or adolescent writing about his juvenile or teenage experience. What identifies this particular young narrator is his illegitimacy. He is described at the end of the novel as "a member of an accidental family", a phenomenon characteristic, in Dostoevsky's view, of society at the time he was writing' (1994: vii).

3 The following passage illustrates the gist of how Dostoevsky perceived the difference between the principle of individuality of Western bourgeoisie and his understanding of collectivism: 'Fraternity, brotherhood. Now this is a most curious concept and, it must be admitted, constitutes the principal stumbling block in the West. The Western man speaks of brotherhood as of the great moving force of humanity, and does not realize

that brotherhood cannot come about if it does not exist in fact. What is to be done? Brotherhood must be created at all costs. But it turns out that brotherhood cannot be created, because it creates itself, is given, exists in nature. It was, however, found to be absent in French and in Western nature generally; what was found to exist instead was the principle of individuality, the principle of isolation, of intensified self-preservation, of self-seeking, of self-determination within one's own personality or self, of contrast between this self, the whole of nature and the rest of humanity; and this contrast was considered as an independent and separate principle completely equal and equivalent in value to all that existed apart from itself.

Now such a contrast could not produce brotherhood. Why? Because within brotherhood, true brotherhood, it is not the individual personality, not the self, that should lay claim to its right of equality in value and importance with all the *rest*, but all this *rest* should *itself* approach the individual, the separate self laying this claim, and should itself without being asked, recognize the individual as its equal in value and rights, i.e. the equal of all else that exists in the world. Nay more, the individual who rebels and makes claims should much rather sacrifice both his personality and the whole of himself to society and not only not claim his rights, but on the contrary, hand then over unconditionally to society. But the Western individual is not used to this kind of procedure: he demands by force, he demands rights, he wants to *go shares*. And, naturally, no brotherhood results. There is, of course, the possibility of regeneration. But such a regeneration takes thousands of years, for ideas of this kind must, first of all, become completely ingrained and assimilated in order to become reality.' (2016: 66–7)

# 4

# 'Hamlet' in *Demons* (1871–2)

*What art represents, it misrepresents.*

(Morson, 1981: 8)

In describing the atmosphere of *Demons*, John Jones evokes 'a sensation, a crawling sensation of the *time being out of joint*; there is more *Hamlet* to *The Possessed* than what is personal to Stavrogin' (1983: 278–9). The text of *Demons* is a very complex thread of references, an 'allegorical palimpsest' (Valentino, 1997: 47). Thus, the references to Hamlet/*Hamlet* and Russian Hamletism should be systematized to follow the hints Dostoevsky intentionally leaves. There are three groups of Shakespearean references in the following order of appearance: mentioning Shakespeare's works and heroes (the figures of Hamlet and Othello); comparing Stavrogin to Prince Hal and Hamlet, and Lebyatkin to Falstaff; utilizing Shakespeare as a tool for examining an ideal. However, these scarce references are not themselves sufficient to support my main hypothesis that Stavrogin is one of Dostoevsky's Hamletian characters and that Shakespeare's *Hamlet* is such an important hypotext[1] for *Demons*. From a theoretical perspective, these references imply that the connection between *Hamlet* and *Demons* is neither marginal nor accidental nor follows a pattern of banal Shakespearean references and allusions, as can often be found in Russian narratives between the 1820s and 1870s. On the contrary, I will demonstrate that there exists a crucial resonance between Hamlet and Stavrogin's characters and explore how the play echoes within the novel at various transtextual[2] levels. *Demons* can be regarded as a novel with a main character that belongs to a certain type of heroes or anti-heroes based on the figure of Hamlet (given the parallels between Stavrogin and the Danish Prince). I suggest that the character of Hamlet as well as its derivations in Russian Hamletism provides Dostoevsky with a model for representing and constructing subjectivity. Apart from the ones mentioned above, Dostoevsky uses complex and manifold referencing strategies to signal the relationship between *Hamlet* and *Demons*, including hints that are not clearly marked and do not coincide with usual readings of Shakespeare's *Hamlet*. Furthermore, Hamletian motifs and themes transcend the borders of literary works of the period and participate in the flux of the political, ideological and cultural discourse of the phenomenon of Russian Hamletism. Additionally, in criticizing Hamlet's solipsism, despair and nihilism, Dostoevsky addressed what he regarded as the negative influences of Western individualism, particularly the lack of ethical responsibility towards the singularity and uniqueness of another being.

In the first part of *Demons*, Dostoevsky introduces an episode about writing a book that would be 'so to speak, a picture of the spiritual, moral, inner life of Russia for an entire year' (2006: 129). The young aristocratic lady Lizaveta Nikolaevna Tushina, inspired by the company of Nikolay Stavrogin (with whom she is in love) and Peter Verhovensky (the leader of a false revolutionary network and master manipulator), resolves to 'work for a common cause' (2006) and communicates to Ivan Shatov (a former revolutionary turned into Slavophile) that she wants to create a book, one collected out of a selection of facts from yearly newspapers and journals published in Russia. Shatov understands her in a specific way: 'So the result would be something with a tendency, a selection of facts with a specific tendency' (2006). But she naively insists on objectivity: 'there's no need for any tendency. Just impartiality – that is the only tendency' (2006). However, Shatov, a much more astute and cautious reader, replies: 'But there's nothing wrong with a tendency [. . .] and it's impossible to avoid, as soon as at least some selection reveals itself. The selection of facts will in itself indicate how they are to be understood. Your idea isn't bad' (2006). This whole episode could and should be read as a nod Dostoevsky gives to his readers: an instruction, or a manual for reading and interpreting *Demons*. It is a metafictional moment at its best. Russell Scott Valentino supports this approach by claiming, in 'The Word Made Flesh in Dostoevskii's *Possessed*', that *Demons* is maybe more than anything else a book teaching us how to read:

> *The Possessed* is a work about literature, about creating literature, and most important, about literary interpretation, it is the work's treatment of allegory per se that makes explicit the purpose such an insistence on its relation to other texts must inevitably promote. *The Possessed* represents an attempt to teach – or perhaps reteach – its readers how to read, to lead them back from the brink of sacramental ethereality into the concrete world of literature as such. (1997: 49)

Hence, the traces of literary sources as the author's deliberate choices suggest avenues for interpretation. This metafictional dimension constitutes a significant facet in my approach, revealing Dostoevsky's cautionary stance against manipulation, misinterpretation and deception: utilizing the discourse of the novel, against the seduction of 'the devil'. Dostoevsky implies that to confront the demonic, one must become a very discerning, astute and critical reader. The reader must not only discern the narrator's identity but also scrutinize their potential motives, evaluate the tone, consider contexts and, above all, refrain from uncritically accepting the apparent value or meaning of a text without meticulous analysis. In other words, Dostoevsky instructs the reader's ability to dismantle the ideology behind the text. The implicit reader envisioned and endorsed by the novel is thus trained to combat confusion, naivete and delve in mystery and contradiction. It is thus crucial to underscore the significance of Shatov's remarks as a hermeneutical model for reading *Demons*, one we should also have in mind when analysing the sources of Dostoevsky's work. Shatov's response claims two things. First, he contends that avoiding intentionality in selection (and creation) is impossible, and moreover, that this inherent impossibility should be acknowledged. Second, Shatov asserts that both selection and interpretation are inherently always already a political and aesthetical act.

My analysis starts with the subtext of *Demons* in the form of its preparatory materials, progressing to the exploration of the paratextual elements before reaching the text of the novel which serves as a foundation for uncovering subtle hints, trails and latent imprints dispersed across multiple layers. Linear intertextual and interdiscursive disseminations of Russian Hamletism and the Russian reception of *Hamlet* are approached diachronically and as examples of author-directed intertextuality. Additionally, I explore the synchronic network of Dostoevsky's ideas concerning the Hamlet-figure, by directing attention towards the subtext of the novel. Since this material was not intended for publication by the author, the connections and interpretations are reader-related. The subsequent step scrutinizes the paratextual layer, encompassing epigraphs, chapter titles and an omitted chapter, aimed at revealing the underlying ideology governing the narrative's organizational principles. This layer is approached from a reader-perspective, identifying dissipated motifs and connecting the network of Hamletian themes to discern the most fitting approach to the narrative. Lastly, the textual analysis delves into the isotopy network, exploring its convergence with the Hamlet-ideologeme, aspects of Russian Hamletism and *Hamlet*, both from reader and author-directed perspectives. This endeavour aims to unravel both overt and implicit functions of Hamletian references in *Demons*.

## Shakespeare in the *Notebooks* for *Demons*

In order to understand and complicate the debate on how Dostoevsky perceived Shakespeare and what is the meaning of his references to Shakespeare, the *Notebooks* for *Demons* are of utmost importance and can be treated as a subtextual layer. In the preparatory materials there are four crucial instances. First, the future Stepan Trofimovich Verkhovensky, who is called Granovsky in the drafts,[3] asks: 'And so the entire question is – Shakespeare or Christ or petroleum [the symbol of the Commune – K.S]?' (PSS, 11: 369), and answers: 'Vive Shakespeare and *à bas le pétrole!*' (11: 371). However, there are three options in this question, as Kovalevskaya notices: 'Shakespeare is opposed to BOTH Christ and petroleum' (2014: 79). I agree with her that the 'way' Shakespeare embodies is not 'the religious way emblematized by Christ, and not the atheistic, science-based way emblematized by petroleum' (2014). Also, characteristically for Westernizers, Stepan Trofimovich offers his answer in French. The second example focuses on Dostoevsky's most often quoted words on Shakespeare as a prophet. However, Levin has identified that this passage, erroneously attributed to Dostoevsky (Lantz, 2004: 393), was actually written by the historian Granovsky, whose lines Dostoevsky planned to attribute to Stepan Verkhovensky. Thus, it represents a 'Western' perspective on Shakespeare that will be put in question.

> On Shakespeare:
>
> This is non-tendentious, and eternal, and it has survived.
>
> This is not a simple reproduction of everyday life, in which, as many scholars assert, exhausts the whole reality.
>
> The *whole of reality* is not exhausted by everyday life, for a great huge part of it is present in it in the form of a *still latent, unexpressed, future Word*. From time to time there appear prophets who *divine and express* this integral word. Shakespeare is a prophet, sent by God, so as to reveal to us secrets about man, about the human soul. (*Notebooks*, 1968: 375, my emphasis)

This passage epitomizes Romantic Bardolatry, perpetuating the idea of a divinely inspired Shakespeare's genius. As such it is neither original nor particular for Russian reception. There are two other reasons why this note should not be taken as a straightforward expression of Dostoevsky's attitude. First, in his 'Pushkin Speech', Dostoevsky argued that Pushkin was the prophetic writer, rather than Shakespeare. Second, following this note, Dostoevsky adds an invented dialogue between two anonymous voices regarding themes of prophecy and divinity: '"A prophet and anointed, you can't say that, Sir." "Do you know what the word anointed means?" Thou shall not be saved unless thou hast sinned' (1968). How should we understand these paradoxical statements? It seems that Dostoevsky intuits that closeness to 'divinity' and a capability to see through human souls, revealing their secrets, is something that requires anointing, i.e. smearing '(a person who is sick, dying, or infirm) with blessed oil, as part of the sacrament of extreme unction' or accepting '(a person) into the Christian Church by performing this action' (OED). In other words, this prophetic capability of Shakespeare deserves blessing, but it also represents the sin of human transgression in placing him closer to the divine. Shakespeare is understood as this dual entity that is simultaneously in contact with the demonic and marked by sainthood. This dynamic encapsulates the Shakespearean demonic *destructive creation* that Dostoevsky has in mind when he claims: 'Thou shall not be saved unless thou hast sinned' (1968). It is a prerequisite to be saved. Luigi Pareyson might help us to understand this complex position explaining that Dostoevsky's conception of God 'is certainly closer to the ones who are desperate for having denied Him, than to the ones who believe to have always affirmed him' (cited in Farafonova, 2022: 28). Stefano Aloe also contends that Dostoevsky's portrayal of great atheists diverges from orthodox atheism. Aloe further elaborates, 'in keeping with Dostoyevsky's penchant for paradox that these great atheists doubt ceaselessly, struggle inwardly and even seem tempted to yield to the recognition of faith' (2016: 63, my translation). A pertinent excerpt from *Demons* underscores the complexity: 'But wasn't it you [Stavrogin] who told me that if someone *proved to you mathematically that the truth is outside Christ, you would better agree to stay with Christ than with the truth*? Did you say that? Did you?' (*Demons*, 2006: 249, my emphasis).[4] In this pivotal argument, belief is starkly juxtaposed not only against rational proof but, crucially, to the rational (mathematical) concept of truth. Aloe maintains that Dostoevsky's atheists 'do not oppose God out of weakness; rather, weakness and fragility would signify yielding to the solace of faith before grappling with the *aporia* of disbelief previously identified by their reasoning' (2016: 63, my translation). Despite claiming atheism, Stavrogin also says: 'If I had belief, I would no doubt repeat it now as well; I wasn't lying, speaking as a believer' (2006: 249). To explain this phenomenon, Aloe references Lukács, 'who observes the proximity of Dostoyevsky's atheists to God. According to Lukács, for Dostoyevsky as for Kierkegaard, the paradox lies in arriving at faith not through adherence to Christianity but rather through disbelief' (2016: 63, my translation). The proximity of blasphemy to faith opens another dimension to nihilism, which stands in opposition to religious ontology, when viewed through a secular, psychological lens. In moments of profound bleakness and numbness, when one is close to being lifeless and in a state of torpor, there emerges a primal urge towards (self-) destruction that by contrast offers a heightened sense of reality and vitality.

A similar emphasis on a Western perspective epitomized in Shakespeare is present in the third example, when the Prince (the future Stavrogin) reads Shakespeare's works. 'The Prince. He touched upon Shakespeare, got to talk about him, brought in Russia for comparison, and suddenly said: "Oh, well, how and where could we compare ourselves to anything so colossal?"' (*Notebooks*, 1968: 200). The Prince draws the comparison that underscores the lack of a direct equivalent in Russian culture, perpetuating the introjected inferiority complex from the West. However, as we will see in the 'Pushkin Speech', it is not the opinion Dostoevsky held himself.[5] The Romantic myth of Shakespeare as a divinely inspired prophet resonates deeply within Dostoevsky's work – although it is an assumption that is only partially accurate. His appropriation of Shakespeare's anthropological ideology is similarly paradoxical. His remarks signal a paradoxical vision that deconstructs both a Romantic and a Realist interpretation of the Bard. To Dostoevsky, Shakespeare embodies a paradoxical identity – an 'anointed' prophetic figure that is a blend of a specific form of demonic and sainthood. This statement underscores the significance of *free faith* in any process of interpretation, thus, of Shakespeare's value as well. As George Pattison explains, 'the process of interpretation cannot be separated from our moral orientation', therefore responding adequately 'to the appeal of the text is thus to embark upon an ethical and not just aesthetical education' (Pattison, 2001: 253). The faith to which Dostoevsky summons his reader 'cannot be labelled arbitrary or capricious: it is necessarily difficult, responsible and profoundly moral' (2001), meaning that Shakespeare's value, as the value of anything else, should be a test of one's capacity to judge in accordance with *free faith*.

## 'Hamlet' on the paratextual level

As previously mentioned, the title of the second chapter, 'Prince Harry. Matchmaking', refers to Shakespeare's *Henry IV*. As a paratext, the title represents 'an "undefined zone" between the inside and the outside, a zone without any hard and fast boundary' (Genette, 1997: 2). The subtle hint in the chapter title invites the reader to delve deeper into the parallels with Shakespeare's 2 *Henry IV*, especially concerning the all-prevailing theme of rumours. Namely, Varvara Petrovna, Stavrogin's mother, devises a secret scheme to marry Stepan Trofimovich to Dasha Shatova in order to conceal rumours about Stavrogin's possible affair with her. This detail offers yet another indication of Dostoevsky's penchant for metafictional commentary. The parallels between Prince Hal and Stavrogin have been addressed, as mentioned before. However, the linking of Dostoevsky's novel with the personification of Rumour from 2 *Henry IV* has not been analysed to my knowledge.

Rumours play a pivotal role in *Demons*. Morson provides a comprehensive analysis of the function of rumour, claiming that it predominates the narrative: 'No matter what happens, rumors circulate countless versions. Indeed, rumors serve as one of the prime movers of action in the novel' (1994: 122). Moreover, rumours define the main ideology of the narrative in which 'truth itself may serve as a *dodge because anything is possible and possibilities carry more weight than actualities*' (1994, my emphasis). Furthermore:

Nothing is ever as it seems, and the novel ends with many mysteries unresolved and the plurality of possibilities unreduced to singularity. *The Possessed* offers a haze of stories about a haze of stories. It might almost be said that rumor is the main character of *The Possessed*. [. . .] as the book progresses it becomes apparent that rumors seem to spread on their own, even in situations in which there was no one to spread them. (122–4)

I include one example of how rumours gradually and subtly transition from mere gossip in the narrators' discourse to being integrated in the narrative as accepted truths, becoming aspects of character portrayal, seemingly factual and objective. In one of the first instances when the narrator describes Stavrogin, he refers to how 'people said his face resembled a mask' (*Demons*, 2006: 43). The full quotation is as follows:

I was not alone in my surprise: the whole town was surprised, having *already been informed*, of course, of *the whole of Mr. Stavrogin's biography*, and even in such *detail* that it *was impossible to imagine where it could have come from*, and, what is most surprising, *half of which turned out to be true. All our ladies lost their minds over the new visitor.* They were sharply divided into two parties – one party adored him, the other hated him to the point of blood vengeance; but both lost their minds. Some were especially fascinated by the possibility of some fatal mystery in his soul; others positively liked his being a killer. [. . .] *People said his face resembled a mask*; however, they *said much else as well*, about his great physical strength, among other things. (43–4, my emphasis)

In the next example, the narrator directly quotes the same phrase, that his *face resembled a mask*, but the focalization is different. Instead of people, it is the viewpoint of 'vicious-tongued ladies', which indicates slander:

But one thing struck me: before, even though he had been considered a handsome man, his face had indeed 'resembled a mask', as certain vicious-tongued ladies of our society put it. Whereas now – now, I don't know why, but he appeared to me, at very first sight, as decidedly,

unquestionably handsome, so that it could in no way be said that his
face resembled a mask. (181–2)

The progression from a rumour to a perceived fact is followed by
another refutation by the narrator. As Morson argued, readers are left
in a state of uncertainty whether Stavrogin's face resembled a mask.
It raises questions whether he truly is handsome, whether offended
women deny that fact or whether his true appearance is a fabrication
created by the people in the province. Undoubtedly, the use of rumours
makes undecidability the novel's crucial narrative characteristic.
This conclusion is reinforced if we compare the text of Shakespeare's
Prologue from 2 *Henry IV* with the logic of the narrative: 'Enter
RUMOUR, painted full of tongues', 'From Rumour's tongues / They
bring smooth comforts false, worse than / true wrongs' (2 *Henry IV*,
Prologue). Similarly to the dynamics of rumour in *Demons*, Rumour's
discourse in 2 *Henry IV* demystifies the logic of spreading 'false reports'
in order to strengthen the position of the ruling class and spread discord
in the play:

> *Rumour is a pipe*
> Blown by surmises, Jealousie's conjectures,
> And of so easy and so plain a stop
> My well-known *body to anatomize*
> Among my household? (2 *Henry IV*, Prologue, my emphasis)

Moreover, the motif of the 'pipe', occurring in Hamlet's provocative
response to Rosencrantz and Guildenstern, 'Do you think I am easier
to be played on than a pipe?' (*Hamlet*, 3.2.361), in which he reveals
his awareness of their manipulative intentions and the impossibility to
control him, can be connected to the logic of political conspiracy in the
Prologue of 2 *Henry IV*, as a false hint for the 'still-discordant wav'ring
multitude' to 'play upon it' (2 *Henry IV*, Prologue). Loren M. Blinde, in
her article 'Rumored History in Shakespeare's 2 *Henry IV*', suggests that
'Rumor serves both as 2 *Henry IV*'s organizing principle and its guiding
spirit' (2008: 34). The fact that in *Demons*, Dostoevsky mentioned

Shakespeare's 'immortal chronicle' (2006: 42), referencing the play can provide a reason to compare these two mechanisms of rumours. Blinde develops her arguments that Shakespeare reveals 'the *theatricality* inherent in the *"making" of history*' and by doing so he highlights 'the fundamental sense of unreliability' of history and constructing 'a theory of history that transcends notions of true and false' in which 'alternative histories are alive and viable' (2008: 34, my emphasis).

> Upon my tongues *continual slanders ride,*
> The which in every language I pronounce,
> *Stuffing the ears of men with false reports.*
> *I speak of peace while covert enmity*
> *Under the smile of safety, wounds the world:*
> (2 *Henry IV*, Prologue, my emphasis)

I am not necessarily suggesting that 2 *Henry IV* directly influenced Dostoevsky in this regard, but I rather wish to highlight the striking similarity in the critical accounts of both the play and the novel, which can serve as a paratextual ideological lens for approaching the novel's text. Blinde's article can be helpful in illuminating the functioning of rumours in *Demons*. She claims:

> The events do not themselves constitute stories; they need Rumor to *unfold the events* so that they come together *as stories.* Importantly, the stories' endpoints are yet undetermined, and in being the one who unfolds the stories from beginning to end Rumor confirms his place as *storyteller* as well as *meaning-maker.* (2008: 38, my emphasis)

Blinde states that 'Shakespeare's achievement with Rumor centers on the paradox that rumor *makes meaning through misunderstanding*' (42, my emphasis), whereas truth seeks 'believability: a rumor is tantalizing, and therefore vital, if it hints at something that could be true, at some kind of secret knowledge' (43). I argue that Blinde's description, even in a more precise way than Morson's, corresponds to the novel's narrative. Rumour is the storyteller that is not necessarily in the position of the narrator, but rather functions on the level of the discourse, or to use an older term, as an implicit author – rumour is the demonic storyteller. It traverses through different levels of narration and manipulates information to create meaning in accordance to a preconceived intention, as if it 'possesses' characters and narrators in different moments of the novel. This principle of storytelling is shared by Peter Verhovensky and by Stavrogin in his confession. It is the same mechanism of Peter Verhovensky's conspiracy and, in general, the way information circulates in the novel. It might be the reason why Stavrogin does not want to print his confession – there is a possibility it would always remain just a rumour for others. Although Stavrogin decides not to publish it by the end of the omitted chapter 'At Tikhon's', the narrator, when introducing the confession's document, comments: 'One may suppose it is now known to many' (*Demons*, 2006: 690), again undermining the certainty of information. Finally, Blinde points to the most pertinent characterization when put in the context of *Demons*, 'Rumor is possessed' (Blinde, 2008: 53), and it is the possessor in *Demons*.

Beyond the parallelism in the Prologue by Rumour, the comparison and intertextual connection to Hal is extensively demonstrated in scholarly criticism (Leer, 1962). I would instead wish to point out another trajectory of parallels that extends from Hal and his homology with Hamlet and, consequently, Stavrogin. Namely, in *Hamlet and the Concept of Character* (1992), Bert O. States indicated similarities of character and ways of representing subjectivity in the examples of Hal from *Henry IV* and Hamlet, as well as a crucial resemblance in plot: 'Both *Hamlet* and *Henry IV* plays are, to a striking degree, variations on the theme of the education of the prince, featuring in each case, a prince who, for reasons of his own, hangs back from responsibility and spends himself in forms of behavior that are socially errant or erratic' (159). The description of Stavrogin's behavior perfectly aligns with these comments. States explains the common denominator between Hall and Hamlet as the enigma of character. 'But with Hal and Hamlet Shakespeare was apparently dealing with a different kind of character crisis that required a new dramaturgic relationship between speech and behavior' (164). States here analyses the mechanism of reception of these characters: 'The *net effect of our juxtaposition* of these opposing signals [projections of behavioral signals of character's intelligible behavior], as they accumulate over theatrical or reading time, is the illusion of deepening character born out of our attempt *to join* the images, to find the thing between them, or beneath them, that will bring them on a *line*' (163, my emphasis). Adding Stavrogin to this characterization again seems plausible. Lastly, when concluding that the challenge might lie in representing a rich and contradictory inner life, States invokes Dostoevsky's creative practice at the end of the paragraph:

> The thing about Hal and Hamlet is that a sense of a *subtextual life* consists in Shakespeare's having left a *gap* not so much in our expectations as in the articulation of gap's psychological contents. As I have said, it is not an unbridgeable gap but one that *fixes our attention on a region of character that isn't being specified* and therefore *remains open and profound* in the sense that you *can't set limits on it.* One of the quickest ways to create an impression of depth in real life is to remain silent when you're expected to speak or to say or do something that is odd, under the circumstances, a principle that at the bottom of Dostoevsky's whole oeuvre. (165, my emphasis)

I argue that Stavrogin is the most evident example of this creative practice, being a character that is mostly silent, behaving in strange and mysterious ways, and is ultimately structured around a gap at the centre of his psychological motivations. All three characters, Stavrogin, Hal and Hamlet, are thus constructed around an enigma.

To conclude, paratexts offer two most important ideological entry points into the text of the novel. First, the logic of rumours organizes the narrative and switches focalizations, creating an essentially unstable meaning of the text that we might characterize as undecidability. Second, the homologies between Hal, Hamlet and Stavrogin, encapsulated best in the gap in the representation of their psychological content, resonate with the feature of performative subjectivity. Thus, the analysis of the novel considers the essential uncertainty of any information and any meaning, as well as the nature of lacunary presences, across the narrative, the story and the use of intertextual and interdiscursive connections with *Hamlet*, suggesting that the text of *Demons* is a network of gaps in *mise-en-abyme*.

## 'Hamlet' on the textual level of *Demons*

As we have seen, *Hamlet* had different meanings for Dostoevsky throughout his life and across various works, as well as in different stages of writing *Demons*. The utilization of Hamletian meanings underwent transformation from beginning to the end. For example, the type of Hamlet associated with Stavrogin from the subtext (the preparatory materials) differs from Hamletian variation in the final version of the novel. In order to understand the relevance of the Hamlet-figures and Hamletian references in the character of Stavrogin, we also have to consider all Hamletian echoes in the novel. Stavrogin, as the ideological centre, contains and disseminates all other relevant thematic threads. As such, his ideas become deformed and fragmented reflections in the thoughts and behaviour of the other characters. We are not directly informed about his ideological positions or his arguments from his speech; on the contrary, the narrative presents his previous beliefs or ideas as radicalized or appropriated by Kirillov and Shatov.

Here is an example of the dynamic of the exchange of ideas between Shatov, who claims to be completely influenced by Stavrogin, and Stavrogin, who insists that Shatov unwillingly made changes to his ideas by merely appropriating them: "As for your thoughts and even your very words, I haven't changed anything, not a word." "I wouldn't say you haven't," Stavrogin remarked cautiously. "You took it ardently, and have altered it ardently without noticing it'" (*Demons*, 2006: 251). In this example we can identify Stavrogin's awareness of the dynamic of appropriation. Namely, already by 'taking' someone's idea, one unconsciously alters it to one's own ideology. Stavrogin subtly warns about the dangers of dialogue and the impossibility to control the meaning of an idea once it is shared. Another important distinction could be noted – the Hamlet-ideologeme, with its alterations of references to the text of *Hamlet* and Russian Hamletism, is ascribed to various characters, not only Stavrogin. Namely, apart from the main hero and Kirillov, as stated in the introduction, Stepan Trophimovich displays some nuances of Russian Hamletism, and we can find echoes of Hamletian motifs typical for Dostoevsky in the character of Shigalyov, in the episode in which he outlines his utopian totalitarian system.

## Stepan Trofimovich Verkhovensky

Stepan Trofimovich is coloured by many features of Russian Hamletism given in a parodic tone adequate to the prominent critique of Hamlet-figures in Russian culture in the 1860s. He could be interpreted as a travesty of a Russian Hamlet with his intertextual connections with Granovsky and Turgenev strengthening this link. In the world of the novel, he is the first disseminator of Shakespeare's work. The subsequent scene exemplifies Dostoevsky's remarkable humoristic approach to the ideological axis of Stepan's character in connection to Shakespeare and the demonic:

> 'Messieurs, the last word in this matter is *all-forgiveness*. I, an obsolete old man, I solemnly declare that the spirit of life blows as ever and the life force is not exhausted in the younger generation. [. . .] The whole perplexity lies in just what is *more beautiful*: *Shakespeare or boots, Raphael or petroleum?*'
>
> 'Is he *an informer*?' grumbled some.
>
> *Compromising questions!*
>
> '*Agent provocateur!*'
>
> 'And I proclaim,' Stepan Trofimovich shrieked, in the last extremity of passion, 'and I proclaim that *Shakespeare and Raphael are higher than the emancipation of the serfs, higher than nationality, higher than socialism, higher than the younger generation, higher than chemistry,*

> *higher than almost all mankind, for they are already the fruit, the real*
> *fruit of all mankind, and maybe the highest fruit there ever may be!* [. . .]
> it [mankind] only *cannot live without beauty*, for then there would be
> *nothing at all to do in the world!* The whole secret is here, the whole of
> *history* is here!' (*Demons*, 2006: 485–6, my emphasis)

While satirically referring to the 'Shakespeare or petroleum' debate,
Dostoevsky acknowledges arguments against Shakespeare by subtly
drawing a motivational link between Stepan's lofty declarations and
his parasitical status in Russian society. The important question here is
not whether Shakespeare and Rafael are 'the real fruit of mankind', but
rather what is to be done with such ideals. Stepan Trofimovich, however,
does not raise that question. His focus is on what is more beautiful. His
indirect guilt is underscored because all the characters he has educated
on Shakespeare, die or commit suicide. As Stepan passionately worships
the profound and to him, undeniable supreme civilizational value and
beauty of Shakespeare, the entire ideology is starkly demystified by an
anonymous voice from the audience. This representative of the people
sheds light to Stepan's indirect involvement and culpability not only for
the murders that have occurred in the novel (Fedka killing Stavrogin's
wife and her brother), but also his irresponsibility towards Fedka as
another human being whom he has treated like an object for sale, and,
even worse, gambled over in a game being the petty, spoiled gentleman
he is.

> Here in town and in the vicinity we've now got *Fedka* the Convict, an
> escaped convict, wandering around. He robs people, and just recently
> *committed a new murder.* Allow me to ask: *if you had not sent him to*
> *the army fifteen years ago to pay off a debt at cards – that is, if you had*
> *not quite simply lost him in a card game* – tell me, would he have wound
> up at hard labor? Would he go around putting a knife in people, as he
> does now, in his struggle for existence? *What have you got to say, mister*
> *aesthete*? (487, my emphasis)

This episode can be regarded as a marvellous, simple and effective
criticism of Russian Hamletism, paradoxically using Shakespeare as an

epitome of moral and aesthetic values. It holds relevance within the novel as Dostoevsky simultaneously portrays Shakespeare as a symbol of highest value while debasing him within the narrative of *Demons*. However, my suggestion is that he does not criticize the work or value of Shakespeare's plays, given his well-known and profound appreciation for the English writer. Instead, he warns that even the loftiest values might be and often are misused for petty, vain and seemingly inconsequential deeds. This type of misuse, lacking honesty and respect towards values, ultimately leads to a *danse macabre* ending in the world of the novel.

Moreover, being a mentor to almost every important character from the succeeding generation (Stavrogin, Liza, Shatov, Dasha and indirectly Peter), Stepan Trofimovich is the ideologue of their intellectual horizons, who has taught them the story of Prince Hamlet and has been the first to introduce the comparison between Stavrogin and Hal, paving the way for the likening of Stavrogin with Hamlet by his son, Peter Stepanovich. Stepan Trofimovich is described like a stage actor *manqué*,[6] a quasi-scholar[7] who is a representative of the generation that praised the Romantic cult of Shakespeare, while being severely criticized for his social and emotional parasitism. As such, he is a hysterical and neurotic representative of Russian liberal idealism. Being himself a 'child' in need of a friend, he is clearly described by the narrator to be responsible for 'education and moral development' that 'somewhat unsettled his pupil's [Stavrogin's] nerves' (*Demons*, 2006: 40–1). He has instilled in Stavrogin melancholy, the 'sensation of that age-old, sacred anguish which the chosen soul, having once tasted and known it, will never exchange for any cheap satisfaction' (41). In that sense, apart from representing socio-political themes related to superfluous men and Russian Hamletism, Stepan is the point of conjecture from which other Shakespearean and Hamletian motifs are dissipated. On the other hand, as many critics have pointed out, Stepan is the first disseminator of the demonic – a connection that is matched with the idea that Hamletism is one of the sources of the demonic. Yuri Corrigan explains Stepan's role in his chapter 'On the Education of *Demons* and Unfinished Selves', describing his demonic pedagogy as: 'the flimsy, depthless, possessive and possessed personality of the tutor, who in his hunger *to dissolve himself in others*, develops a pedagogical practice with destructive consequences for the wounded, ravenous, and "unfinished" selves that grow up in his care' (2017: 87, my emphasis). Corrigan further argues that 'Stepan's prevailing impact upon the youth lies not in the transmission of ideas, but rather in the concerted *invasion of the self* that he both pursues and embodies' (2017, my emphasis). However, while Corrigan's ideas shed light only on the example of Stepan, we can extend the treatment of the same dynamic of the demonic in the novel as a 'dual activity of the demon – as both possessor and possessed' (101). In the following part we will see examples of the demonic pedagogy of Stepan Trofimovich and how it spreads in the novel. The first time Hamlet as a figure is mentioned in the novel occurs when Liza Tushina meets Stepan Trofimovich as an adult and reminisces about his lessons:

> You see, I remember all your lectures by heart! [. . .] And do you remember telling me the story of Prince Hamlet? And do you remember describing to me how poor emigrants were transported from Europe to America? It was *all untrue*, I learned it all later, how they were transported, but how *well he lied to me then*, Mavriky Nikolaevich, it was *almost better than the truth*! (*Demons*, 2006: 107, my emphasis)

Liza Tushina emphasizes how she was seduced by storytelling, as conveyed and interpreted by Stepan. Although the transportation of emigrants is referred to as a pack of lies, nothing can assure the reader that Stepan Trofimovich retold the story of Prince Hamlet accurately. In addition, the notion of storytelling as a vehicle for truth is being put in question once more. Liza enriches this motif by implying that there was something better than truth to it, maybe unconsciously suggesting the performative and seductive function of a story. The next example confirms the seductive power of storytelling. The comparison between Stavrogin and Hal is based on rumours, but the narrator nevertheless appropriates the name of Prince Harry. It is as if rumours, over the course of the narrative, transition into accepted truths and subtly permeate the narrative as dominant meaning:

> But very soon rather strange *rumors* began to reach Varvara Petrovna: the young man, somehow madly and suddenly, started leading a wild life. [. . .] Stepan Trofimovich assured her that these were merely the first stormy impulses of an overabundant constitution, that the sea would grow calm, and that it all resembled Shakespeare's description of the youth of *Prince Harry*, carousing with Falstaff, Poins, and Mistress Quickly. This time Varvara Petrovna did not shout 'Nonsense, nonsense!' as it had lately become her habit to shout quite often at Stepan Trofimovich, but, on the contrary, paid great heed to him, asked him to explain in more detail, herself took Shakespeare and read *the immortal chronicle* with extreme attention. But the chronicle did not calm her down, *nor did she find all that much resemblance.* She waited feverishly for answers to certain of her letters. The answers were not slow in coming; soon the fatal news was received that *Prince Harry* had almost simultaneously fought two duels, was entirely to blame for both of them, had killed one of his opponents on the spot and crippled the other, and as a consequence of such deeds had been brought to trial. (41–2, my emphasis)

However, Varvara Petrovna remains unconvinced and fails to recognize the similarities between her son and Shakespeare's hero. In this long paragraph, we once again notice the merging of motifs such as rumours, the comparison to Shakespeare's hero as an interpretation of Stavrogin's behaviour, a parallelism between the genre of *Henry IV* and *Demons*, and lastly, the narrator's appropriation of this comparison. Dostoevsky uses complex narrative strategies to interlink hidden sources and create a subtextual connection of motifs. Catteau highlights that 'Stavrogin himself, as Pyotr Stepanovich Verkhovensky reports, gives the name of Falstaff to his clownish drinking companion, Captain Lebyadkin. Here again, the myth of Stavrogin-Prince Harry, the young rake who is destined to a glorious future, is sanctioned by the public voice. The subjective dialogue between the writer and his predecessors becomes objective; it emerges, in the finished novel, from the literary awareness of the characters' (1989: 199). By giving his characters' an awareness of their literacy, Dostoevsky creates them as a conflicted map of literary influences and sources. 'This again was an original approach to literary comparison; the comparison was not presented directly by the novelist, as if to give the reader a clue, but was a myth created by the other characters in the novel' (1989). When Stavrogin calls Captain Lebyatkin his own Falstaff, we notice that he also appropriates this method of interpreting or misinterpreting himself through literature, comparing himself to Prince Hal. Lebyatkin claims: 'And though you [Stavrogin] used to call me your Falstaff from Shakespeare, you meant so much in my fate!' (*Demons*, 2006: 263). The same principle is appropriated by Peter Stepanovich in an example that warrants closer consideration due to a particular contradiction. Initially, in attempting to reassure Varvara Petrovna about Stavrogin, Peter Stepanovich seem to lack familiarity with Shakespeare's works and fails to recognize Falstaff as a character from one of his plays:

> 'Once again I ask your forgiveness, Varvara Petrovna. Nikolai Vsevolodovich used to call this gentleman his Falstaff – that must be some former character,' he suddenly explained, 'some burlesque everyone laughs at and who allows everyone to laugh at him, so long as they pay money.' (186)

Later in the same conversation, Peter Stepanovich develops the comparison between Stavrogin and Hamlet, claiming that it suits Stavrogin better than the parallelism with Hal, implying his familiarity with both Shakespearean works. Not only does this inconsistency mirror Peter's manipulative rhetoric, but it also undermines the validity of the comparison between Stavrogin and Hamlet. Peter Verkhovensky insists:

> No, this was something higher than whimsicality and, I assure you, even something holy! A man, proud and early insulted, who had arrived at that 'jeering' which you mentioned so aptly – in short, a Prince Harry, to use Stepan Trofimovich's magnificent comparison

at the time, which would be perfectly correct if he did not resemble
Hamlet even more, at least in my view. (189)

Moreover, this methodology is misappropriated in Peter Stepanovich's
manipulations and seductive deceits, mimicking Stepan's pathetic
rhetoric. Similar to the dissemination of rumours, all these characteristics
gradually, almost imperceptibly, integrate into the narrative thread –
the narrator adopts Stephan's comparison, and the focalization shifts.
However, the problematic aspect of Stepan's transmission of ideas lies
in the same method of his appropriation of values for selfish ends. They
serve for expanding his persona, without genuine regard to the meaning
and value of the objects or ideas he shares, or the people he shares them
to. Indirectly, Dostoevsky suggests that this behaviour is much more
dangerous than mere superficiality; rather, it is a deeply selfish and
ethically dubious use and misuse of ideas and values, under the guise
of nobility, worshipping beauty and art, all in the name of the highest
civilizational values.[8] Nevertheless, since the chapter 'At Tikhon's' was
omitted, Dostoevsky needed to ascribe to someone else than Tikhon the
main ideological opposition to the demonic discourse. Thus, instead of
having Tikhon claiming that 'In sinning, each man sins against all, and
each man is at least partly guilty for another's sin. There is no isolated
sin' (606), Stepan Trofimovich undergoes a transformation towards the
end of the novel, reaching a similar conclusion. The most important
aspect of Stepan Trofimovich's role, placed at the novel's conclusion
in the chapter 'The Last Peregrination of Stepan Trofimovich', is
acknowledgement of his own guilt and a willingness for reconciliation
with everyone. He proposes it as a future programme on his deathbed:
'Oh, let's forgive, let's first of all forgive all and always [. . .] *Let's* hope that
we, too, will be forgiven. Yes, because we are guilty one and all before
each other. All are guilty!' (645, my emphasis). At the novel's conclusion,
another aspect of the Hamlet-isotopy reverberates. In Stepan's version,
the 'Let be' project becomes a programme of forgiveness for all and
the acceptance of complete culpability, alongside responsibility. In that
sense, his transformation aligns with the cited epitaph from the Gospel

of Luke and with Dostoevsky's project of letting go to madness and healing from his 1838 letter. It might be read as a way of overcoming the demonic Hamletian despair:

> The one constant thought that there exists something immeasurably more just and happy than I, fills the whole of me with immeasurable tenderness and – glory – oh, *whoever I am, whatever I do*! Far more than his own happiness, it is necessary for a man to know and believe every moment that there is somewhere a perfect and peaceful happiness, for everyone and for everything [. . .] The whole law of human existence consists in nothing other than a man's always being able to bow before the immeasurably great. If people are deprived of the immeasurably great, they will not live and will die in *despair*. The immeasurable and infinite is as necessary for man as the small planet he inhabits. My friends, all, all of you: long live the Great Thought! The eternal, immeasurable Thought! For every man, whoever he is, it is necessary to bow before that which is the Great Thought. (665, my emphasis)

Stepan's conclusion (*whoever I am, whatever I do*) can be read in comparison to the crucial aspect of the Hamlet-ideologeme: the undecidability of heroes about what to be and what to do as letting go of identity and agency. Moreover, from all Hamletian characters that are wrapped up in their lies and the performativity of their lies, Stepan is one of the rare characters in Dostoevsky's opus that despite perpetuating the same mechanism at least recognizes the gravity of alienating from the possibility of attaining the truth:

> My friend, *I've been lying all my life*. Even when I was telling the truth. I never spoke for the truth, but only for myself, I knew that before, but only now do I see. . . . Oh, where are those friends whom I have insulted with my friendship all my life? And everyone, everyone! Savez-vous, *perhaps I'm lying now; certainly I'm also lying now. The worst of it is that I believe myself when I lie.* The most difficult thing in life is to live and not lie . . . and . . . and not believe one's own lie, yes, yes, that's precisely it! (652, my emphasis)

## Kirillov

In Kirillov we encounter another aspect of the Hamlet-isotopy alongside dissipated motifs of Russian Hamletism. Kirillov becomes an ideologue of the problem of suicide in order to prove the idea of free will. His suicide can also be read as a variation on the 'Let be' project, in aiming to demonstrate free will and the idea of the benevolence of all beings. 'Everything is good . . . . Everything. Man is unhappy because he doesn't know he's happy; only because of that. It is everything, everything! Whoever learns will at once immediately become happy, that same moment' (Demons, 2006: 237). He kills himself in order to demonstrate what he holds as truth, his idea of man-god, transcending the limits of human consciousness. Or at least, this is his intention. However, being wrapped in the confines of rationalistic logic, deemed to be demonic, Kirillov's utilization and extremization of Stavrogin's ideas becomes another fragmented and distorted radicalization of a potentially positive notion. Rowan Williams argues that he represents 'the demonic aspect of visionary ecstasy' (2008: 90). While John Jones claims that 'the novel frees Stavrogin from "to be or not to be" and all other trammels of the notebooks, and transfers them to Kirillov' (1983: 280), I suggest that this phrase is semantically expanded into the dilemma between belief and disbelief, but also, that it belongs to both Kirillov and Stavrogin simultaneously. Transferring it to Kirillov does not absolve Stavrogin from it. Rather, as we have seen concerning the examples of Shatov's appropriation of Stavrogin's ideas, Kirillov attunes it to his own ideology. Within Kirillov's discourse we can trace the Hamletian 'to be or not to be' logic, contextualized in the direction of why should one commit suicide. In fact, he claims that the difference between *to be* and *not to be* is the biggest deceit. And, lastly, Kirillov, more explicitly than Stavrogin, discards the difference between living and killing oneself. In the conversation with Peter Verkhovensky, he repeats three times that after attaining freedom of will, 'it makes no difference whether *one lives or does not live. That* is the goal to everything' (*Demons*, 2006: 115, my emphasis), echoing distantly the 'to be or not be' phrase. In his programme, we can also identify a distorted version of Dostoevsky's 'Let be' project articulated in his letter – a project aimed to bring people to consciousness and heal them:

> 'It is my duty to proclaim unbelief,' Kirillov was pacing the room. 'For me no idea is higher than that there is no God. The history of mankind is on my side. Man has done nothing but invent God, so as to live without killing himself; in that lies the whole of world history up to now. I alone for the first time in world history did not want to invent God. Let them know once and for all.' (617–8)

However, in this case, the logic of 'Let be' is demonized and Kirillov acknowledges that the undercurrent of his system, instead of absolute goodness, is a deep despair concerning the condition of the world. Kirillov claims:

> And if so, if the laws of nature did not pity even This One [Christ], did not pity even their own miracle, but made Him, too, live *amidst a lie and die for a lie*, then the whole planet is a lie, and stands upon a lie and a *stupid mockery*. Then the very laws of the planet are a lie and a *devil's vaudeville*. Why live then, answer me, if you're a man. (618, my emphasis)

Moreover, the actual scene of his suicide, preceding his frenzied bite of Peter Verkhovensky's finger, undermines all the positive or emancipatory aspects of his ideological system. His suicide will ultimately be exploited to justify acts of crimes and destruction, in accordance with Peter's plan and conspiracy. Dostoevsky's irony is at its strongest when Peter Verkhovensky persuades Kirillov to falsely claim responsibility in his suicide note for murdering his only friend Shatov. In that way, despite the magnanimity of Kirillov's intentions, the novel discards his ideology and behaviour as demonic and destructive.

## Shigalyov

The first description of Shigalyov immediately evokes some aspects of the Hamlet-isotopy and a number of motifs we find in other Hamletian characters. Like Raskolnikov and Ivan Karamazov, he is the author of an article in which he presents his system of beliefs. Also, his mood and character are fairly gloomy and pessimistic. And lastly, the invocation of the Apocalypse is given in a grotesque and absurd manner: 'He looked as if he were *expecting the destruction of the world*, and not just sometime, according to prophecies which might not be fulfilled, but quite definitely, round about morning, the day after tomorrow, at ten twenty-five sharp' (*Demons*, 2006: 136, my emphasis). Shigalyov is connected with themes of future social organization that should reinstate justice in the world and the dichotomy between words versus action. The connection with *Hamlet* is rather intensified because of motifs of despair, madness and the paraphrase of the 'to be or not to be' quotation, while the link with Russian Hamletism has a satirical twist, since the question about Shigalyov's despair being a private or a public matter is raised in a humoristic and farcical tone. Shigalyov starts explaining his theory:

> Having devoted my energy to studying the question of the social organization of the future society which is to replace the present one, I have come to the conclusion that all creators of social systems from ancient times to our year – have been dreamers, tale-tellers, fools who contradicted themselves and understood precisely nothing of natural science or of that strange animal known as man. [. . .] But since the future social form is necessary precisely now, when we are all finally going to act, so as to stop any further thinking about it, I am suggesting my own system of world organization. [. . .] 'Besides that, I announce ahead of time that my system is not finished.' (More laughter.) (402)

In Shigalyov's system, we have a different fragment of the Hamlet-isotopy – a demonstration of how abstract and rational logic only leads to despair because of the impossibility of solving the dilemma between absolute freedom and complete slavery. In an attempt to solve the problem of a social system through mere thoughts, action becomes trapped in the absurdity of its logic. The parallels deepen when considering despair and the dead end of radical rationality, or the demonic of a Hamlet-Stavrogin trajectory. It is important to note that the motif of an earthly paradise echoes Stavrogin's dream of the Golden Age. But, while Stavrogin is deeply aware of the paradise lost, Shigalyov's socialist utopia and the programme of restoring a Golden Age on earth through action are doomed to be caught up in their own contradictions:

> I got entangled in my own data, and my conclusion directly contradicts the original idea from which I start. Starting from *unlimited freedom*, I conclude with *unlimited despotism*. I will add, however, that apart from my solution of the *social formula*, there *can be no other.* (2006, my emphasis)

Dostoevsky uses parody by adding a voice from the audience who acknowledges that Shigalyov's system, simply, ends in despair – equating despair with contradiction:

> 'If you yourself weren't able to hold your system together, and arrived *at despair*, what are we supposed to do?' one officer observed cautiously.
>
> 'You're right, mister active officer,' Shigalyov turned abruptly to him, 'and most of all in having used the word "despair". Yes, I kept arriving at despair; nevertheless, everything expounded in my book is irreplaceable, and there *is no other way out*; no one can invent anything.' (403, my emphasis)

At that point, Hamletian references are intensified by adding madness, and even more importantly, by placing an echo of the 'to be or not to be' phrase alongside the motif of despair:

> 'Is he *crazy*, or what?' voices asked 'So it all comes down to Shigalyov's *despair*,' Lyamshin concluded, 'and the essential question is whether he *is to be or not to be* in *despair*?'
>
> 'Shigalyov's proximity to despair is a personal question,' the high-school boy declared.

'I suggest we vote on how far Shigalyov's despair concerns the common cause, and along with that, whether it's worth listening to him or not,' the officer gaily decided. (2006, my emphasis)

Dostoevsky's criticism of Russian Hamletism is again at its subtlest and its best in the ridicule over voting whether Shigalyov's despair is a common or private cause. Shigalyov nevertheless retains proximity to the Hamlet-isotopy in a serious manner by concluding his presentation with the suggestion of a final decision, a final solution: *as a final solution of the question, the division of mankind into two unequal parts.* One tenth is granted freedom of person and unlimited rights over the remaining nine tenths. [. . .] 'What I propose is not vileness but *paradise, earthly paradise*, and there can be no other on earth' (403–4, my emphasis). According to how Stavrogin's ideas can be appropriated and changed, Peter Verkhovensky has further vulgarized Shigalyov's system, naming it Shigalyovism,[9] distorting and mocking his ideas, in favour of his own political aspirations. Shigalyovism becomes a farcical and absurd rendering of socialism in his intervention. He explains in his own words: 'Each belongs to all, and all to each. They are all slaves and equal in their slavery [. . .] The first task is to bring down the level of education, science and talent [. . .] Cicero's tongue is cut off, Copernicus' eyes are put out, Shakespeare is stoned – this is Shigalyovism' (417)'.

As with Stepan Trofimovich and Kirillov, in the example of Shigalyov we can trace the same motifs: madness, despair, 'to be or not to be' phrase; all ideas that initially came from Stavrogin's consciousness (at least at the discursive level of the narrative, although not necessarily on the level of the story). All three characters at the level of the text confirm the initial idea that the Hamlet-ideologeme creates a dissipated network of motifs that are kaleidoscopically diffracted and multiplied after emanating from Stavrogin. That brings this book to the next hypothesis, that Stavrogin as a discursive formation in the novel, that is, not as a character on the level of the story but as a palimpsestic textual construction that is antimimetic (self-referential). These ideas will be explored in the following chapter and might provide an answer to why

*Hamlet* as a play, Russian Hamletism and Dostoevsky's understanding of the figure of Hamlet are relevant for Stavrogin.

# Notes

1   'Hypertextuality refers to any relationship uniting a text B (which I shall call the hypertext) to an earlier text A (I shall, of course, call it the hypotext), upon which it is grafted in a manner that is not that of commentary' (Genette, 1997: 5).

2   Transtextuality is 'the textual transcendence of the text, [. . .] all that sets the text in relationship, whether obvious or concealed, with other texts' (Genette, 1997: 1). Transtextual levels include intertextuality, paratextuality, architextuality, metatextuality and hypertextuality (hypotextuality).

3   Timofeyev Granovsky (1813–55) was a famous historian, writer and Westernizer and one of the prototypes for Stepan Trofimovich.

4   Dostoevsky attributes to Stavrogin a variation of his own confession of faith in the mentioned letter to Madame Fonvizina. The famous excerpt goes as follows: 'I want to say to you, about myself, that I am a child of this age, a child of unfaith and skepticism, and probably (indeed I know it) shall remain so to the end of my life. How dreadfully has it tormented me (and torments me even now) – this longing for faith, which is all the stronger for the proofs I have against it. And yet God gives me sometimes moments of perfect peace; in such moments I love and believe that I am loved; in such moments I have formulated my creed, wherein all is clear and holy to me. This creed is extremely simple; here it is: I believe that there is nothing lovelier, deeper, more sympathetic, more rational, more manly, and more perfect than the Savior; I say to myself with jealous love that not only is there no one else like Him, but that there could be no one. I would even say more: *If anyone could prove to me that Christ is outside the truth, and if the truth really did exclude Christ, I should prefer to stay with Christ and not with truth.*' (*From Letters of Fyodor Mikhailovitch Dostoevsky to His Family and Friends*, 1914: 70–1, my emphasis)

5   A perspective more akin to Dostoevsky's personal view might be provided
    by interpreting the Shakespeare portrait which, in 2014, Boris Tikhomirov
    found drawn among his preparatory materials, the *Notebooks of Demons*,
    which reinforces the significance of Shakespeare's work for the creation
    of the novel (2014: 90). Konstantine Barsht explains: 'A portrait drawing
    completed in 1871-1872 displays features clearly similar to those of
    William Shakespeare, and is found among the sketches related to the
    writer's work on Chapters one and two of Part 3 of *The Devils*' (2017: 65).
    The portrait is not given frontally, but exposes Shakespeare's profile, which
    might indicate that Dostoevsky regarded Shakespeare as someone hiding
    his true face, in accordance to a poetics of veiling, as Kovalevskaya argues
    (2014: 75).

6   'I will say straight off: Stepan Trofimovich constantly played a certain
    special and, so to speak, civic role among us, and loved this role to the
    point of passion – so much so that it even seems to me he would have
    been unable to live without it. Not that I equate him with a stage actor:
    God forbid, particularly as I happen to respect him. It could all have been
    a matter of habit, or, better, of a ceaseless and noble disposition, from
    childhood on, towards a pleasant dream of his beautiful civic stance. He
    was, for example, greatly enamored of his position as a "persecuted" man
    and, so to speak, an "exile"' (*Demons*, 2006: 8).

7   'And yet he was such an intelligent man, such a gifted man, even, so to
    speak, a scholar – though as a scholar, however . . . well, in a word, he did
    very little as a scholar, nothing at all, apparently' (*Demons*, 2006: 8).

8   The example in which Stepan mentions Shakespeare is an apt description
    of this mechanism.

9   Pevear, the translator of *Demons*, explains how the word 'shigalyovism'
    entered Russian language implying 'a form of socio-political demagogy
    and posturing with a tendency to propose extreme measures and total
    solutions' (*Demons*, 2006: 727).

# 5

# 'Hamlet' in Stavrogin

*Stavrogin is a Surrealist* avant la lettre.

(Benjamin, 2005: 214)

Nikolay Vsevolodovich Stavrogin, the central protagonist of *Demons*, has inspired a wealth of critical commentary due to his alluring, yet elusive, features, called by Mochulsky 'Dostoevsky's greatest artistic creation' (1973: 463). He is a paradoxical character bearing a name that is a combination of the Greek word *stavros* for cross and Russian *rog* for horn, implying an oxymoronic symbolism of sanctity and the demonic. He begins as a well-mannered and educated young aristocrat, marked by striking physical beauty, sharp intellect and a fearless, arrogant attitude.[1] However, Stavrogin's arc from a figure of potential to an embodiment of moral collapse, spiritual decay, existential nihilism and despair, accompanied by self-loathing, controlled, yet intense rage, cynical self-awareness of his own faults and psychological disintegration, culminates in complete disillusionment with life and his suicide. As an embodiment of a supremely extraordinary character, he is usually seen as a powerful symbol of a tragic decline. However, the motivation behind his behaviour remains mysterious, for other characters and readers alike. Moreover, since Dostoevsky symbolically connects the fate of Stavrogin with the historical fate of Russia, the problem of his identity overlaps with the problem of Russian national identity. Although critics offer various interpretations of his elusive and immoral behaviour, he is almost unanimously regarded as an anti-hero. While Western critics tend to focus on his existential dilemmas, Russian scholarship more often centres on his spiritual emptiness and metaphysical uprootedness within the context of Eastern Orthodox

Christianity.[2] In a previous publication, I tackled the issue that most scholars approach him as a philosophical or religious concept, often overlooking his fictionality and the aesthetic principles that underpin his character (Bjelica, 2020: 235). Namely, at the heart of most critical analysis of Stavrogin is the notion of a coherent character, rendered in a manner consistent with the protocols of realist fiction (Frank, 1969; Davison, 1983; Danow, 1988; Pope and Turner, 1990; Corrigan, 2017). Despite his characteristics, traditional criticism is mostly concerned with the psychological interpretation of Stavrogin, attempting to reveal the mystery behind his behaviour, often projecting psychological, philosophical and artistic motivations. 'Nonetheless, from whatever perspective we approach him, Stavrogin contains paradoxical elements that inspire ambivalent sensations. But what if this ambivalence lacked proper context? What if his attractiveness lies somewhere beyond or before language?' (2020). Following a hermetic comment by Walter Benjamin that 'Stavrogin is a Surrealist *avant la lettre*' (2005: 214), I suggested that Dostoevsky's creation of Stavrogin 'resembles a surrealist collage' (2020: 235). There are many reasons why Benjamin's reading of Stavrogin cannot be completely sustained by Dostoevsky's text, as I demonstrated (2020). However, I also argued that Benjamin's insight brings to light another aspect of Stavrogin's 'radical ambivalence that is slowly breaking and cracking the layers of realism' (236).

This view is an expansion of Leatherbarrow's portrayal of Stavrogin as an 'ectoplasm summoned up from the European literary tradition and trailing clouds of literary allusion' (2000: 14). Apart from Hamlet and Prince Hal, 'Stavrogin is compiled of a long list of literary heroes or historical figures appearing like allusions or subtexts – from [. . .] Byron, Pushkin's Onegin and Boris Godunov, Lermontov's Pechorin, Rousseau, Grigorij (Grishka) Otrep'ev, a vampiric hero from Ann Radcliff's gothic novels, Dickens's Steerforth, Bakunin, Nikolay Speshnyov' (Bjelica, 2020: 235). As Leatherbarrow observes, Stavrogin 'emerges gradually and confusingly out of the "reading" and "misreading" of him by other characters and indeed the reader himself, such readings being sustained by the literary, cultural and social expectations that each brings to the process' (2000: 3) and is 'exposed to similar attempts on the part of others to label, objectify or, in Bakhtinian terms, "finalize" him in the light of expectations fed by "explanatory models"' (2000). However, this process only reveals a multiplicity of his non-identities because most of the intertextual links to above-mentioned literary figures are surrounded by narrative irony. Leatherbarrow observes that Dostoevsky uses evasive narrative strategies that serve his aesthetic purpose – to reveal things indirectly. He is 'essentially a non-character, an ever-shifting and indefinite composite whose "meaning" is derived from the readings and misreadings of others' (15).

Apart from other relevant reasons for considering Stavrogin a Hamletian hero, Letherbarrow's view of Stavrogin as a non-character and this strange ever-shifting composite proves to be the most relevant argument to my hypothesis about the kaleidoscopic quality of this particular 'Hamlet' of Dostoevsky. Moreover, Stavrogin is structurally homologous to the way Dostoevsky engages with Hamlet/*Hamlet* and Russian Hamletism, being a palimpsest of literary references and numerous prototypes, a character that is antimimetic and created as an intertextual and interdiscursive network. Attempts to 'finalize' Stavrogin parallel the hermeneutic intention of Russian Hamletism to explain the mystery behind Hamlet's character in accordance with expectations of the Russian readership. Analogously to how Shakespeare's text resists this objectification, Dostoevsky's text resists a unified reading of Stavrogin. However, in the 'Introduction' to *The Notebooks for the Possessed*, Edward Wasiolek competently suggests that even Dostoevsky 'did not understand Stavrogin, and did not know who he was' (1968: 14), but was rather seduced and enchanted by his own creation. Wasiolek's description most profoundly and accurately encapsulates the enigma of Stavrogin:

> The Stavrogin of the novel has passed *beyond words* and passion, creation and destruction, faith and unfaith. His lips are sealed by the confidence that *no word is worth speaking* and *no act is worth doing*. About him is a babble of voices and a riot of action, and he alone seems

> *to be meaning in his unmeaning.* He is *wise with wisdom that wisdom is*
> *not wise*, and *strong in his fate that all fate can be shaken.* Peter may be
> mysterious, *Stavrogin is mystery.* (1968, my emphasis)

Wasiolek's comment is in accordance with the antimimetic approach
to Stavrogin, that is, eschewing interpretation of psychological traits
and motivation of the character. Stavrogin's mysteriousness and the
rhetoric of the demonic might also be seen as an aspect of his Russian
Hamletism, which I claim is deliberately crafted by Dostoevsky as
part of the construction of his character, that contains all previously
mentioned Hamletian traits and ideas, echoed, fragmented and/or
distorted in various ways. These themes include problems of suicide,
despair, weakness and paralysis of will that at times borders utter
indifference, isolation from and disgust with the world and people,
radical scepticism and negation. But apart from these prominent and
crucial topics for Stavrogin, other parallels include his Hamletian
quest for meaning and the search for his own identity. Both Hamlet
and Stavrogin are melancholic heroes, enigmatic and elusive, resisting
interpretations and political appropriations by other characters,
provoking them with *an antic disposition* that might be a part of
their histrionic nature, a political strategy or both. They are gifted by
hyperconsciousness or the 'sudden demon of irony' (*Demons*, 2006:
180) as Varvara Petrovna quotes Stepan Trofimovich's characterization
of Stavrogin's erratic behaviours; they see ghosts or hallucinations, and
can be said to have been uprooted from a Symbolic order they belonged
in. Lastly, they are obsessively trying to be a free subject in control of
their destinies, while their self-consciousness and self-knowledge are
intertwined with the epochal problems.

I suggest that Stavrogin is a Hamletian hero *par excellence.* Subtextual
and intertextual links to other novels participating in the Hamlet-
isotopy network become more apparent when we focus on the central
position of the 'To be or not to be' dilemma within his character. Also,
to fully grasp the semantic potential of the 'Let be' nexus of motifs and
themes, it is imperative to analyse how references to Hamlet/*Hamlet*,

the Hamlet-ideologeme and Russian Hamletism signify in *Demons*. As demonstrated throughout the book, Stavrogin's connections to Russian Hamletism are evident in his bridging of Byronism with the archetype of the superfluous hero, and with figures such as Pushkin's Onegin and Aleko, Lermontov's Pechorin, Turgenev's Bazarov, to name a few. He represents the next stage in the evolution of Russian Hamletism, where indifference, hopelessness, boredom, disgust and scepticism are intensified. He combines the Romantic demonism of Lermontov's Pechorin with sceptic and nihilistic overtones of Turgenev's demonism. In Dostoevsky's prose, predecessors to Stavrogin include characters like the man from the underground, Raskolnikov, Prince Myskhin and Nastasya Filippovna, who, like other Hamletian figures, are caught between contradictory arguments. However, Stavrogin emerges as the most extreme example, embodying radically opposed ideas simultaneously. The Hamlet-ideologeme is the ultimate ideologeme of Stavrogin's identity, as can be supported by the already quoted description from the preparatory materials: as 'a gloomy, passionate, demonic, and disorderly character, *without any sense of measure*, with a lofty question, all the way to "to be or not to be"? To live or to exterminate oneself?' (*Notebooks*, 1968: 266, my emphasis). Moreover, references to Hamlet/*Hamlet* that are relevant for Stavrogin can be identified by following the two already mentioned spheres of parallels between the heroes and the plots. Bradley J. Irish, in his article '"Something After?": *Hamlet* and Dread' (2019), delineates how the play is structured around two sets of characters engaging in different modes of interaction unfolding the action. The first mode is the interrogatory mode, in which 'Hamlet interrogates the veracity of the ghost's claim, while Claudius (with the help of Polonius, Rosencrantz, and Guildenstern) in turn interrogates the cause of Hamlet's melancholy and madness' (Irish, 2019: 240). The same structure can be noticed in Dostoevsky's novel. As Morson demonstrates, *Demons* 'interweaves two plots, the story of Pyotr Stepanovich's conspiracy and the story of Stavrogin's search for meaning' (1999: 126). Like Hamlet, Stavrogin is the bearer of the interrogatory mode. He is exploring the veracity of his own arguments while all other characters (Varvara Petrovna, Shatov, Kirillov, Liza Tushina, Dasha Shatova, the narrator and the whole society) are trying to interpret his melancholy, mysterious behaviour and supposed madness.[3] According to Irish, the second mode in *Hamlet* is the operational mode in which 'Hamlet attempts to secure his revenge against Claudius, while Claudius (with the help of Laertes) in turn attempts to restore order to his court by eliminating Hamlet' (2019: 240). While in *Demons*, the operational mode concerns Peter Stepanovich's attempts to appropriate Stavrogin for political machinations, orchestrates a false revolutionary conspiracy, manipulating other characters in hope of positioning Stavrogin as their new, charismatic leader, while Stavrogin, on the other hand, attempts to confess and seek atonement. Lastly, an 'additional set of relations includes Hamlet's self-interrogation that is deferring the operational mode' (2019), while Stavrogin's self-interrogation defers his actions and undermines his atonement, leading him to suicide. Stavrogin, while striving to find a mission worthy of his potential (as he claims to Daria Shatova: 'I've tested my strength everywhere. You advised me to do that, "in order to know myself"', (*Demons*, 2006: 675)), fails to overcome his despair, nihilism and atheism. Thus, these two works exhibit a dual plot structure that aligns itself along with two distinct modes: the interrogatory and the operational. To sum up, the interrogatory mode includes the protagonists' (Hamlet's and Stavrogin's) search for identity (meaning and truth, metaphysical roots, and self-knowledge), while the operational mode involves the political aspect – the chaos of intrigues, surveillance mechanisms, and question of sovereignty, reflecting a broader metaphysical and ontological crisis of values.

    In the following part I analyse this kaleidoscopic structure around the enigma of Stavrogin, first, at the subtextual level (the preparatory materials), second, by analysing the paratextual elements in the ommited chapter 'At Tikhon's', and lastly, on the textual level of the novel.

# Revealing 'Hamlet' on the subtextual level

The subtext of *Demons* consists of the novel's preparatory materials and provides the most important information about the character of the Prince, who later evolves into Stavrogin. In the *Notebooks*, themes connected with Stavrogin resonate with elements of the Hamlet-isotopy. Direct references include three instances. First, Dostoevsky depicts Stavrogin as being possessed by an idea, notably referencing *Hamlet*: '(He is terribly fascinated by something – *Hamlet* for instance.) January 2, 1870' (*Notebooks*, 1968: 57). Second, Stavrogin embodies the existential dilemma summed up in *to be or not to be*:

> The Prince is a somber, passionate, demoniac, and dissolute character who knows no moderation; facing the ultimate question he has reached 'to be or not to be'? Should he go on living, or should he destroy himself? He cannot, in good conscience and judgement, go on living as before, yet he goes on doing the same things as before and commits the rape. (266, my emphasis)[4]

Third, the juxtaposition of *words, words, words* and meaningful action is evoked: 'Words, nothing but words' (367). Beyond these explicit references, the Hamlet-isotopy is present in the following: Stavrogin is a sceptic bordering on cynicism, tirelessly probing existence in pursuit of proof of God's existence, wielding the profound knowledge of all philosophical *pro* and *contra* arguments. The narrative strategy of the novel, gleaned from the preparatory materials, posits that *Stavrogin is everything*, as Dostoevsky wrote in 1870 – a multifaceted figure encompassing contradictory roles and identities.

> For Stavrogin is, at one and the same time, the absolute incarnation of being – the universal man; a more perfect Christ, who, remember, 'had no beauty that we should desire him' (Isaiah 53.2-3) etc. – AND that spirit of ruinous decreation. Stavrogin is unforgettably expressive of a fault at the heart of being, of its consummation in nothingness. (Fernie, 2013: 108)

His identity is a constant existential self-experiment confronting the omnipotent gaze of God, using masks and performing different and contradictory roles. He is a source of ideas that mutually cancel one another. His main interlocutors are not other characters in the novel, to whom he says little to nothing, but, rather, otherness itself, the divine 'Other' represented in the Christian God. As Fernie notes, he is 'the *pro* and *contra*: he is the full spiritual span of our humanity' (113). In the preparatory notes, Dostoevsky reflects on his future hero:

> N.B. This man is possessed by *an idea*. This idea grips him and gains mastery over him; however, its action is qualified by the fact that it does not so much rule over his mind as it does *become embodied* in his person, becoming part of his nature, always with suffering and anxiety. And, once it has been lodged in his nature, it demands to be transformed into action without delay. [. . .] He has suddenly become a terrible *sceptic*, distrustful, and inclined to assume the worst – a phenomenon consistent with a strong character. To make *a decision* for him means to burn all bridges and to do what is to be done. This kind of person may well experience doubt before he makes his mind, as long as he isn't quite convinced; but once he has begun to doubt, his *passionate nature* will turn him into a sceptic to the point of cynicism. (*Notebooks*, 1968: 174, my emphasis)

In comparison with the final version in the novel, one quote from the preparatory materials could serve as a guiding principle about the essence of Stavrogin's Hamletian idea:

> 'The Prince (theme): 'I've come to you <asking you to> prove God to me.'
>
> 'Why do you need Him so suddenly? Aren't you an educated man?'
>
> The Prince: 'Yes, I do know, more or less, all the *pro* or *contra*; also that there is no proof, and rather many more facts suggesting His superfluity. But that is not the point. I have been told that you are the one that of those who really do believe. Well, you must have something to tell me why you believe, if you actually, do believe. I have never

met a man who actually believed. Tell me anything. Forgive my rude, feverish impatience.' (348)

The motifs reminiscent of Hamletian 'pro and contra' contemplations are recurrent in the Hamlet-isotopy but now explicitly within the religious context. The Prince embarks on a fervent quest for evidence of God's existence, oblivious to the fact that the dialectical logic of *pro* and *contra* is binary, and fails to encompass the multifaceted truth of religious experience. Engaged in a project of self-fashioning and experimentation with epochal ideologies, Stavrogin employs a performative, histrionic attitude to probe vast possibilities of thought and action. Performativity and seduction become his means of exploration and exploitation of others: 'The Prince, in his effort to investigate *everything*, even pretends to be a nihilist, makes friends with Nechaev and tries to elicit some information from him' (175, my emphasis). As the work on the novel continued, Dostoevsky reduced the Prince to less and less content; stripping him of ideas, characteristics, desires and interests. Confronted with his essential uprootedness, Stavrogin becomes depleted of ideas, adrift amidst an endless meandering between *pro* and *contra*, bereft of the primary cause. Much like his literary counterparts, the underground man and Raskolnikov, Stavrogin harbours a Hamletian, yet heightened, sense of revulsion and loathing towards his contemporaneity. These reflections of his are absent in the final version of the novel; moreover, he is reluctant to express his ideology or beliefs, beyond terse, enigmatic comments. His acute self-awareness, coupled with a critical consciousness of national, epochal and generational currents, results in a nihilistic resignation and disillusionment – he has lost hope or any illusion that there is anything to be said or done. 'I opened my eyes and I saw too much – I couldn't stand that rootlessness of ours' (176). He has emptied himself of any particular idea:

March 15 <1870>. – The Prince is a person who is easily bored. A product of this Russian age. He looks down on people and knows how to remain independent, i.e., he keeps away from the gentry, as well as from Westernisers, and from the nihilists, and from Golubov.[5] Yet there remains for him the question: what is he himself? The answer for him is 'Nothing'. He is very intelligent and therefore realizes that he is in fact not a Russian. (180)

This example presents an interesting paradox – Stavrogin is a typical product of the Russian age that is not Russian at all. However, he realizes that he is not Russian once he understands he is *Nothing*. Paradoxically, as such *nothing*, he assumes a central role within the novel. Dostoevsky is quite adamantly straightforward about this aspect: 'N.B. Everything is contained in Stavrogin's character. Stavrogin is EVERYTHING' (269–70). Thus, although he perceives himself as *nothing*, he becomes a space which contains everything within the novel – which might be one way of interpreting Dostoevsky's elusive use of the word 'everything' in this context. Moreover, Dostoevsky explicitly designates Stavrogin as the focal point: 'AND SO, THE WHOLE PATHOS OF THE NOVEL LIES IN THE PRINCE; HE IS THE HERO. All the rest moves around him, like a kaleidoscope [. . .] A boundlessly lofty figure' (182). These three qualifications (Stavrogin's self-perceived significance as nothingness, his capacity to encompass everything for others and being the central hero around whom all the rest moves as in a kaleidoscope) are the crucial metaphors for the way his character is constructed. As a representative of a Russian gentlemen educated on European principles and a typical product of his age, he cannot deny his uprootedness and nihilism.

> Does anyone (of the Pan-Slavs or even Slavophiles) believe, and finally, even the question: *is it possible to believe*? And if not, then what does it mean to shout about the Russian people's strength in Orthodoxy? This, consequently, *is the only question of our times*. There the *disintegration*, atheism began earlier; with us, later, but it will begin certainly with the entrenchment of atheism. [. . .] It emerges, consequently, that the whole matter lies in the pressing question: *can one believe, being civilised, i.e. a European, i.e. believe absolutely in the divinity of the Son of God, Jesus Christ?* (for all faith consists only of this) [. . .] *And so, here lies the enigma. . .* (Cited in Mochulsky, 1973: 430, my emphasis)

The central theme of the novel might be defined as the exploration of whether a Russian, educated on European civilizational principles, can believe in Jesus Christ and atone for his sins. More precisely, the question is whether the true Russian Hamlet, with the wholesome 'broadness' of his soul (as depicted in Dostoevsky's description of Grigoryev and Dmitry Karamazov's confession), drawn to both belief and disbelief, can truly and simple-heartedly believe in Jesus Christ. As Dostoevsky writes in the preparatory materials for the novel, that is the most pressing question, foregrounding the narrative's thematic gravity. This theme is an expansion of Russian Hamletism. However, no one to my knowledge before Dostoevsky highlighted Orthodoxy as the main context in which *Hamlet*, as a product of Western tradition and culture, is being appropriated in the Russian context. We can draw parallels to *The Idiot*, wherein Ippolit's Hamletian confession includes a description of Holbein's Dead Christ, another work of art belonging to European civilization that can destroy someone's belief, as Dostoevsky claimed. Apart from this aspect, as already noted in the Hamlet-isotopy, the question 'to be or not to be' can be translated into 'to believe or not to believe', as a background for the development of other Hamletian motifs, references and quotations. The epistemological concerns are transformed into religious and spiritual dilemmas. In that sense, Dostoevsky's 'Hamlet' becomes a figure struggling for salvation despite the demonic Hamletian logic. The fact that Stavrogin inevitably fails is the most severe criticism of Russian Hamletism.

In conclusion, the portrayal of Stavrogin in the preparatory materials parallels aspects of Dostoevsky's Russian Hamletism. This argument gains the strongest support from the clearest reference to the 'to be or not to be' phrase. In comparison to other Hamletian characters, Stavrogin not only emerges as the most immoral character, yet paradoxically, he also harbours the most fervent dream[6] about paradise on earth. He is most radically stretched between belief and disbelief in very practical terms, while simultaneously functioning as the main ideologist. In the following part we shall see how Dostoevsky solved these issues in the omitted chapter of *Demons*, the one which was censured.

## The omitted chapter 'At Tikhon's'

The text of *Demons* confronts us with another lacuna on an editorial level. The whole chapter 'At Tikhon's', including Stavrogin's confession to the eccentric monk Tikhon, was omitted in the *Russian Messengers's* first edition and Dostoevsky did not publish it later when he had a chance. Instead, he made crucial changes both to the *fabula* and to the overall poetical and ideological resolution of the novel by attributing the central position to Stepan Trofimovich's spiritual transformation at the end of *Demons*. The history of the omitted chapter 'At Tikhon's', in which Stavrogin visits the monk and brings his confession to read it, perpetuates the patterns of lacunary presences in the novel. Building upon insights gathered from the preparatory materials up until now, one can argue that Stavrogin's visit to Tikhon serves as his final test of the feasibility of genuine faith, representing the culmination of his struggle with the main dilemma of the Hamlet-ideologeme – indecisiveness about what to be and what to do. The dual, or rather, multifaceted forms of himself, akin to the devil's undertaking of various forms, are a sign of undecidability among numerous possibilities that prove to be just impossibilities. Stavrogin approaches his own hallucination of the devil with the same suspicion, treating it as a fragment of his own imagination. He tells Tikhon: 'It's I myself in various aspects and nothing more [. . .] of course I do, I see it, just as I see you . . . and sometimes I see it and am not sure I see it, though I do see it . . . and sometimes I'm not sure I see it, and I don't know what's true: he or I . . . it's all rubbish. And you, can't you somehow suppose that it's actually a demon?' (*Demons*, 2006: 686–7). Paradoxically, he immediately admits to believe in the true incarnation of the devil, despite acknowledging the possibility that it might merely be a part of one of his various, fragmented selves: 'I believe in the demon, believe canonically in a personal demon, not an allegory, and I have no need to elicit anything from anyone, there you have it' (687). Is Stavrogin a similar demonic impostor? He could be, since he hypothetically has the qualities for such

a role, yet he lacks the ambition to fulfil it. The others are projecting
their desires in attempts to appropriate him for this role. However,
he leaves them disillusioned in their desire to impose predetermined
identities upon him. The entire ideological framework surrounding
Stavrogin is a construct of others' desires and projections, stemming
from his enigmatic essence, transformed into a mythic aura around
his character. Even Tikhon, it appears, might have fallen into this trap
of perception. When Tikhon recalls encountering Stavrogin earlier,
the latter dismisses that, adding: 'Perhaps you simply heard about
me and formed some idea, and so you confused that with seeing
me' (582). As Dostoevsky remarks, Stavrogin is kaleidoscopically
present in the perception of other characters – they extract an aspect
of him, distort it and then multiply it as if looking at him through a
kaleidoscope. The novel functions metonymically – a part of Stavrogin
becomes appropriated and serves a purpose for fuelling diverse and
often contradictory ideologies – somewhat paralleling the function
of *Hamlet* in Russian culture in the nineteenth century. Stavrogin is
aware of the mechanism of the rumours and the power of projections.
He understands how preconceived ideas or insinuations develop into
solid beliefs, even if untrue – as if he was metafictionally aware of the
narrative logic. He is the only character aware of the complexity of
the kaleidoscopic mechanism on the existential level. Being aware of
this paradoxical mechanism, Stavrogin recognizes that it shapes his
understanding and perception of himself and others. He perceives all
other characters as metonymic extensions of his ideas or perceptions,
albeit in an abstract sense. In this regard, Stavrogin truly is 'everything',
his network of ideas reach all characters, and there is no idea within
the narrative that eludes him. However, he tells Tikhon: 'Listen, I don't
like spies and psychologists, at least those who try to pry into my soul.
I don't invite anyone into my soul, I don't need anyone, I'm able to
manage by myself' (587).

In his confession Stavrogin writes how he did not enjoy meanness,
but rather found pleasure in 'intoxication from the tormenting
awareness of my baseness' (693). Intoxication and transgression are

the only means to experience vitality, once uprooted and disconnected from the others. But a more perilous intoxication is his inability to let go of his personality and his hyperconsciousness:

> All this so that everyone will know that this feeling never subjected the whole of me, but there was always full consciousness left (and it was all based on consciousness!). And though it possessed me to the point of recklessness, it never came to the point of forgetting myself. [. . .] I am convinced that I could live my whole life as a monk, despite the animal sensuality I am endowed with and which I have always provoked [. . .] I *am always master of myself when I want to be.* And so, let it be known that I do not want to seek irresponsibility for my crimes either in the environment or in illness. (2006, my emphasis)

The main issue stemming from the Hamlet-isotopy that is pertinent to this discussion revolves around the impossibility of letting go of reason, autonomy, and selfhood, which is a feature of the demonic. Stavrogin's impossibility to detach himself from logic, and his incapability of discerning the difference between moral polarities, manifests themselves in his remaining on an aesthetic level of impressions. Besides, Dostoevsky accentuates the criticism of hyperconsciousness typical of Russian Hamletism. By insisting on his autonomy from the influences of the environment or the effects of illness, Stavrogin serves Dostoevsky to develop further the argument from *Notes from Underground*. The similar performative compulsion towards self-abasement is evident in Stavrogin's accounts of the worst crimes that culminate in the episode about the rape of the girl Matryosha, which has led to her suicide. Apart from the enhanced cynicism of tone in describing the sadistic seduction of the young girl, Stavrogin's level of emotional detachment is represented in the choice of details he retells: 'When I kissed her feet, she recoiled all over and smiled as if in shame, but with some *crooked smile*' (695, my emphasis): even in such an appalling scene, his focus is on the aesthetic aspect of her smile. It appears he was ultimately disgusted by and afraid of the passion he incited in the girl:

Finally, there suddenly occurred an odd thing, which I will never forget and which *caused me astonishment*: the girl threw her arms around my neck and suddenly began kissing me *terribly herself*. Her face expressed complete admiration. I almost got up and left – *so unpleasant was it in such a tiny child* – out of pity. (695–6, my emphasis)

In this disturbing part of the confession (the main reason why the chapter was censored), the description of lust incited in a child is deeply problematic. The little girl also becomes possessed. As a result of Stavrogin's actions, she commits suicide, claiming beforehand that she killed God. If we follow the logic of the quest for meaning and values, this episode is the ultimate test for Stavrogin since it completely discourages him from the belief that anything can remain innocent and pure in the world, since even a child could be seduced and possessed by passion. Paradoxically, just a few paragraphs later, Stavrogin reports about his Golden Age dream of restoring paradise on earth, confirming the lost illusion. Although the narrator characterizes Stavrogin as a bad writer, the juxtaposition of these two episodes, the extreme difference in the moral dimensions they include, the imposed tone, and style, all reveal a skilful seducer and storyteller. We might add that Dostoevsky wrote Stavrogin's confession as a continuation of the motifs from the underground man's parodic attack on Russian Hamletism. He describes his dream:

Here *European mankind remembered its cradle*, here were the first scenes from mythology, its earthly paradise. [. . .] A wondrous dream, a lofty *delusion! The most incredible vision of all that have ever been, to which mankind throughout its life has given all its forces, for which it has sacrificed everything, for which prophets have died on crosses and been killed, without which people do not want to live and cannot even die . . .* (703, my emphasis)

The dream was inspired by an actual painting by Claude Lorrain called *Acis and Galatea*, which was one of Dostoevsky's favourite pieces in the *Gemäldegalerie* in Dresden. The painting itself depicts a scene supporting the idea that this idyll is a delusion. 'Namely, two lovers are in the front in the picture. But in the back, there is the giant Polyphemus that later kills Acis out of jealousy' (Bjelica, 2020: 237). Stavrogin recalls how after the episode of the dream situated at the Greek archipelago, he envisions Matryosha through hallucination – both traumatic symptoms of the Real.

> I saw before me (oh, not in reality! and if only, if only it had been a real vision!), I saw Matryosha, wasted and with feverish eyes, exactly the same as when she had stood on my threshold and, shaking her head, had raised her tiny little fist at me. And nothing had ever seemed so tormenting to me! The *pitiful despair* of a helpless ten-year-old being with a still unformed mind, who was threatening me (with what? what could she do to me?), but, of course, *blaming only herself!* [. . .] No – what is *unbearable to me is only this image alone*, and precisely *on the threshold*, with its raised and threatening little fist, only that look alone, only that minute alone, only that shaking head. I am making this *statement on my own, and have no accuser*. (*Demons*, 2006: 703, my emphasis)

These visions result in Stavrogin's definitive split. 'Both images deepen the ambivalent chasm and disturb the idealistic vision of innocence and harmony. Stavrogin is the witness to both images and he doesn't allow the ambivalence, eternally new, to be disregarded. His sharp, ruthless knowledge and self-knowledge is a product of him being a witness to it' (Bjelica, 2020: 237). Stavrogin's gaze into the Real becomes a part of the story in that he transcends human limits by committing crimes and rape. Let us remember that the Real stands for everything that cannot be included in the Imaginary and Symbolic. The Real:

> is manifest only as a symptom, a recalcitrant element within the subject's discourse which analysis tries to identify but cannot grasp, experiencing it only as 'an essential encounter – an appointment to which we are always called with a real that eludes us' (Lacan, 1979: 53). Therefore, the real may only be located negatively, through reference to the compulsive attempts made to represent it within the signifying network. (Armstrong, 1996: 231)

The other symptom of the traumatic encounter with the Real is the gap in representation. The gaze into the Real is 'an impossible vision which subject desires but can never attain, for it would dissolve the subject/object split, which founds and orders the symbolic and imaginary optic fields' (1996). This traumatic experience, echoing Lacan's understanding of the Real, cannot be transferred either in language or symbolic representation, manifesting itself in the hallucinations of the girl Matryosha and the devil. At the narrative level, this trauma is manifested in the radically ambivalent, contradictory and paradoxical textual construction of Stavrogin, a character symptomatically structured by a gap in representation. His inner emptiness cannot be, and is not, transferred on the level of the story but is given instead only in form of dream visions and hallucinations. Rather than expressing remorse and seeking atonement, Stavrogin's confession is a demonstration of his incapacity to confront guilt and claim responsibility for his sins, as Tikhon rightly notices. He emphasizes this by accusing Stavrogin of exaggerating his self-accusations and dismisses his over-elaborated honesty as a posture. Stavrogin refuses this interpretation: "Portray? I tell you again: I was not portraying myself and especially was not posturing" (*Demons*, 2006: 706). But Tikhon is the only one to mention that behind this cynical façade there lies an essential trauma: 'This document comes straight from the need of a mortally wounded heart.' (2006) Tikhon exposes Stavrogin's self as performative act in front of the mirror and imaginative audience, similar to that of the man from the underground and Raskolnikov's: 'But it is as if you *already hate beforehand all those who will read what is described here and are challenging them to battle. If you are not ashamed to confess the crime, why are you ashamed of repentance?* Let them look at me, you say; well, and you yourself, how are you going to look at them?' (2006, my emphasis). Lastly, by criticizing the style of the confession he reveals Stavrogin's intention. Tikhon's insight could further be read as a metafictional commentary on the acts of reading and analysing the text – instructing the reader to discern stylistic nuances:

Certain places in your account are *stylistically accentuated*; as if you admire your own psychology and seize upon every little detail just to astonish the reader with an unfeelingness that is not in you. What is that if not the proud challenge of a guilty man to his judge? (2006, my emphasis)

Tikhon unmasks Stavrogin's confession as deliberate provocation and demystifies his projection of the omnipotent and omnipresent gaze. Stavrogin's provocation is directed towards God, paradoxically implying a belief in the concept of the omnipotent witness and judge. In emphasizing 'Let them look at me', Tikhon reveals the sense of being under surveillance and being gazed upon *a priori* – which signals a deeply rooted, suppressed sense of guilt, but, paradoxically, a feeling of self-importance and arrogance in assuming that he is watched upon with such scrutiny. As a mechanism of defence from Tikhon's interpretation, Stavrogin uses the dynamic of the self as a performance, since a protean and fluid self enables him to evade the judgement and transparency – he lies about lying, embodying the ultimate liar's paradox: "'Perhaps I don't suffer nearly as much as I've written here, and perhaps I've really heaped too many lies on myself,' he added unexpectedly' (707). However, Tikhon subverts this logic of the liar's paradox, rendering individual judgement of truth or falsehood inconsequential within the framework of belief in which the individual *a priori* bears guilt for everyone: 'In sinning, each man sins against all, and each man is at least partly guilty for another's sin. *There is no isolated sin*. And I am a great sinner, perhaps more than you are' (711, my emphasis). Thus, while Stavrogin seeks to transcend the confines of the given Symbolic order by transgressing all possible limits, by the way of immorality and fluidity of identity, Tikhon offers an alternative path in destroying limits between subjectivities. Famously, the first to notice Stavrogin's dependence on others (other characters but also the Other) was Mikhail Bakhtin in *Problems of Dostoevsky's Poetics*:

In actual fact the style of Stavrogin's Confession is determined above all by its *internally dialogic orientation vis-a-vis the other person*. Precisely this sideward glance at the other person determines the breaks in its style and its whole specific profile. Tikhon had precisely this in mind when he began directly with an 'aesthetic critique' of the style of the confession. [. . .] Tikhon's critique is very important, for it doubtless expresses the artistic intention of Dostoevsky himself. (Bakhtin, 1999: 243, my emphasis)

Following Tikhon's critique, Bakhtin notices that Stavrogin's attitude towards himself and others resembles the vicious circle which had caught the man from the underground as well – they pretend to ignore others while constantly having them in mind and fundamentally depending on them. However, the style of Stavrogin's confession appears to be monologic on the surface:

No one else's word, no one else's accent forces its way into the fabric. There is not a single reservation, not a single repetition, not a single ellipsis. No external signs of the overwhelming influence of another's word appear to register here at all. Here, indeed, *the other's word has penetrated so deeply within, to the very atoms of the construction, the conflicting rejoinders overlap one another so densely* [. . .] But nevertheless even the careless ear can catch in it *sharp and irreconcilable voices* interrupting one another, as was pointed out immediately by Tikhon. (244–5, my emphasis)

Tikhon further suggests that belief is beyond thoughts and words, ungraspable by man's will and reasoning, and infinite – the only way out of the diabolical interchangeability of truth and lies, good and evil, 'for there are *no words or thoughts in human language to express all the ways and reasons of the Lamb*, "until his ways are openly revealed to us." Who can *embrace him who is unembraceable*, who can *grasp the whole of him who is infinite!*' (*Demons*, 2006: 711, my emphasis). However, Tikhon himself succumbs to the same fallacy of judgement and interpretation by remarking, seemingly being possessed himself: 'that you, poor, lost youth, have never stood so close to the most terrible crime as at this moment!' (713). Unfortunately, this reaction incites in Stavrogin the same revolt and defiance, who angrily denounces:

"'Cursed psychologist!" he broke off suddenly in a rage and, without looking back, left the cell' (714), rejecting the role of an object of interpretation and investigation, being aware of the impossibility to be healed. Stavrogin's quest for meaning encompasses both self-identity and the world devoid of metaphysical, national and existential roots. He seeks an Absolute value, without moderation. Despite his final attempt to attain an identity, or at least proof of true belief, if not proof, of God's existence (which would grant the Absolute value for stabilizing his identity), his confession and conversation with Tikhon remained trapped within the logic of interrogation, rumours and surveillance.

## Stavrogin in the text

In the projection of the first aspect of the Hamlet-ideologeme, Stavrogin is the bearer of otherness and the character that has gazed into the Real, bringing the story to a crisis and sowing disruption and destruction of meaning. The model of a fully present, unitary knowledge has been imposed upon Stavrogin. The text itself demonstrates his obsessive quest for the character's identity; both by himself and by other characters. Yet, in his giving up or letting go at the end of the novel Stavrogin anticipates a self-awareness about the impossibility of a unified subject. As already argued, Stavrogin refuses to be inscribed in the domain of the Other, but he constantly fails in his attempts at this refusal. Stavrogin as a theoretician of Russian Hamletism provides the subtlest deconstruction of issues and connections between action and being, and the undecidability between 'to be or not to be'. His biggest anxiety is to be pinned down or explained by another character, since he will be reduced to a signifier easily appropriated and modified in the other's discourse.

What has *Hamlet* to do with Stavrogin and how did the nexus of Hamletian motifs develop into this variation of Dostoevsky's 'Hamlet'? It developed into Stavrogin's answer to the Hamlet-ideologeme (the undecidability of what to be and what to do) and its consequences. Stavrogin in the text of the novel has renounced words, acts and self-identity after gaining the paradoxical knowledge once he had gazed into the Real – wisdom is not wise enough, while no act will contribute to the change of power structures, or the dynamic of the interpersonal relations and the possibility of true belief – in other words, it is impossible to 'set it right' (*Hamlet*, 2.1.187). Dostoevsky masterfully created a mystery – a hero with a seductive penetrating silent gaze after staring into the abyss, torn between nihilism and the Absolute. As G. Wilson Knight in *The Embassy of Death: An Essay on Hamlet* (2001) notices, 'He [Hamlet] is an inhuman – or superhuman – presence, whose consciousness – somewhat like Dostoevsky's Stavrogin – is centred on death' (38). Stavrogin is the bearer of the Apocalypse,[7] the stasis of time in which everything is dead and petrified. As his mother observed him while he is sleeping and caught unguarded without a mask for others, the narrator describes 'his face was pale and stern, but as if quite frozen, motionless; his eyebrows were slightly knitted and frowning; he decidedly resembled an inanimate wax figure' (*Demons*, 2006: 212).

In a similar vein to T. S. Eliot's naming Hamlet as the Mona Lisa of literature, Thomas Mann analogously characterized Stavrogin as 'possibly one of the most weirdly attractive creatures in world literature' (1945: v). However, I argue that it is not the content ascribed to him by Dostoevsky that makes him so seductive, but the structure. Or more precisely, it is not his spiritual emptiness, erotic seductiveness or mysterious allure that is compelling and charismatic, but the emptiness of the unknown, the otherness in Stavrogin that cannot be represented. Thus, I suggest that Lacan's concept based on his interpretation of *Hamlet* – the organization of the illusion[8] – might be understood as performative subjectivity: an organized illusion both for oneself and for others. The structural centre of Stavrogin is unknown to others and appears as an empty void. However, onto that void others (characters, and on another level critics and readers) project meanings depending on the organization and rhetoric of the narrative – the organization of the illusion of a character. The formula can be 'everything and nothing' – embodying the paradox of acting and being, questioning the realness of reality – a feature that is hauntingly present in the play and all of Dostoevsky's Hamletian characters. Moreover, in Dostoevsky's work, it is often a source of anxiety, dread and the demonic. Most radically in Stavrogin, we might interpret it as a consequence of him being aware of the artificiality of his character. His main action is a certain way of self-effacement, a practiced desire to be nobody, which ends with suicide. As his suicide note shows ('Blame no one, it was I.' ["Nikogo ne vinit', ya sam."] (*Demons*, 2006: 678)), he wanes into nonexistence and silence in a manner of a Lacanian *aphanisis* – or the fading of the subject under the signifier, reducing himself only to the pronoun 'I' [ya] – paradoxically, he kills himself by saying 'I am'. This fading might be understood in terms of the 'demonic kenosis':

> In a process we might call 'demonic kenosis', Stavrogin empties his own ideas and ideologies into the minds of his followers, who, in their turn, project his teachings back onto Stavrogin in an attempt to transform him into a living symbol of the ideas they have made their own, only to discover that Stavrogin is but an empty impostor, symbolizing nothing but nothingness. (Børtnes, 1998: 116)

Again, I argue for an aporetic logic to Stavrogin: thus, he is not 'but an empty impostor'. Instead, he is *also* an empty impostor. The negative void does not exclude the shadows of all the possibilities in him – that is why his structure can be described as an organization of an illusion and why he is such a vivid and compelling character. I suggest that the way Dostoevsky uses the comparison between Hamlet and Stavrogin, if taking into account the established interpretation of the novel and different layers of signification, can offer a plausible argument for this statement. Namely, Peter Stepanovich's comparison should be interpreted from another perspective as well:

> No, this was something higher than whimsicality and, I assure you, even something holy! A man, proud and early insulted, who had arrived at that 'jeering' which you mentioned so aptly – in short, a

Prince Harry, to use Stepan Trofimovich's magnificent comparison
at the time, which would be perfectly correct if he did not resemble
Hamlet even more, at least in my view. (*Demons*, 2006: 189)

The whole comment is made in front of the gathered group of people
in Varvara Petrovna's salon, and it is the first scene in which all
important characters are present together. This is the first time Peter
Stepanovich has entered the novel's society. He uses the opportunity
to start implementing his plan and creating an air of mystery around
Stavrogin in order to solidify the myth around his persona and use him
as leader of his organization. Thus, the idea of holiness perfectly fits into
laying the basis for developing an idol of Stavrogin and Peter's intended
ideological manipulation. Further on, the myth around the figure of
the noble sufferer Hamlet fits even more as an aesthetically pleasing
justification of any ethically problematic behaviour. It is interesting that
Peter Stepanovich is the character that implements this comparison in
the narrative, while, as we have seen, his whole generation is familiar
with the story of Prince Hamlet. Also, it is exactly the comparison that
pleases Varvara Petrovna, since it flatters her lofty aspirations for her
son:

'And if Nicolas had always had at his side' (Varvara Petrovna was half
singing now) 'a gentle Horatio, great in his humility – another beautiful
expression of yours, Stepan Trofimovich – he would perhaps have been
saved long ago from the sad and "sudden demon of irony" that has
tormented him all his life. (The phrase about the demon of irony is
again an astonishing expression of yours, Stepan Trofimovich.) But
Nicolas never had a Horatio, or an Ophelia. He had only his mother,
but what can a mother do alone and in such circumstances? You know,
Pyotr Stepanovich, I can even understand, and quite well, how a being
such as Nicolas could appear even in such dirty slums as those you
were telling about. I can imagine so clearly now this "jeering" life (your
remarkably apt expression!), this insatiable thirst for contrast, this dark
background of the picture, against which he appears like a diamond –
again according to your comparison, Pyotr Stepanovich. And so he

meets there a creature offended by everyone, a cripple, half crazy, and perhaps at the same time with the noblest feelings!' (189–90)

This example might thus be read as a critique of the Russian Hamletism mania by Dostoevsky, rather than the basis for a parallelism between Hamlet and Stavrogin. Moreover, it shows how parasitic liberalism uses the lofty symbols for justification of problems, as we can see in Varvara Petrovna's response, as she was more than eager to take over suggestions and develop them much further, in a rather comical and exaggerated way. If we consider Peter Stepanovich's mechanism of implanting ideas by merely employing hints, this example then perfectly fits into his manipulative and cynical programme. Thus, at the centre of Stavrogin's character, there is a kaleidoscopic network of different literary characters, allusions and layers. *Hamlet* and Russian Hamletism remain on the level of potential significance yet to be discovered by the reader, if s/he manages to deconstruct the actual rhetoric of the novel. Stavrogin is smart and sees through this dynamic and Peter Stepanovich's rhetoric. His deferral of action and utter disappointment with the dynamic of appropriation and the inevitability of 'impurity' of thoughts, ideas and others is essentially Hamletian. However, in accordance with Dostoevsky's creative practice, the writer puts in the mouth of a clearly negative character the crucial comment that should be taken into account about Stavrogin – the hidden source of *Hamlet*. And precisely in this mechanism Dostoevsky reveals the biggest danger of demonic rhetoric. Namely, the fact is that Peter Stepanovich is, also, right. And this mechanism reveals the demonic rhetoric in a way that it reveals the paradoxical interconnectedness of good and evil. The idea is to demonstrate the seductive power of the demonic in its mechanisms of taking something with values and appropriating it for its own means and goals. Thus, Dostoevsky is not necessarily criticizing *Hamlet* or the hero per se, but the misappropriation that violates not only the values of the appropriated object but also its own dubious agenda. It seems to be a subtle distinction, but it points to the ideology of the demonic that possesses its objects. In a way, Hamlet becomes an empty signifier to which the speaker/narrator ascribes the needed or fantasized meaning, and thus giving it a performative function that goes beyond the criteria whether something or someone is Hamletian or not. No one to my knowledge has pointed out that this mechanism mirrors the ideology of the narrative and the ideology of demonic possession, which is another point of conjecture between Stavrogin and the role of *Hamlet* in the meaning of the novel. This brings me to one of the most important consequence of this interpretation – that Hamlet is a sign and source of the demonic and that it is one of the many examples in the novel by which Dostoevsky criticizes not only the manipulative appropriation but also crucial disregard of the singularity and specificity of any particular situation, individual and context. In Dostoevsky's rendering of Russian Hamletism, his writing can paradoxically bring one closer to belief through dismantling the demonic.

The 'Let be' project aims at overcoming the demonic. In Stavrogin's case, it is an attempt to go out of the Symbolic order in which his identity is just an infinite chain of signifiers without a root, pinned down in someone else's discourse. Kirillov guesses this dialectic in the already quoted sentence: 'if Stavrogin believes, he does not believe that he believes. And if he does not believe, he does not believe that he does not believe' (*Demons*, 2006: 616). If we presume that 'to be or not to be' is Hamlet's signature as understood in Russian reception, a formula of his subjectivity, and, moreover, a sign of dialetheic logic of 'to be and not to be', then the above-mentioned conundrum about Stavrogin's belief might be regarded in a similar way. Namely, it is also the crucial sentence that articulates the logic behind his subjectivity; the formula of his being. Accordingly, Stavrogin both believes and does not believe at the same time. In Stavrogin's case 'Let be' might be seen as an attempt to make a leap beyond the binary logic of the novel – the logics of interrogation, intrigues, the demonic and the solipsistic performativity of the self. In a way, a leap beyond the novel's logic can be an emblematic summary of the behaviour of Hamletian characters in Dostoevsky's novels, especially Stavrogin, in his solipsistic testing of human limits and provocations to God in order to receive and find proof of his existence. Stavrogin is playing with others in his scandals, biting a gentleman's ear, publicly kissing another man's wife and pulling the nose of Gaganov. Moreover, he treats many others recklessly: he kills a couple of men, leads a few women to misery and death out of his caprice. And lastly, Matryosha is like a toy for Stavrogin. He is directly responsible for raping her and for her suicide, indirectly responsible for the killing of his wife and Lebyatkin, and partially for Shatov's murder. As Kasatkina claims about Stavrogin, he is essentially an absolute ironist who needs to test, touch, influence and violate others to be assured of their existence (Kasatkina, 2019: 144, 149, my translation). The main limit in his transgressions remains the violation of children as described in the Bible. It is his main reference point for testing human limits in comparison to the Absolute.

> 'Christ, incidentally, will not forgive', Stavrogin asked, and a light shade of irony could be heard in the tone of the question, for it is said in the book: 'Whoso shall offend one of these little ones' – remember? *According to the Gospel, there is not and cannot be any greater crime.* In this book! (*Demons*, 2006: 711, my emphasis)

That is the point of no return. In Stavrogin, 'Let be' represents letting go in a way of giving up. He is on the other side of the threshold, seeing hallucinations; thus the line between 'to be or not to be' for him is blurred – the dilemma loses its significance. In comparison with Hamlet, figures in Russian Hamletism, and other Hamletian characters, Stavrogin is a hero that has committed many crimes, and even has committed the worst crime, perhaps only because he had wanted to test the concepts and beliefs presented by the Bible. As such, he is the development of the trajectory of the Hamlet-isotopy in the direction of seeking repentance, testing belief with the strongest atheism and consciously trespassing the limit only to descend into otherness.

## Stavrogin's suicide

Stavrogin goes beyond the undecidability between what to do and what to be. In this light, Stavrogin's suicide might be read as a denunciation of others and the logical consequence of his solipsism. He alone is guilty and responsible and renunciates any connection with others. The narrator suggests that he is not a good storyteller/writer.[9] However, I argue that he is a careful and intelligent reader – he certainly understands that he cannot express his whole life: 'I've told you a lot of my life. But not all. Even to you – not all!' *(Demons,* 2006: 674) and he knows that the story swallows the storyteller because it will be appropriated by the reader – thus he stops telling the story of his own narrative identity: '. . . only in your presence could I speak of myself aloud. Nothing follows from that' (2006). His last letter to Dasha Shatova summarizes his ideological and existential position – the ultimate fusion of all traits of Dostoevsky's Russian Hamlets – driven to its extremes:

*Nothing binds me to Russia – everything in it is as foreign to me as everywhere else.* [. . .]

I've *tested my strength everywhere.* You advised me to do that, *'in order to know myself'.* This testing for myself, and for show, proved it to be *boundless,* as before all my life. [. . .]

But *what to apply my strength to* – that I have never seen, nor do I see it now [. . .] *I am as capable now as ever before of wishing to do a good deed, and I take pleasure in that; along with it, I wish for evil and also feel pleasure.* But both the one and the other, as always, are *too shallow, and are never very much. My desires are far too weak; they cannot guide.* [. . .] As always, *I do not blame anyone. I've tried great debauchery and exhausted my strength in it; but I don't like debauchery and I did not want it.* [. . .] Do you know that I even looked at these negators of ours with spite, *envying them their hopes?* But your fears were empty: I could not be their comrade, because I shared nothing. Nor could I do it out of ridicule, for spite, and not because I was afraid of the ridiculous – I cannot be afraid of the ridiculous – but because, after all, I have *the habits of a decent man and felt disgusted.* [. . .] Your brother told me that he who loses his ties with his earth also loses his gods, that is, all his goals. *One can argue endlessly about everything, but what poured out of me was only negation, with no magnanimity and no force. Or not even negation. Everything is always shallow and listless.* Magnanimous Kirillov could not endure his idea and – shot himself; but I do see that

*he was magnanimous because he was not in his* right *mind. I can never
lose my mind, nor can I ever believe an idea to the same degree as he did.
I cannot even entertain an idea to the same degree.* I could never, never
shoot myself!

*I know I ought to kill myself, to sweep myself off the earth like a vile insect;
but I'm afraid of suicide, because I'm afraid of showing magnanimity.
I know it will be one more deceit – the last deceit in an endless series
of deceits. What's the use of deceiving oneself just so as to play at
magnanimity? There never can be indignation or shame in me; and so
no despair either* [. . .] (675–76, my emphasis)

Stavrogin's letter reveals some intriguing parallels with Dostoevsky's
Hamletian letter from 1838 and the Hamlet-isotopy that was derived
from it. The first parallel lies in the confessional mode to a trusted
individual. Stavrogin's confession could be interpreted as a response
to the question posed by young Dostoevsky: 'But what will become of
me, if everlasting idleness is to be my only attitude towards life? I don't
know if my gloomy mood will ever leave me' (1914: 3). Additionally,
Dostoevsky's concluding remarks in the letter fits as a commentary to
Stavrogin's entire character: 'It is terrible to watch a man who has the
Incomprehensible within his grasp, does not know what to do with it,
and sits playing with a toy called God!' (1914) Stavrogin emerged as
a character that has the capacity to perceive 'the Incomprehensible',
and yet is toying with that knowledge. His existential position, a
response to the first isotopy of the *crisis*, bears striking resemblance
with Nietzschean Dyionisian man and his Hamlet.[10] All of them have
gazed beyond illusions, 'into the true essence of things, they have
acquired knowledge and they find action repulsive, for their actions
can do nothing to change the eternal essence of things', arriving to
a conclusion that 'it as laughable or shameful that they should be
expected to set to rights a world so out of joint' (Nietzsche, 1999: 40). It
is this knowledge that 'kills action; action requires one to be shrouded
in a veil of illusion' (1999),[11] leaving Stavrogin completely numb and
inactive. Stavrogin express the problem of indefinite argumentation as
identified in the second Hamlet-isotopy of *negativity* stating that 'One

can argue endlessly about everything' (*Demons*, 2006: 676), but also further radicalizes his position by stating that 'I know it [suicide] will be another delusion – the last in an endless series of delusions' (2006). The rational logic, being fictitious, has an Ouroboros structure – it will only eat its own tail and can offer no stable basis for identity: 'I can never lose my reason and I can never believe in an idea' (2006). The effects of such a realization are the dissolution of reality, indulging in immorality and personifying demonic indifference between good and evil, which leads to self-destruction and destruction of others. Everything is possessed by Stavrogin's *sudden demon of irony*, even his dream of the Golden Age – a theme belonging to the isotopy of the *lost ideal*. The next isotopy, 'to be or not to be' question, is paradoxically rendered. It is articulated best in his capability of 'wishing to do a good deed, and I take pleasure in that; along with it, I wish for evil and also feel pleasure' (2006), while this complete disillusionment colours his extended rumination over whether to kill himself or not. Not a single idea or emotion is strong enough to lead him to either decision: 'Everything is always shallow and listless' (2006). He feels as if his life is not worth living, repeating the motif of self-debasement in comparing oneself with an insect: 'I know I ought to kill myself, to sweep myself off the earth like a vile insect' (2006). However, his logic penetrates another veil of illusion – killing oneself in circumstances of being unequivocally guilty of so many vile and repulsive crimes would imply a demonstration of repentance which he does not feel. Also, it will be an act he will not be able to explain or defend any more. Once he kills himself, the meaning of his suicide will be available for others to interpret and use accordingly to their own needs, desires, and projections. Thus, he concludes: 'I'm afraid of suicide, because I'm afraid of showing magnanimity. I know it will be one more deceit – the last deceit in an endless series of deceits. What's the use of deceiving oneself just so as to play at magnanimity?' (2006). The *confession* isotopy is manifested in his own deconstruction of a possibility to confess to Dasha Shatova when he claims that 'I've told you a lot of my life. But not all. Even to you – not all!' (2006), only to finish the letter with a statement highlighting the futility of his confession: 'only in your presence could I speak of myself aloud. Nothing follows from that' (2006). Lastly, the *let be* isotopy may be viewed in his nihilistic giving up on any meaning, life, hope and faith; as Nietzschean Hamlet he accepts the tragic 'wisdom of the wood-god Silenus' (Nietzsche, 1999: 40), that it is best for a man that he has never been born and since he is born, to die as soon as possible.[12]

Out of thirteen paragraphs, seven begin with the pronoun 'I' (Ja), and it is used in seventeen sentences in this rather short letter. This might indicate the actual tragedy of his solipsism: the incapability to let go of himself and the aporetic demonic logic. His almost obsessive need for honesty that we find in other Hamletian characters (man from the underground and Raskolnikov especially) reveals itself to be a perpetual mechanism of performing different subject-positions, in which the self gets even more detached from itself in language. By spilling one's heart in words in a Hamletian manner, he is creating an organized illusion that others will fill, but he will not achieve an equivalence between being, words and action. Identity remains in the sphere of the undecidability of what to do and what to be. Stavrogin is stuck in the Hamlet-ideologeme: for him, even the conclusion about undecidability is a part of an endless chain of deceits and illusions. Another motif that is repeated in Stavrogin's letter is magnanimity. We encounter it six times and we can also locate it throughout the novel. As nobility in *Hamlet*, magnanimity is irrevocably lost. Therefore, the question of what to do in order to be free becomes the question of 'to be or not to be'. However, in Stavrogin's case, the background of the question expands to the dilemma between belief and disbelief, which remains unsolvable in all Hamletian characters in Dostoevsky's work. In concordance with the demonic rhetoric, the decision to believe is impossible in the scope of rational logic. Stavrogin is the vehicle of questioning the radical extremes of to be or not to be, manifesting the potentiality of everything and realization of nothing, and containing both aspects at the same time until succumbing to suicide. With his suicide, he aims at retaining a sense of authority over his identity and taking full responsibility for his guilt. We might regard him as a character trying and failing in confession, or even better, realizing that confession is per se impossible – since language always depends on the other who will change, alter and adapt the meaning according to themselves. In search for a stable identity in the disturbed order and unwillingness to accept any of the given options, Stavrogin's story about himself shrinks to one sentence: *Blame no one; it was I*. This gesture may be regarded as equivalent to Hamlet's lines 'This is I, Hamlet the Dane' (*Hamlet*, 5.1.246-7) and 'The rest is silence' (5.2.342) with the following outcome: letting go of being and taking responsibility for that choice and act. Stavrogin remains persistent in his need to be a concise, but decisive, author of his autobiography (identity/subjectivity). However, Stavrogin fails in his attempt to be free. 'Our medical men, after the autopsy, completely and emphatically ruled out insanity'[13] (*Demons*, 2006: 678). It is the last sentence in the novel, by which the doctors overtake the control over the narrative of Stavrogin's story.

In order to understand how Stavrogin's suicide resonates with Dostoevsky's profound criticism of Russian Hamletism, at the end, I turn to a marginal episode in the novel about an eighteen-year-old boy who shoots himself because he got drunk and spent his family money:

> On the table lay a note, in his handwriting, saying *no one was to blame for his death*, and that he was *shooting himself* because *he had 'caroused away'* four hundred roubles. The phrase 'caroused away' stood just so in the note: in its four lines there were *three grammatical errors*. (326, my emphasis)

Three motifs stand out and are repeated in the episode of Stavrogin's suicide as well. First, the fact that the boy takes all the blame for his actions; second, the suicide; and third, the presence of grammatical errors. When read in comparison to Stavrogin's suicide it suggests that the hero of the novel is not an isolated and peculiar case, but rather interconnected with the youth of the nation, despite his sense of uniqueness and alienation. However, another motif reverberates even more strongly. One of those who had gone to see the body of the young boy comments, repeating the leitmotif of the novel, the moral, national and religious uprootedness: "'Why have we got so many people hanging or shooting themselves – as if we'd jumped off our roots, as if the floor had slipped from under everyone's feet?" The *raisonneur* was given unfriendly looks' (327–8). By connecting these two separate episodes and motifs, we might come to the conclusion that Stavrogin is just a metonymical representation of a network of suicides all over Russia. Again, he is the point in which the political, ethical and spiritual dimensions of the epoch intersect and the most profound tool for criticizing Russian Hamletism. One might even suggest that the *raisonneur* who received unfriendly looks is a mark of Dostoevsky's self-ironic signature – a hint towards the future statement in the *Diary of a Writer*. With it, Dostoevsky elaborates on one of his main endeavours: to identify the underlying motif behind the disintegrated Russian society and answer the *accursed Hamletian questions*. He addresses contemporary problems in Russia; yet, the passage is intricately connected with *Demons* and the Hamlet-isotopy. Moreover, it can be interpreted as a declaration of his intentions with writing *Demons* – his hidden signature:

> One feels that here something is not so; that an enormous part of the Russian order of life was left entirely without observation and without a historian. At least, it is clear that the life of our *middle-upper stratum* of nobility, so graphically depicted by our belles-lettrists, already constitutes an *insignificant and segregated little corner of Russian life*. Who will be the historian of the other little corners, apparently, quite numerous? And if, in this *chaos* which has long prevailed – but which is particularly noticeable at present – in our social life, as yet, the *normal law and guiding thread* cannot be discovered, perhaps, even by an artist of *Shakespearean magnitude*, – who is going to *elucidate at least a fraction* of this chaos, even *without the hope of finding the leading thread*? (*Diary of a Writer*, 1919: 592, my emphasis)

In *Demons*, Dostoevsky attempted to elucidate the leading thread by interconnecting all the most important epochal problems in the character of Stavrogin, making him a figure to serve his cathartic *project* of healing. By portraying him a Hamletian character, Dostoevsky warns of a cluster of civilizational ideas that, when taken to extremes, result in destructive behaviour. The connection to Shakespeare's *Hamlet* does not straightforwardly enrich Stavrogin for readers; rather, a simple appropriation of a Hamletian model appears to be outdated, destructive and futile.

# Notes

1  The first description of Stavrogin, in the chapter 'Princ Harry. Matchmaking' goes as follows: 'He was a very handsome young man, about twenty-five years old, and I confess I found him striking. I expected to see some dirty ragamuffin, wasted away from depravity and stinking of vodka. On the contrary, this was the most elegant gentleman of any I had ever happened to meet, extremely well dressed, of a behavior such as is to be found only in a gentleman accustomed to the most refined decorum. [. . .] He was not very talkative, was elegant without exquisiteness, surprisingly modest, and at the same time bold and confident like no one else among us. Our dandies looked at him with envy and were totally eclipsed in his presence. I was also struck by his face: his hair was somehow too black, his light eyes were somehow too calm and clear, his complexion was somehow too delicate and white, his color somehow too bright and clean, his teeth like pearls, his lips like coral – the very image of beauty, it would seem, and at the same time repulsive, as it were. People said his face resembled a mask; however, they said much else as well, about his great physical strength, among other things. He was almost a tall man. Varvara Petrovna looked at him with pride, but also with constant uneasiness. He spent about half a year with us – listless, quiet, rather morose; he appeared in society and observed all our provincial etiquette with unswerving attention. He was related to our governor through his father, and was received in his house as a close relative. But several months passed, and the beast suddenly showed its claws.' (*Demons*, 2006: 43–4)

2  For an introduction to a comprehensive bibliography on Stavrogin, see Leatherbarrow (ed). *Dostoevsky's The Devils: A Critical Companion* (1999).

3   After suddenly and without apparent reason Stavrogin had bit a respectable citizen to his ear, 'it turned out that he was in an acute state of brain fever. [. . .] All three of our doctors gave the opinion that the sick man *could already* have been in delirium three days earlier, still in possession of consciousness and cunning, but not of common sense and will – which, by the way, was confirmed by the facts' (*Demons*, 2006: 51).

4   John Jones comments, having in mind the development of Stavrogin during the writing of the novel: 'Nevertheless Stavrogin does contemplate suicide, and the notebook entry 'to be or not to be' bears the date 16 August, so it belongs to the summer when the 'tendentious' political story gets tugged back into great-sinner orbit, growing physically and imaginatively larger and more formidable all the time. Dostoevsky's main troubles were with Stavrogin himself, his new-found 'chief character'. His first and continuing urge was to drive him towards crisis and clarity, which involved, one might almost say which meant, finding a *podvig* that would satisfy his idea of Stavrogin. And thus suicide comes in.' (1983: 279)

5   Golubov is the prototype for the character of Tikhon from the final version of the novel.

6   This is the slightly changed version of the dream that was later attributed to Versilov in *An Accidental Family* since the whole chapter was censored.

7   As a hint that the Book of Revelation is an important text for him, Stavrogin mentions it in a conversation about the possibility of life after death with Kirillov: 'In the Apocalypse the angel swears that time will be no more' (*Demons*, 2006: 217), and again in the conversation with Tikhon.

8   See Lacan's evaluation of the mystery behind Shakespeare's play: 'That the drama of Shakespeare exists behind Hamlet is secondary with regard to what makes up *the structure of Hamlet*. It is this structure which corresponds *to the effect* Hamlet has, and this all the more that Hamlet himself, as the authors put it metaphorically, all the more that Hamlet himself is a character whose depths we do not know and not simply because of our ignorance. He is effectively a character who is composed of something which is the vacuum for situating – because this is the important thing – our ignorance. *A situated ignorance is different to something purely negative.* This situated ignorance, after all is precisely

nothing other than this presentification of the *unconscious*. It gives to Hamlet *its import and its force*.' (1979: 190–1, my emphasis)

9  The narrator functions as the editor of the document of Stavrogin's confession, commenting on the quality of the writing and style: 'I have allowed myself only to correct the spelling errors, rather numerous, which even surprised me somewhat, since the author was after all an educated man, and even a well-read one (judging relatively, of course). In the style I have made no changes, despite the errors and even obscurities. In any case, it is apparent that *the author is above all not a writer*.' (*Demons*, 2006: 588, my emphasis)

10  For a recent analysis of the similarities between Dostoevsky and Nietzsche, see *Nietzsche and Dostoevsky: Philosophy, Morality, Tragedy* (2016) and '"Feeling of Thought": Nietzsche's and Dostoevsky's Experience with Nihilism' (2018).

11  Nietzsche explains the similarities between Dionysiac man and Hamlet as follows: 'The reason for this is that the ecstasy of the Dionysiac state, in which the usual barriers and limits of existence are destroyed, contains, for as long as it lasts, a lethargic element in which all personal experiences from the past are submerged. This gulf of oblivion separates the worlds of everyday life and Dionysiac experience. But as soon as daily reality re-enters consciousness, it is experienced as such with a sense of revulsion; the fruit of those states is an ascetic, will-negating mood. In this sense Dionysiac man is similar to Hamlet: both have gazed into the true essence of things, they have acquired knowledge and they find action repulsive, for their actions can do nothing to change the eternal essence of things; they regard it as laughable or shameful that they should be expected to set to rights a world so out of joint. Knowledge kills action; action requires one to be shrouded in a veil of illusion – this is the lesson of Hamlet, not that cheap wisdom about Jack the Dreamer who does not get around to acting because he reflects too much, out of an excess of possibilities, as it were. No, it is not reflection, it is true knowledge, insight into the terrible truth, which outweighs every motive for action, both in the case of Hamlet and in that of Dionysiac man. Now no solace has any effect, there is a longing for a world beyond death, beyond the gods themselves; existence is denied, along with its treacherous reflection in the gods or in some immortal Beyond. Once truth has been seen, the

consciousness of it prompts man to see only what is terrible or absurd in existence wherever he looks; now he understands the symbolism of Ophelia's fate, now he grasps the wisdom of the wood-god Silenus: he feels revulsion.' (1999: 40).

12  In Nietzsche's own words: 'Wretched, ephemeral race, children of chance and tribulation, why do you force me to tell you the very thing which it would be most profitable for you not to hear? The very best thing is utterly beyond your reach not to have been born, not to be, to be nothing. However, the second best thing for you is: to die soon' (1999: 23).

13  [Nashi mediki po vskrytii trupa sovershenno i nastojchivo otvergli pomeshatel'stvo.] The same word [pomeshatel'stvo] is used for describing Shygayov's madness.

# Conclusion

*A poet is not an apostle; he drives out devils only by the power of the devil.*

(Kierkegaard, *Fear and Trembling*, 1983: 61)

## *Demons* – The most Hamletian novel

Apart from being the most Hamletian novel among Dostoevsky's works, *Demons* is the best manifestation of his kaleidoscopic poetics. In analysing why *Hamlet* is relevant and how it signifies in Stavrogin and *Demons*, I have reached the conclusion that *Hamlet* is one of the Western sources of the demonic. Or more precisely, in the scope of the narrative, the story about Hamlet is used as a vehicle to demonstrate the dynamic of the demonic. Analogously with the Russian readership, characters are inflicted with Russian Hamletism as one of the many appropriations of Western values. Stavrogin, a Russian gentleman educated in a European manner, is stuck as the abstract theoretician of Russian Hamletism and enclosed in the solipsism of testing his own theories.

The core conclusion of this book is thus that Dostoevsky viewed Shakespeare's *Hamlet* through a lens of demonic qualities, marking his entire literary output as an important yet insufficiently explored phase in *Hamlet* criticism that reinterprets Hamletian themes and associates them further to demonic figures in world literature such as Faust or Don Juan. In the first part of the book my intention was to dismantle the relations between *Hamlet* and Dostoevsky's work, identifying the gap in criticism and the lack of adequate approach to analysing all the complex levels of their interaction. I arrived at the conclusion that Dostoevsky's letter to his brother Mikhail, although written when the author was only sixteen years old, contains and anticipates all the important topics that intersect with his future interpretations of *Hamlet* and his use of Hamletian motifs. Following the Hamlet-isotopic network throughout the palimpsestic layers of interaction between *Hamlet* and *Demons*, this study has offered an original method of comparative reading of Shakespeare's and Dostoevsky's work. I demonstrated that the isotopes from one of the layers sometimes explain or amplify the importance of the motifs in other layers, and sometimes they are in contradiction. They have a dynamic relationship that mirrors the design of a kaleidoscope, leaving the reader to choose whether to take all of them into account, or to make a selection of motifs that might participate in the creation of his/her reading. The general conclusion is that the ideological background of *Demons* provides a possible guiding principle for interpretation. Unfortunately, that ideological outcome is not helpful for the reader. It claims that no meaning is certain, that storytelling is based on misunderstanding and that everything is possible and impossible with equal significance.

What is the version of Dostoevsky's 'Hamlet' that emerges from the relations of the analysed layers? How does *Hamlet* signify in *Demons*? I have suggested a possible answer: in terms of the form, *Hamlet* signifies as a lacunary presence. In terms of the content, however, references to *Hamlet*/Hamlet and Russian Hamletism demonstrate the dynamic of the demonic and overcoming of it. The paradox of the demonic lies in its mixing of truth and lies, good and evil. For example, in helping Kirillov write his suicide note, Peter Verkhovensky insists: 'so that they'll believe you, you must be as obscure as possible, precisely like that, with just hints. You must show only a little corner of the truth, exactly enough to get them excited. They'll always heap up more lies for themselves, and will certainly believe themselves better than us, of course' (*Demons*, 2006: 620–1). I suggest that the comparison between Stavrogin and Hamlet might be this kind of a misleading hint in *Demons*. Or maybe, a hint lies in the fact that in Dostoevsky's work, Hamlet may be seen to be an empty-worded obscurantist and that the popularity of the play across centuries comes exactly from the structural formation that allows anyone to create their own story about him.

Additionally, the symbolic mechanism of the demonic possession on the level of the plot corresponds with appropriating the other, the foreign and the unknown into a new cultural context in which the native culture is rewritten and its uniqueness is potentially violated. The fact that in this process neutrality and freedom are impossible – as Shatov warned – might be Dostoevsky's hint for the interpretation of the novel. Selection and organization of facts imply a tendency, a specific ideological and critical position that cannot be overlooked. On the other hand, the rhetoric of the demonic blurs and hides its sources, making it impossible to create a stable meaning. Thus, Dostoevsky is not addressing the ideological issue about the 'purity' of Russian culture or literature in regard to Western influence, nor the indisputable quality of Shakespeare's art, but rather a necessity of a clear and honest explanation of one's position and intentions in the process of selection and organization of facts, ideas, motifs, as the only way of getting closer to avoiding manipulation or misuse (that might come from good intentions as well). On a different level, of the same importance is an honest and respectful relation to any other singularity. Because of this reason, I suggest that the phrase 'Let the other be' might be read as one of Dostoevsky's signatures – a metafictional concept that interconnects his work and poetics.

## Demonic

In his Hamletian characters (Mr. Golyadkin, the man from the underground, Raskolnikov, Ippolit, Nastasya Filippovna, Stavrogin, Kirillov, Versilov, Arkady Dolgoruky, Dmitry, Ivan and Alyosha Karamazov, Shigalyov), Dostoevsky executes a cynical vivisection of the self and of one's own arguments, meanders of self-irony and self-debasement. These arguments belong to a broader dialogue between the demonic and issues of Russian Hamletism. They are driven to their extreme logical consequences, amplified and radicalized, yet equally strongly criticized by Dostoevsky himself. However, in most cases, the result is that Hamletian heroes are profoundly alienated from the materiality of the others' existence and their national identity. The others are understood as a sheer abstraction, aesthetic and rhetorical objects at disposal to be used and misused in testing ideas, which only amplifies the way that reality feels like a dream and expands the alienation of the Hamletian heroes from the people, the nation and its values of Christian Orthodox mysticism, as professed by Dostoevsky. This radical doubt about the very existence of reality is extended to the sense of the self as a non-existent entity and a sensation of a dream without a dreamer, which is the most radical form of scepticism. Epistemological conundrums become ontological uncertainties because everything simultaneously might be and not be – which is the challenge of the demonic. Thus, in the most severe criticism of Russian Hamletism, Dostoevsky attributes it to the demonic, because as demonstrated in the world of *Demons*, everything is open to being possessed by the demonic, from the little girl Matryosha to the highest civilizational value of Shakespeare's art.

How could values of Western humanism be demonic? A recent book by Ewan Fernie, *The Demonic: Literature and Experience* (2013), eloquently demonstrates in which ways Western culture and the demonic are deeply interconnected: 'Modern Western civilisation is intimately related to the demonic, and some of our most valuable artistic, religious and philosophical works – from Shakespeare to Thomas Mann [. . .] and from Hegel to Dostoevsky – repeatedly confess this' (3). According to him, the demonic is a 'profoundly vital *experience* [. . .] the womb of possibility [. . .] the paradox of life that is opposed to life' (22). Moreover, Fernie highlights the resonance between demonic negativity and Western modern subjectivity, vis-à-vis *Hamlet*: 'modern subjectivity emerges when the subject sees himself as "out of joint", as excluded from the "order of things", from the positive order of entities' (Žižek cited in Fernie, 2013: 9). Additionaly, it is important to note that the term 'demonic' should not be narrowly construed solely as a religious attribute associated with the devil or as an exclusively theological concept. Rather, readers are encouraged to comprehend this intricate phenomenon as a quality that deeply ingrains Western civilization and subjectivities, extending beyond mere theological implications.

Within Dostoevsky's body of work the concept of the demonic holds significant complexity. In his insightful study *A Devil's Vaudeville: The Demonic in Dostoevsky's Major Fiction* (2005), Leatherbarrow analyses Dostoevsky's demonology, highlighting that the core value of the devil is the symptom of moral decline and his key weapons are disguise, deceit and ambiguity. He distinguished three distinct cultural sources in Dostoevsky's work: the Russian folk tradition of devilish figures, the 'appropriation of a demon figure by European Romanticism and its reconfigurations in the 19th century' and the framework of Russian Orthodox demonology (Leatherbarrow, 2005: 2). I propose an additional fourth source: the demonic as emblematic of the particular discursive formations within Western European civilization, originating in Cartesianism and blooming in the capitalist bourgeois society of the nineteenth century. More precisely, its roots lie in the values of egoism, a culture of rationalistic individualism and a self-interest-driven violence towards others – a worldview that underscores many anthropocentric perspectives and foundational principles of modern rationalistic subjectivity. This framework includes scepticism and disbelief which within the context of Russian culture in the 1870s gave rise to nihilism, atheism, alienation, despair and, finally, terrorism. Furthermore, the notion of demonic possession holds significant metaphorical weight, suggesting a control over someone and their loss of autonomy through being possessed by some external influence. Seen from that perspective, the demonic may represent an infatuation with Western European civilization that brings disillusion and despair into a non-Western context and *vice versa*. Moreover, we should bear in mind that the cultural practice of demonization as 'the action of portraying a person or thing as wicked and threatening' (*OED*), is often used to justify the need to civilize someone or something. The first step of demonization is often a form of othering, a projection defence mechanism based on fear and misunderstanding. Thus, demonization as a racist practice is often present in 'civilizational' projects – and this mechanism is something Dostoevsky acutely warns against. One way of deconstructing the process of demonization is using the epitome of a Western modern hero such as Hamlet and demonstrating the inherent violence behind this type of dealing with 'the other'.

*Demons* prominently demystifies the dynamic of the demonic. Richard Pevear, one of the translators of *Demons* into English, has pointed out that the demonic is not as simple concept as it might seem. Starting from the title, he rightly notices that the notion of demon does not refer to the possessed but the possessor and argues that neither Stavrogin nor any other character is a demon. Stavrogin cannot be the demon since 'the title is plural' (Pevear, 2006: xiii). More importantly, he claims that 'Dostoevsky called the novel *Demons* [. . .] precisely because the demons in it do not appear, and the reader might otherwise overlook them. The demons are visible only in distortions of the human image, the human countenance, and their force is measurable only by the degree of the distortion' (xiv). He concludes that 'demons, then, are ideas, that legion of isms that came to Russia from the West: idealism, rationalism, empiricism, materialism, utilitarianism, positivism, socialism, anarchism, nihilism, and, underlying them all, atheism' (xvii). Although I do not completely agree with the straightforwardness of this position, what is more interesting in view of my discussion is Pevear's reference to 'an evil or alien idea coming to inhabit a person, misleading him, perverting him ontologically, driving him to crime and insanity' (xviii) and that demons are not visible themselves, implying that they are a certain type of absence that has its effect on characters. From the perspective of Dostoevsky's overall work, one of the biggest problems with his Hamletian characters lies in their pursuit of meaning and their demonic desire for identity; they strive to be the sole creators and authors of their narratives. Hence, while Hamletian characters in Dostoevsky's work teeter on the brink of a paranoid dread of being objectified by the 'gaze' of others and 'the Other', they themselves engage in a similar process of objectification of others – by de-realizing their individuality, reducing them to abstract ideas and concepts. Rowan Williams asserts that for Dostoevsky, this urge for autonomy and self-authorship is inherently demonic. The perspective of ethical responsibility towards others is crucial because 'the demonic always "de-realizes" or "disincarnates", distracts us from the body and the particular' (Williams, 2008: 82). Herein lies another paradox: one cannot exist apart from relational networks, yet within them, one's complete self, one's irreplaceable singularity, remains elusive, probed to be recreated as an illusion, projection and fantasy. There is no possibility it can be seen in his/her wholeness. Furthermore, my premise is that the *demonic* may be interpreted as the inevitable distortion of a subject's identity in the process of translation into another's discourse. More precisely, because of this Dostoevsky's Hamletian characters are obsessed with the fear of being appropriated by another's discourse, subjected to interpretation beyond their control and manipulated by the gaze of 'the Other'. From a Lacanian viewpoint, the demonic signifies the process of objectification, resulting in fragmentation between the Symbolic, the Imaginary and the Real. This reduction of a person to the dynamic of the Symbolic necessarily represents a misinterpretation compared to the wholeness and uniqueness of any tripartite psyche, opening the space for intended misuse, misrepresentation and manipulation of the 'newly' constructed identity of another. While it can be argued that the subject can only be known through the symbolic distortions of others, Dostoevsky dramatizes this issue while suggesting a 'project' to overcome this dynamic. However, as Leatherbarrow notes, fictional narrative can be regarded as demonic itself[1] while the reader is demonized by reading because he/she forms a demonic pact with the writer. 'Thus, the construction of Dostoevsky's novels is founded upon a clash of Orthodox and novelistic sensibilities, where the desire to affirm God's creation is paradoxically achieved through the demonically incited novel form relying on narrative invention' (Leatherbarrow, 2005: 25).

## To be or not to be – Let be

Dostoevsky's creative, philosophical and spiritual endeavour can be depicted as an arc transitioning from an attempt to create a coherent narrative about what it means *to be or not to be* in *a time out of joint* to acceptance and letting go as summarized in his version of Hamlet's 'Let be' (*Hamlet*, 5.2.201–2). How should we in the end interpret his ambiguous and elusive sentences? 'I have a new plan: to go mad. That's the way: for people to lose their heads, and then be cured and brought back to reason!' (Dostoevsky, 1914: 5). The keyword of my reading is *pust'* 'particle let' (Wheeler, ORD, 1984: 653), the third person of the verb *pustít'*, means 'to let go; to set free; to let; to allow, permit; to let in, allow to enter; to start, set in motion, set going; to set working; to set, put; to send; to start, launch, set going, set in train; to put forth, put out' (ORD, 1984: 652). Although the double aspect of letting go as passively allowing something to happen and actively putting it in motion is lost in the translation by Ethel Colburn Mayne, I concentrate on the original, which includes the semantic potential of the English verb 'let'. Also, the paradoxicality of the whole 'project' reflects the two opposing ways we can interpret *let* in English. The verb 'let' is an antagonym, a Janus word, containing two contradictory meanings simultaneously.[2] According to *OED*, 'let' means to 'leave or allow or make something happen" but also "to leave undone, omit to do; to omit or cease to speak of; to quit, abandon, forsake' (*OED*). However, there is another nuance of direct confrontation to something: 'to hinder, prevent, obstruct, stand in the way of (a person, thing, action, etc.); to hinder, to be a hindrance; to delay, tarry, wait' (*OED*). 'Let be', however, means, 'a. to leave undisturbed, not to meddle with; to abstain from doing (an action); to leave off, cease from; b. to cease to speak of' (*OED*). When read compared to *pustít'* in the sentence from the letter, 'let be' may be understood in two connected ways. First, as letting people go mad, abstaining from interfering as it will be the only way for them to heal – thus, passively observing. The active aspect of letting be is allowing oneself to be mad, letting go of reason and action. Second, letting go of oneself might be read as a type of selflessness that was Dostoevsky's ultimate ideal, the ideal which would, if not restore justice and paradise on earth, then mimic the conditions that are prerequisite for it. In 'Pushkin Speech' he explains:

And can one person found his happiness on the unhappiness of another? Happiness is found not only in the pleasures of love, but also in the *higher harmony of the spirit* [. . .] Can you imagine that you are erecting the edifice of human destiny with the goal of making people happy in the end, of giving them peace and rest at last? And now imagine as well that to do this it is essential and unavoidable to torture to death just one human creature; moreover, let that creature be not an entirely worthy one, a person some may find even ridiculous – *not some Shakespeare*, but simply an honorable old man [. . .] And so you need only to disgrace, dishonor and torment him and build your edifice on the tears of this dishonored old man! Will you consent on those terms to be the architect of such an edifice? *That is the question* [. . .] Tell me, could Tat'iana, with her noble soul and her heart that had suffered so much, have settled the matter in any other way? (*Pushkin Speech* as cited in Bowers, Doak, Holland, 2018: 472, my emphasis)

In explaining why Pushkin's Tatiana is the ultimate symbol of Russian people, its wisdom and moral superiority, Dostoevsky defends her choice not to run away with Onegin, reformulating the ultimate question *to be or not to be* into *let be*:

this is how a pure Russian soul settles it: '*Let it be* that I alone have no happiness; *let* my unhappiness be immeasurably greater than the unhappiness of this old man; finally, *let no one*, not even this old man, ever learn of my sacrifice and appreciate it; but *I do not want to be happy after having destroyed another!*' This is the tragedy: it unfolds, and the line cannot be crossed; it is already too late, and so Tat'iana *sends Onegin away*. (2018, my emphasis)

The main dilemma that was underlying the paradox of Hamletian subjectivities is here resolved in a way that individuality should not be based on violation of another being. Thus, if we turn back to *let be* as an answer to the Hamletian *to be or not to be* dilemma, we can read it as a paradoxical letting go of reason, logic and epistemological inquiry, as well as letting go of reasonable action, as the way of overcoming the binary division between to be and not to be, achieving a form of healing which would mean a higher state of self-awareness and ethical consideration of others. But most importantly, it entails a sacrifice of individuality in accordance with Dostoevsky's understanding of personality. The underlying implicit criticism of the behaviour of Shakespeare's Hamlet lies in the observation that if he had acted responsibly towards the happiness and well-being of others (primarily Ophelia, Gertrude, Polonius, Rosencrantz and Guildenstern), their deaths could have been avoided. As it is, they were sacrificed to Hamlet's self-reflection and solipsism. However, I emphasize that Dostoevsky's 'Let be' project does not arise from Shakespeare's play or Hamlet's line 'Let be'. Dostoevsky's project should be read alongside the already-mentioned Heidegger's reflection on letting be: '*To let be is to engage oneself with beings* [. . .] To let be – that is, *to let beings be as the beings that they are* – means *to engage oneself with the Open and its openness into which every being comes to stand*, bringing that openness, as it were, along with itself' (GA9: 188/144, cited in Davis, 2007: xxvii). Thus, the most important interpretative intervention of this book is to ascribe the 'Let be' project to Dostoevsky as his way of reading *Hamlet* and constructing his poetics that include an openness to 'being' beyond rational knowledge, beyond *doxa*, to letting 'beings be as the beings that they are'. Dostoevsky's anthropology rests upon the idea of freedom of choice and a pivotal moment in which one decides what to become; a type of choice that necessitates letting go of oneself.

In Dostoevsky's 'project' we might notice a violent aspect of rage and fury in the proces of letting go into madness that in *Demons* results in the bloodshed and murders of almost all the characters at the end of the novel. More significantly, the title of the novel *Demons* (Besy), is equivalent to the Russian verb besyatsya (besít') (to rage, to be furious). I connect Dostoevsky's 'Let be project' with the epigraph for *Demons* from the Gospel of Luke: 'Then people went out to see what happened, and they came to see Jesus, and found the man from whom the demons had gone, sitting at the feet of Jesus, clothed and in *his right mind*; and they were afraid. And those who had seen it told them how he who had been possessed with demons was *healed*.' (Luke, 8:32–36, my emphasis). The biblical quotation refers to Jesus expelling demons from a man and driving them into a herd of pigs which jumped into a lake and drowned. The paratext of *Demons* demonstrates the ideological lens of the 'project' of healing the society from demons described in the quotation – which is precisely the theme of the novel. The realization of the healing project in the novel could be debated, but of relevance is that the letter about *Hamlet* contains a similar idea as the abstract summary of the plot of *Demons*.

Dostoevsky transforms *to be or not to be* into a question of theodicy to which he answers with *Let be*. 'Let be' might be read as a performative claim that contains two opposite meanings – what is relevant is what it does, not what it ambivalently means. Its performativity distantly echoes the biblical 'Let there be' from Genesis. Thus, 'Let be' also mirrors the religious aspect of Dostoevsky's thought, or more precisely, the position of man in relation to the divine. As Farafonova concludes: 'The unrest to which man is condemned is a sign of his ambiguous and fatal incapacity "to know certainly and to ignore absolutely." His inability to solve these crucial problems – particularly the problem of God's existence – still being profoundly appealed by them, is fundamental to human nature, and this "knowing ignorance" is constitutive to it' (2022: 51). In this constellation, 'Let be' refers to enduring aporetic uncertainty and the willing participation (letting go) in the 'knowing ignorance' of the experience of otherness. 'In both Dostoevsky's and Pascal's reflections, it is opposed to the "order of the heart", which has its supreme expression in the Christian ideal of *pietas*, or love. It alone is capable of embracing opposites and accepting the paradoxical nature of being and of reason itself' (48). As I already stressed, for Dostoevsky, in Pareyson's opinion, God 'is certainly closer to the ones who are desperate for having denied Him, than to the ones who believe to have always affirmed him' (cited in Farafonova, 2022: 28). As Rowen Williams claims, 'the cliché of the Dostoevskian "holy sinner" is accurate to the extent (and no more) that the sinner who is conscious of sin and suffers because of it becomes a vehicle of the holy, an "iconic" figure, through that act of conscious self-referral to the holy, both as source of judgment and as possibility for the future' (2008: 225). Also, this paradox represents the same logic of being possessed by sin and being healed (saved, anointed) which is in accordance with the ideas represented by the character of Stavrogin and the ambivalent 'Let be'.

To conclude, Dostoevsky's work teaches its readers how to recognize above-mentioned mechanisms of demonic seduction and in Kierkegaardian manner 'drives out devils only by the power of the devil' (Kierkegaard, 1983: 61) through his novels. Rowan Williams perfectly articulates the extent of this problem and the dynamic between the demonic and holiness/lies and truth and how this ambivalence and openness of Dostoevsky's work might be understood in the scope of Orthodox Christianity:

> Kierkegaard, for whom there could – more or less by definition – be no decisive visible form of holiness, given the essential anonymity, or at least utter ambiguity, of incarnation itself. He reminds us that this *failure is itself a theological matter*, a way of illustrating [Simone] Weil's point that *what we can successfully conceive as a representation of the divine* will *inevitably be a falsehood in some crucial respect*. But to some extent, Dostoevsky knows what he is about, knows *what kind of failure he has condemned himself to*. (2008: 10, my emphasis)

Dostoevsky's Christian art might seem like a failure. And indeed, critics often define it as such, as Morson comments that Dostoevsky's novels are an endeavour 'to tell the story of a failure to tell a coherent story, a failure that is itself the best index to a world beyond the reach of ordered vision' (1994: 9). However, I argue with Williams that this seeming 'failure' gives the space for readers to be co-creators of sense and meaning that is otherwise elusive. Dostoevsky's art is based on a spirituality of free faith *despite* despair. Thus, 'Let be' includes the meaning of 'Let *the other* be', implying an openness to otherness and the responsibility towards the otherness of the other – without projecting expectations or judgement:

> The credibility of faith is in its freedom to *let itself be* judged and to grow. In the nature of the case, there will be no unanswerable

demonstrations and no final unprovable biographical form apart from Christ, who can only be and is only *represented in fiction through the oblique reflection of his face in those who are moving toward him* [. . .] And the question will never be resolved as to whether faith's capacity *to survive disillusion and apparent failure* [. . .] is a mark of the power of resourceful self-deceit or the power of truthfulness. A good novel will not pretend to answer this; a novel written for the sake of the credibility of Orthodox Christianity can only set out *the (necessarily incomplete) narrative* and *invite the reader* freely to indwell it and discover whatever is to be discovered. (Williams, 2008: 10–1, my emphasis)

'Let the other be' is thus Dostoevsky's invitation to the reader to open himself/herself to the contradictions and endless explorations of meaning, without succumbing to nihilism and scepticism. In an insightful study, *Dostoevsky's Heavenly Mind* [*Rajski Um Dostojevskog*, 2009], Dragan Stojanović argues that the whole oeuvre of Dostoevsky is founded on a 'heavenly thought'. He explains that *heaven* should not be regarded as a place or 'a specific state but rather a relation: for to make oneself responsible for everyone and everything in the oceanic wholeness of the world, to forgive and expect to be forgiven does not necessarily mean to change the world for the better, but it means to experience it *as if it is better* than it is. That is how it *truly* becomes better' (2009: 229, my translation). Thus, Stojanović identifies Dostoevsky's process of healing and reconciliation in 'bringing heaven to earth', within the ordinariness of experience. He argues that Dostoevsky achieved something special: 'by taking us almost unbearably close to the abyss of nothingness and confronting us with the greatness of losing oneself in insignificance, he also demonstrates the extraordinarily close proximity to heaven, to existence itself; heaven that exactly consists in existing. [. . .] The light of existence is in the foundation of everything' (202, my translation). Vinokurov discusses similar nourishing of the 'sense of wonder' (2000: 36) towards sanctity, beauty and value of the ordinary in life: this is the resource for healing which Dostoevsky offers to all of his Hamletian characters and caricatures, and more importantly, to his readers. It is the seed of rebirth and vitality implied in the ultimate conclusion of Stepan Trofimovich that mirrors Zosima's words – about everyone being guilty and the need for everyone to forgive everyone else – which are the starting points of the healing process from Dostoevsky's project that can also be articulated in an advice to 'live more', given to Stepan by his maid:

> 'Live more,' my friend, as Nastasya wished me on my last name day (*ces pauvres gens ont quelquefois des mots charmants et pleins de philosophie*). I do not wish you much happiness – it would bore you; I do not wish you trouble either; but, following the people's philosophy, I will simply repeat: 'Live more' and try somehow not to be too bored; this useless wish I am adding on my own. Now, farewell, and a serious farewell. (*Demons*, 2006: 491).

Curiously enough, it is exactly this aspect of Dostoevsky's work that inspired one of the most important authors dealing with otherness, particularly relevant to discussing ethics of appropriation in Shakespeare studies (Joubin, 2020: 25–36). It is the philosopher Emmanuel Levinas and his ethical thought that may serve as a lens for reading the 'Live more' advice (Vinokurov, 2000: 36). As Vinokurov states, by 'living more' one realizes 'the simple generosity of the world, that (as Levinas suggests), the world is not mere sustenance but *nourishment* and that life is *love* of life. For Levinas, this realization is necessary so that then I know when and how to wake up from this somnambulant enjoyment of the world outside me, to shake myself into the insomnia of infinite ethical obligation before the face of the other' (2000). However, Dostoevsky is yet more cautious. This dialectical paradoxical subjectivity that is based on the relation with the other is its site of demise at the same time. Levinas's question 'what is an individual if not an usurper?' (cited in Lehnhof, 2014: 490)[3] strongly looms over in these arguments. René Girard demonstrated that in Dostoevsky the interaction between the self and the other 'always runs the risk of disintegrating into violence: or, more precisely, the way in which the structure of the self that grounds the possibility of dialogue is the same structure that grounds the possibility of violence' (cited in Pattison, 2001: 245). This paradox, the inseparable connection between dialogue and violence in the very formation of identity, implies that the rupture, the openness that enables creation, is, at the same time, the entry point of the demonic.

At the end, in order to address the initial question of why there has not been and cannot be a straightforward answer to 'Who is Dostoevsky's Hamlet?', it was essential to consider the manner in which Shakespeare's *Hamlet* and various manifestations of Russian Hamletism are employed by Dostoevsky. According to all demonstrated by now, I come to a conclusion that the question itself may be flawed. Throughout this book, it becomes evident that *Hamlet* simultaneously serves as a source and yet does not. I term the outcome of Dostoevsky's reworking of Hamletian material, as *iconic*. This form of his engagement with Shakespeare, particularly with *Hamlet*, translates the iconic principles of Orthodox Christian holy images to a secular and aesthetic realm of fictional narratives. Icons, as cult objects, reflect and manifest the divine, while providing believers with opportunities for contemplations on themes such as life, death and faith. They offer a narrative context and means for self-identification, as noted by Williams (2008: 200). Through Dostoevsky's reimagining, we witness a complex interplay between these sacred principles and their secular adaptations.

First, the iconic dimension of Dostoevsky's 'Hamlets' is evident in his objectives: his utilization of references or allusions to *Hamlet* (in the way this study established) serves as a vehicle for self-identification and provides a narrative framework for contemplating themes, such as the existence of God and the possibility of an afterlife. Second, icons are considered '"true" images not because they reproduce something absent but because they *express*, and give a *specific vehicle* for, something present' (2008, my emphasis). Similarly, the 'Hamlets' emerging from Dostoevsky's kaleidoscopic writings are not mere reproductions or imitations of the Shakespearean source, but, rather, they serve to convey the reconciliation of the core of the Hamlet-ideologeme manifested in 'let be'. Third, just as icons symbolize 'brokenness healed and plurality reconciled', representing a narrative of disruption and eventual restoration (201), Dostoevsky's portrayal of fragmented and troubled

Hamletian heroes reflects the discord and chaos inherent in the world. As Hudspith explains:

> The icon that is Dostoevsky's œuvre portrays a disfigured subject, and yet it still retains its transfiguring power thanks to its Slavophile organic wholeness, its living form and its sense of hope. As an artist, Dostoevsky is not unlike his Ridiculous Man, whose ideal dream world became corrupted, but who loved it all the more for its fall, and who with that poignant, burning vision in his heart, looks amid the *bezobrazie* toward the future, proclaiming: 'And I shall go on! I shall go on!' (XXV, 119) (2004: 176)

Fourth, while 'Hamlets' in Dostoevsky's novels comprises an ever-shifting, fragmented, distorted and demonized versions of Hamlet-figures that are predominantly negative, the admiration for Hamlet the hero and the veneration of Shakespeare's play remain evident throughout his writings. Dostoevsky's fascination with *Hamlet* persists even through his caricatures, reflecting the notion that 'the divine image establishes itself not by universally compelling attraction but by its *endurance through disruption and defilement*' (Williams, 2008: 208, my emphasis). In essence, 'it is in the nature of images *to be capable of desecration*, and that what makes images sacred is not some magical invulnerability or supernatural protection but their *capacity to retain in themselves the real energy of another world, transmitted* into the world of isolated and death-bound agents' (2008, my emphasis). Despite Dostoevsky's corrosive irony and undeniably negative, disturbing and hauntingly immoral nature of his Hamletian anti-heroes, these characters still captivate and affect readers in a cathartic manner. Lastly, 'the presence of an otherness' (2008) provides a foundation for readers to confront themselves through Dostoevsky's 'Hamlets'. Although this confrontation involves mirroring oneself through kaleidoscopic and distorted fragments, it offers a recognition of a possibility of healing and acknowledges endurance despite the presence of the demonic. The critical, iconic quality of Dostoevsky's novels lies in their transformative effect on the individual reader.

> Murav writes that an icon should be 'a model, not a law, something
> whose meaning cannot be exhausted in advance but must be
> continually interpreted, something that points the way but never
> fully discloses itself' (1992: 148). If art is to be iconic, it should be a
> continuous source of inspiration; rather than provide an answer or
> a prescription, art should interact with man to enable him to strive
> toward the ideal, unattainable in this life, and to achieve this it must be
> unfinalized. (Hudspith, 2004: 171–2)

Ultimately, Dostoevsky's novels do not present a singular or unified
portrayal of Hamlet. Instead, his prose offers a Hamlet-icon – an
array of fragmented Hamlets, each rooted in the unique experience
and interpretations of individual readers. The essence of Dostoevsky's
poetics of reworking sources lies in allowing each reader to find a
'Hamlet' within his work, rather than imposing a Shakespearean lens
that might overshadow Dostoevsky's own creative vision: *Let* a Hamlet
*be* in and through Dostoevsky's work *for* a reader. This approach does
not sustain a Hamletian reading of Dostoevsky but an emanation
and experience of 'a certain Hamlet' through Dostoevsky's work and
it values the personal, transformative experience of engaging with
literature, which can lead to a beautiful, opinion-alternating, profound
encounter with a text.

Both Dostoevsky's engagement with his sources and the focus of
my analysis centre on the effects such strategies have on readers. As
mentioned before, since the very inception of *Hamlet*'s reception in
Russia, two main aspects have been emphasized: modernizing texts to
align with contemporary readers' needs and naturalizing Shakespeare
as 'their own' literary heritage. Dostoevsky aimed to create works that
would spiritually transform his readers and lead them towards a freely
chosen faith, rather than merely producing a pastiche of Shakespearean
references to enhance his novels' standing in the canon of world
literature or offer original readings of Shakespeare's plays. This method
inverts the traditional approach, challenging both the authority of
Shakespeare's texts and studies of Shakespeare as a main authoritative
context for interpretation and meaning-making.

What *Hamlet* signified for the *Russian readership* of Dostoevsky's time may be translated into what Dostoevsky 'Hamlet' could signify for *an Anglophone readership today*. Amidst the gruesome moral and spiritual crisis of the contemporary moment, Dostoevsky reintroduces the complex ethical and philosophical questions Shakespeare's *Hamlet* raises, potentially offering insights on how to transform the kaleidoscopic chaos of an unjust time into a coherent image/face (*obraz/lik*) of an ideal. This transformation would involve piecing together fragmented reflections into a unified face (*lik*), ready to act ethically in service of the other.

# Notes

1   Leatherbarrow aptly explained two reasons why the view about narrative fiction being demonic persisted in Western culture: 'First, it involves falsehood and deception, which are of course the primary weapons of the devil in his attempts to seduce and ensnare the souls of the unwary. Narrative fiction is inspired lying: it involves presenting what has not happened as though it had, and what is not real as though it were. The narrator of such fiction uses the devices of the devil in order to "draw us up into the novel's world through an entire arsenal of snares: confusion, deception, pity, connivance, temptation". Second, the authors of such narratives assume creative *authority,* which should be the prerogative of God alone. The writing of narrative fiction thus travesties divine creation in that the writer creates false worlds and the peoples those worlds with men and women created not by God, but by his own imagination. Thus the traditional analogy of God-as-creator with writer-as-creator is one that supports demonic interpretation, whereby writing, like secular artistic creation in general, represents an importunate assumption of God's role.' (2005: 23)

2   'The words in which a single word has multiple meanings are an instance case of polysemy. In the special case of contronyms, the polysemous terms contain two opposite meanings. This phenomenon is called by linguists in different ways, it is known also as antagonym, enantiosemy, antilogy,

contronym, contranym, autantonym, or contradictanym. In English there are so called Janus words named after the Roman god of doors and beginnings – Janus.' (Murodova and Djumabayeva, 2017: 12)

3  '"What is . . . a solitary individual," Levinas asks, '"if not a growing tree without regard for all that it cuts off and destroys, absorbing the nourishment, the air and the sun, a being which is fully justified in its nature and its being? What is an individual if not a usurper? What does the advent of conscience mean . . . , if not the discovery of cadavers at my side and my horror of existing as a murderer?"' (Levinas, cited in Lehnhof (2014: 490)).

# Epilogue. 'Pushkin Speech'. Dostoevsky in Global Shakespeare

This book has endeavoured to reconstruct Dostoevsky's engagement with *Hamlet* and to explore the distinctive manner in which he employs the concept of Russian Hamletism. While it became evident how Dostoevsky contributed to the nineteenth-century phenomenon of Russian Hamletism, the question arises: can his nineteenth-century interpretation continue to be relevant and inspiring when viewed through the lens of contemporary global adaptations, appropriations, reworking, and transformations of Shakespeare's works? This epilogue aims to address these last issues, mapping Dostoevsky's position within the expansive and multifaceted discourse of Global Shakespeare. Dostoevsky's nuanced and kaleidoscopic understanding of *Hamlet* and Russian Hamletism, interwoven with his own philosophical and theological inquiries, may yield fruitful insights within the diverse spectrum of global readings and a unique lens through which to perceive the intersection of Russian and Western literary, cultural and ideological traditions.

A complex scholarly endeavour to map and organize terminology in Global Shakespeare studies has significantly advanced the field, sparking ongoing debate. Recent emphasis on source studies of Shakespeare underscore the importance of these explorations. Dostoevsky's project may be particularly intriguing because it centres on the dynamic contact between Shakespeare's work and nineteenth-century interpretations, rather than prioritizing Shakespeare or his modernization at any cost. His approach extends to fostering an engagement with the reader. Dostoevsky's oeuvre as a whole can be seen as a critique of the concept of imitation, advocating for the creation of a stable identity distinct from the others, thereby allowing for a deliberate relinquishment of this identity for the sake of others. His most significant contribution, in my view, lies in the realm of ethics of appropriation. Dostoevsky is distinguished by his bravery in tackling uncomfortable topics and recognizing the complex love/hate dynamic that exists between individuals and cultures, particularly the complex and paradoxical dialogue between the so-called Western and Eastern cultures. In order to truly transcend this unhealthy relation, according to his ideas, one must first become fully aware of it. Namely, in order to rewrite his 'Hamlets' he first had to deconstruct his own blind fascination with Shakespeare's *Hamlet*.

For situating Dostoevsky's original engagement with Shakespeare's *Hamlet* within the rich tapestry of Global Shakespeare I selected two pivotal aspects of his career that are particularly representative. The first aspect is his way of engagement with *Hamlet* as a potential source of the demonic, as already delineated in the book. This approach is interwoven throughout his dealings with *Hamlet* and Russian Hamletism, suggesting that the act of appropriating a foreign identity can lead to spiritual and moral disintegration. The second aspect is my interpretation of his famous 'Pushkin Speech', viewed as the final 'project' of 'madness' as he presciently articulated in the postscriptum of his 1838 letter.

First, when discussing ethics of global appropriation, Alexa Alice Joubin recently noted that 'Shakespeare's name and works have been integrated as the "other" within many [. . .] [his work] has become something that is both part of local performance tradition and at the same time a usefully alien presence to inspire new works' (2020: 29). While this is undoubtedly true as this book also bears witness to, Dostoevsky offers a perspective that reveals another side to this interplay. When writing about the ethics of appropriating Shakespeare, Joubin and Rivlin emphasized that citation functions as 'self and mutual recognition', in which 'seeing the others within is the first step toward seeing oneself in others' eyes' (2014: 17). The main premise in the act of citation is that there is 'one's subjectivity, the subject who speaks, and the other's voice that one is channeling, misrepresenting, or appropriating'

(27). Appropriating Shakespeare, as an integrated 'other from within', *vis-à-vis* Dostoevsky, may be interpreted as a demonic and colonizing tool. My reading of *Hamlet* as a source for *Demons* demonstrated that appropriation is always also a misappropriation and misrepresentation, at least in Dostoevsky's view. The integration of the 'other' is inherently accompanied by the violation of both the other and the entity that absorbs it, creating an insoluble conundrum. Dostoevsky's engagement with Shakespeare transcends mere 'appropriation' or 'adaptation'. His strategy can be seen as an 'other within' some dominant perspectives in the discourse of Global Shakespeare adaptation and appropriation studies, as it subverts the naive celebration of cultural exchange and highlights its more sinister aspects of 'an evil or alien idea coming to inhabit a person, misleading him, perverting him ontologically, driving him to crime and insanity' (Pevear, 2006: xviii). In Dostoevsky's approach, we can discern a nuanced warning about and a deconstruction of the attitude in Russian culture that 'ardently' embraced Shakespeare's thoughts and art, integrating him into its cultural heritage, thus making his work an 'organic' part of it's bloodline. Yet, the paradox of such *dialogue* entails the constant lurking danger of devolving into a parody of other's speech, a grotesque caricature, or violation. This dialectic enables the potential for symbolic violence through Shakespeare's cultural hegemony. Exposing these principles in the cultural appropriation of Shakespeare's work in the formation of national identities, Dostoevsky's engagement with Shakespeare may open thought-provoking dialogue. By recognizing this mechanism, Dostoevsky highlighted transcending national ideologies while simultaneously embracing the universal and singular, regardless of how paradoxical it might seem.

'Pushkin Speech' may serve as his contribution to this discussion. It was delivered by Dostoevsky on 8 June 1880 during the festival commemorating the esteemed Russian poet, representing a significant moment in Russian cultural history. This event, imbued with political and historical significance, celebrated literature as a cornerstone of Russian cultural identity and exerted a profound impact on future generations. Dostoevsky's oration and rhetoric, in particular, mesmerized the audience. His charisma and insights, although not entirely unique or original, generated enthusiasm bordering on hysteria among the spectators, even evoking tears. Despite the event's success, Dostoevsky faced considerable criticism. The speech, alongside his reply to attacks, was later incorporated into *The Diary of a Writer*, solidifying Dostoevsky's reputation as the 'prophet' of Russian culture.

Due to its complexity and paradoxical nature, the speech merits thorough analysis through the lens of global Shakespearean interpretations. However, within the confines of this book's epilogue, I concentrate on one of its central themes: Dostoevsky's engagement with foreign sources and influences, particularly his commentary on Shakespeare, and how it resonates or diverges from his view of Pushkin. I read the 'Pushkin Speech' as Dostoevsky's poetic signature, representing a paradoxical approach to transforming the national into the universal. The speech employs elevated rhetoric, hyperbolic exclamations, provocative and contentious opinions, yet it also offers deeply profound insights. It was a performative event that contributed to the creation of the Dostoevskian myth, embodying and enacting the concept of *sabornost* in the moment of its delivery.

For this analysis, I rely on a recent interpretation by Alexandra Smith (2013) that elucidates the speech as an example of Dostoevsky's decolonizing practice. This assertion may appear provocative, as 'Pushkin Speech' was criticized for its nationalistic, anti-semitic, chauvinistic and imperialist rhetoric, blending Russian nationalism with universalism and messianism. While Dostoevsky states that Shakespeare is one of the 'European literatures had creative geniuses of immense magnitude', only Pushkin had 'the capacity to respond to the whole world' (*Pushkin Speech*, cited in Bowers, Doak and Holland, 2018: 476). According to him this type of a relationship with the other is recognized in Pushkin and his understanding of Russian people: 'And it is this capacity, the principal capacity of our nationality, that he shares with our People; and it is this, above all, that makes him a national poet' (2018). On the contrary, he detects Shakespeare's 'colonizing gaze', one that imposes his nationality on other literatures: 'when the European poets dealt with other nationalities they most often instilled in them their own nationality and interpreted them from their own national standpoint. Even Shakespeare's Italians, for instance, are almost to a man the same as Englishmen' while, in his view, 'Pushkin alone, of all the poets of the world, possesses the quality of embodying himself fully within another nationality' (2018). While these claims can be broadly and extensively debated, they nevertheless are an important point in Dostoevsky's overall argumentation because of implying a criticism of a violent appropriative and colonial attitude towards the 'other'. If we apply his statements to his own literary mission, to use Dostoevsky's rhetoric, he accepted the genius of Shakespeare into his soul, knowing instinctively where lied the differences between *Hamlet* and Russian Hamletism, devoting his life work to eliminating Hamletian contradictions and lastly, offering a pan-European and universal vision for everyone.

But how does Smith understand his positions? She offers a Levinasean reading, emphasizing that the speech manifests Dostoevsky's capacity to respond to the 'other', to be in real dialogue with the 'other'. In her view, Dostoevsky's decolonizing gaze can be identified in his projection of Pushkin who's appropriation of 'characters and plots from European literature is based on the ethical principle of respect and answerability that prefigures Levinas' explanation of intersubjective commandment' (Smith, 2013: 138). This decolonizing gaze thus includes recognizing a freedom for the other that is not an object but a *face* to be seen and *speech* to be heard as they are, in their singularity and uniqueness. In accordance with the leitmotif of this book, I conjoin this view to the project of letting the other be as the other it is, ungraspable and incomprehensible. This perspective destabilized ideas of hierarchy and filiation; Shakespeare is completely removed from a pedestal of authority or as being seen as the origin or source of Dostoevsky's engagement. I propose equality to be the core value of comparison and research, in a Levinasean 'face-to-face' manner because Shakespeare is an object of both veneration and desecration, whose underlying presence emanates through Dostoevsky's work. As the analysis of *Demons* demonstrated, in Dostoevsky's view, inherent ethical and political dangers of any appropriation can be resolved only at the level of the spiritual or religious *ideal* of Christianity – in the image of choral voices where every singularity has its place in the harmony of the whole, following the ideas of *sabornost* as a community of people and *tsel'nost* as wholeness of every single person of that community. Despite his problematic rhetoric, I suggest Dostoevsky's contribution lies in the fact that he understood art, if not exclusively, then certainly tangentially alongside the framework of Orthodox Christianity. In this case, this may imply that 'artistic creation as a descent of the Holy Spirit onto the artist-apostle' means 'that the nature of Pushkin's genius was Pentecostal'; with this explanation 'Dostoevsky's understanding of his role and of the messianic potential of Russian literature falls into clear and compelling focus' (Levitt, 2018: 134). Lewitt explains that 'in the Russian Orthodox tradition, the miracle of Pentecost represents a pivotal moment in sacred history and a key to the divine nature of the universe', because it is when 'the Holy Spirit descended upon the apostles in tongues of fire and conferred upon them the miraculous ability to speak and understand foreign tongues, known as "glossolalia"' (2018). Rethinking of the word *global* in 'Global Shakespeare' within the perspective of *glossolalia* all in order to find reconciliation and brotherhood under the Christian faith would imply the following:

> And subsequently, I am certain we (I mean not we, of course, but the Russian people to come) will realize to the very last man that to become a genuine Russian will mean specifically: to strive to bring *an ultimate reconciliation to Europe's contradictions*, to indicate that the solution to *Europe's anguish* is to be found in the *panhuman and all-unifying Russian soul*, to enfold all our brethren within it with *brotherly love*, and at last, perhaps, to utter the ultimate word of *great, general harmony, ultimate brotherly accord of all tribes through the law of Christ's Gospel*! (*Pushkin Speech*, cited in Bowers, Doak and Holland, 2018: 479, my emphasis)

By focusing on this conclusion of the speech, we might extract the following ideas: the concept of 'global' is not an opposite for 'local', but becomes universal, meaning *for* everyone, at everyone's *service*, and not appropriated as *only* someone's cultural capital to be loaned to someone else. In terms of ethics of adaptation and relations, I would summarize the poetic maxim of this speech as *letting the others be* in a choral harmony of voices, providing anyone and everyone a mirror for self-contemplation and enrichment of what they are or may become, where everything, as well as Shakespeare, can truly serve as a universal language that can be 'mobilized by anyone, anywhere, anyhow' (Schalkwyk, 2019: xxiii).

If we understand Dostoevsky's take on the figure of Hamlet and Russian Hamletism as representatives of European contradictions of the nineteenth century, it may be a clarification of what he means by the *ultimate reconciliation to Europe's contradictions*, namely, transcending demonic rationalism, egoistic individualism, immoralism and nihilism. This conclusion may prove original from the perspective of Global Shakespeare because it disrupts the very ideas of adaptation, appropriations and naturalizations of Shakespeare, while emphasizing Shakespeare's iconic qualities that are preserved despite a harsh criticism of *Hamlet*. It is not *Hamlet* that enriches Dostoevsky's work, but, rather, it is Dostoevsky's innovative and idiosyncratic dealing with sources that makes this connection relevant. Moreover, it may pave the way for the readers to utilize Dostoevsky's dealing with Hamlet/*Hamlet* and Russian Hamletism as a model that sustains diachronic and synchronic links between different works; not only Shakespeare's play but also a wide array of discourses across time and geographical space.

Today, Dostoevsky incites a great level of reverence and criticism all across the globe, standing as a strong cultural capital and a global icon himself. Perhaps the name Dostoevsky does not reach the full international and global ideological capacity of a 'business model' (Joubin, 2017: 428) as the brand 'Shakespeare'. However, or precisely because of it, what 'Dostoevsky' as a cultural construct signifies is often misused and wrongly appropriated. Some of Dostoevsky's provocative ideas, such as those presented in his 'Pushkin Speech', provide plausible material for manipulation due to their oxymoronic nature. When taken out of context these ideas may sound problematic. It is important to be mindful about his paradoxical rhetoric that tends to invert one's perspective, to avoid being ensnared with his radical perspective and focus on the dialogic, paradoxical nature of his thought. Nevertheless, as Stefano Aloe thought-provokingly notices, he is too often considered as 'a symbol of something that either belongs to them or to someone else, but as a rule, such people do not read him at all' (2022: 7). There is a dichotomy between the 'cult'/'myth'/cultural construct of 'Dostoevsky', and his texts. Aloe concludes, 'they read around him, under or over his works. If they read him at all. And it is characteristic of such morbidly radical and opposing receptions of the writer that they consistently rely on a dogmatic belief in him as a contemporary and a prophet, thus revealing a considerable misunderstanding' (2022). Rather than endorsing appropriations of his own texts and ideas, Dostoevsky's ethics and aesthetics of authorship promote an openness to wonder and embracing mysteries; a reconciliation of contradictions. Following these premises, adopting Shakespeare, Dostoevsky or anything as 'ours' should not be in terms of a political appropriation but as a participation in an aesthetic and moral experience with *it/them* that fundamentally alters every individual reader. In creating works that witness and echo the force of Shakespeare, Dostoevsky summons readers to let go and accept the profound experience of otherness, alongside the dangers of misunderstanding, misappropriation and manipulation. Accepting him 'as a seminal author who belongs in some way to *everyone* precisely by virtue of his *independence* from everyone' (8, my emphasis), Aloe reclaims Dostoevsky to be a public good for all contemporary readers. Public good is meant to be given freely, to everyone equally. The way it will be received is part of the ethical responsibility of readers – and there's the rub – as the Player from *Hamlet* warns: 'our thoughts are ours, their ends none of our own' (3.2.207).

# Selected bibliography

## Primary sources

Dostoevsky, F. 1914. *Letters of Fyodor Michailovitch Dostoevsky to his Family and Friends,* trans. E. Colburn Mayne, London: Chatto & Windus.

Dostoevsky, F. 1919. *The Diary of a Writer,* trans. B. Brasol, New York: George Braziller.

Dostoevsky, F. 1968. *The Notebooks for 'The Possessed',* ed. E. Wasiolek, trans. V. Terras, Chicago: The University of Chicago Press.

Dostoevsky, F. 1969. *The Notebooks for A Raw Youth,* ed. E. Wasiolek, trans. V. Terras, Chicago: The University of Chicago Press.

Dostoevskii, F. M. 1972–84. *Polnoe sobranie sochinenii i pisem v tridtsati tomakh,* Vol. 30, Leningrad: Nauka.

Dostoevsky, F. 1992. *The Brothers Karamazov,* trans. P. Pevear and L. Volkhonsky, London: Vintage books.

Dostoevsky, F. 1993. *A Writer's Diary: Volume 1, 1873–1876,* ed. and trans. K. Lantz, Evanston, IL: Northwestern University Press.

Dostoevsky, F. 1993. *Notes From Underground,* trans. P. Pevear and L. Volkhonsky, London: Vintage books.

Dostoevsky, F. 1994. *An Accidental Family,* trans. R. Freeborn, Oxford: Oxford University Press.

Dostoevsky, F. 2006. *Demons,* trans. P. Pevear and L. Volkhonsky, London: Vintage books.

Dostoevsky, F. 2007. *The Double* and *The Gambler,* trans. P. Pevear and L. Volkhonsky, London: Vintage books.

Dostoevsky, F. 2008. *The Insulted and Humiliated,* trans. I. Avsey, London: Alma Classics.

Dostoevsky, F. 2012. *The Idiot,* trans. P. Pevear and L. Volkhonsky, London: Vintage books.

Dostoevsky, F. 2016. *Winter Notes on Summer Impressions,* trans. Kyril FitzLyon, London: Alma Classics.

Dostoevsky, F. 2021. *Crime and Punishment,* trans. P. Pevear and L. Volkhonsky, New York: Vintage books.

Dostoevsky, F. 2023. *The Village of Stepanchikovo and Its Inhabitants*, trans. Roger Cockrell, London: Alma Classics.

Shakespeare, W. 2016. *King Henry IV: Part 2*, J. C. Bulman (ed), The Arden Shakespeare, London: Bloomsbury Publishing.

Shakespeare, W. 2017. *Hamlet*, The Arden Shakespeare: Revised edn, ed. Ann Thompson and Neil Taylor, London: Bloomsbury.

Shakespeare, W. 2021. *Complete Works: The Third Series*, ed. R. Proudfoot, A. Thompson, D. Scott Kastan, H. R. Woudhuysen, The Arden Shakespeare, London: Bloomsbury Publishing.

## Secondary sources

Akhter, J., Abdullah, S., Muhammad, K,. 2015. 'Hamlet as a Superfluous Hero', *International Journal of Literature and Arts*, 3 (5), 120–8. https://doi.org/10.11648/j.ijla.20150305.18

Alekseev, M. P. 1965. (ed) *Shakespeare and Russian Culture* [*Shekspir i russkaja kul'tura*], Moskva-Leningrad: Nauka.

Aloe, S., ed. 2012. *About Dostoevsky: Writer's Philosophical Vision and Perspective* [*Su Fëdor Dostoevskij: visione Filosofica e Sguardo di Scrittore*], Napoli: La scuola di Pitagora editrice.

Aloe, S. 2016. 'How did Dostoevsky Understand Atheism? ['Cosa Intendeva Dostoevskij per Ateismo?'] *Numen*, Juiz de Fora, 19 (1): 55–68.

Aloe, S. 2022. 'Complicated and Necessary: Reading Dostoevsky in a Time of Trouble', *Dostoevsky Studies*, 25: 7–9. https://doi.org/10.13136/1013-2309/1329

Armstrong, P. 1996. 'Watching Hamlet Watching: Lacan, Shakespeare and the Mirror/Stage', in T. Hawks (ed.), *Alternative Shakespeares: Volume 2*, 217–38, London: Routledge.

Artemyeva, T. 2014. 'Intellectual Communication of Russian Orthodoxy from the Enlightenment to Modernity', in K. Tolstaya (ed.), *Orthodox Paradoxes: Heterogeneities and Complexities in Contemporary Russian Orthodoxy*, 23–36, Leiden: Brill.

Ascroft, E. 2016. 'Decentering the Dialogic: Lacan with Bakhtin', *The Dostoevsky Journal*, 17 (1): 24–43.

Bakhtin, M. M. and Medvedev, P. N. 1978. *The Formal Method in Literary Scholarship*, trans. A. J. Wehrle, Baltimore: The John Hopkins University Press.

Bakhtin, M. M. 1999. *Problems of Dostoevsky's Poetics*, ed. and trans. C. Emerson, Minneapolis: University of Minnesota Press.

Barsht, K. 2017. *The Drawings and Calligraphy of Fyodor Dostoevsky: From Image to Word*, trans. S. C. Frauzel, Calligrammi, Minneapolis: Lemma Press.

Belknap, R. 1984. 'Shakespeare and *The Possessed*', Paper Read at the Fifth International Dostoevsky Symposium: Dostoevsky Studies, Vol. 5, 63–9. Toronto: University of Toronto.

Benjamin, W., 2005. *Selected Writings, Volume 2, Part 1*, M. Bullocks (ed), trans. M. W. Jennings, Cambridge, MA: The Belknap Press of Harvard University Press.

Benson, S. 2017. *Heterodox Shakespeare*, New Jersey: Fairleigh Dickinson University Press.

Best, S. and Marcus, S. 2009. 'Surface Reading: An Introduction', *Representations*, 108 (1): 1–21.

Bigliazzi, S. 2022. 'Doing Things with Paradoxes: Shakespearean Impersonations', in M. Duranti and E. Stelzer (eds), *A Feast of Strange Opinions: Classical and Early Modern Paradoxes on the English Renaissance Stage*, 41–76. SKENÈ. Texts and Studies.

Bjelica, P. 2020. 'The Ambivalence of Stavrogin: Benjamin's Reading of Dostoevsky's Character as a Precursor of Surrealism', in M. Tagliani, V. Canciani and F. Tommasi (eds), *Humanities: Approaches, Contamination and Perspectives*, Nordest Nuova Serie, 191, 231–9. Verona: Cierre edizioni.

Blinde, L. M. 2008. 'Rumored History in Shakespeare's *2 Henry IV*', *English Literary Renaissance*, 38 (1): 34–54.

Boborykina, T. A. 2021. 'No Longer an Adolescent, Not Yet a Prince', *Dostoevsky and World Culture. Philological Journal*, 4 (16): 88–122. (In Russ.) https://doi. org/10.22455/2619-0311-2021-4-88-122

Boborykina, T. A. 2023. 'Words, Words, Words: Books in the Books of Dante, Shakespeare, Pushkin, Dostoevsky', *Dostoevsky and World Culture. Philological Journal*, 4 (24): 147–71. (In Russ.) https://doi. org/10.22455/2619-0311-2023-4-147-171

Booth, W. C. 1999. 'Introduction', in *Problems of Dostoevsky's Poetics*, ed. and trans. C. Emerson, Minneapolis: University of Minnesota Press.

Børtnes, J. 1998. 'Religion', in M. V. Jones and R. Feuer Miller (eds), *The Cambridge Companion to the Classic Russian Novel*, 104–129, Cambridge Companion Series, Cambridge University Press.

Bowers, K., Doak, C. and Holland, K. 2018. *A Dostoevsky Companion: Texts and Contexts*, Boston: Academic Studies Press.

Brancher, D. 2016. 'Universals in the Bush: The Case of Hamlet', in I. Habermann and M. Witen (eds), *Shakespeare and Space: Theatrical Exploration of a Spatial Paradigm*, Palgrave Shakespeare Studies, London: Palgrave Macmillan.

Bulman, J. C. 2017. *The Oxford Handbook of Shakespeare and Performance*, Oxford: Oxford University Press.

Catteau, J. (1989), 2009. *Dostoyevsky and the Process of Literary Creation* [La Creation Litteraire chez Dostoievski] (1978), trans. Audrey Littlewood, Cambridge; New York: Cambridge University Press.

Cherkasova, E. 2009. *Dostoevsky and Kant: Dialogues on Ethics*, Amsterdam: Rodopi.

Chiesa, L. 2007. *Subjectivity and Otherness: A Philosophical Reading of Lacan*, Cambridge, MA: MIT Press.

Corrigan, Y. 2017. *Dostoevsky and the Riddle of the Self*, Evanston, IL: Northwestern University Press.

Cox, R. 1969. *Between Earth and Heaven: Shakespeare, Dostoevsky, and the Meaning of Christian Tragedy*, New York: Holt, Rinehart and Winston.

Cutrofello, A. 2014. *All for Nothing: Hamlet's Negativity*, Cambridge, MA, London, England: The MIT Press.

Danow, D. K. 1988. 'Stavrogin's Teaching's: Reported Speech in the Possessed', *The Slavic and East European Journal*, 32 (2): 213–24.

Davis, B. W. 2007. *Heidegger and the Will: On the Way to Gelassenheit*, Evanston, IL: Northwestern University Press.

Davison. R. M. 1983. 'The Devils: The Role of Stavrogin', in M. V. Jones and G. M Terry (eds), *New essays on Dostoevsky*, 95–115, Cambridge: Cambridge University Press.

Đermanović, T. 2023. *Dostoevsky between the East and the West* [Dostojevski između Istoka i Zapada], Belgrade: Lom.

Desmet, C., Iyengar, S. and Jacobson, M. 2020. *The Routledge Handbook of Shakespeare and Global Appropriation*, London: Routledge.

Dryzhakova, E. 1979. 'Dostoevsky's Hamlet' [Gamlet Dostoevskogo] *Novyi zhurnal*. Kn., 136 (Sent.): 61–79.

Eco, U. 1980. 'Two Problems in Textual Interpretation', *Poetics Today*, 2 (1a): 145–61.

Evans, D. 1996. *An Introductory Dictionary of Lacanian Psychoanalysis*, London and New York: Routledge.

Evdokimova, S. and Golstein, V. 2016. *Dostoevsky beyond Dostoevsky: Science, Religion, Philosophy,* Boston: Academic Studies Press.

Farafonova, D. 2022. 'Dostoevsky and Pascal: The Paradox of Two Abysses', *Dostoevsky Studies,* 24: 41–60.

Fernie, E., ed. 2005. *Spiritual Shakespeare,* London and New York: Routledge.

Fernie, E. 2013. *The Demonic: Literature and Experience,* London and New York: Routledge.

Foakes, R. A. 1993. *Hamlet versus Lear: Cultural Politics and Shakespeare's Art,* Cambridge: Cambridge University Press.

Frank, J. 1969. 'The Mask of Stavrogin', *The Sewanee Review,* 77 (4): 660–91.

Frank, J. 1986. *Dostoevsky: The Stir of Liberation, 1860–1865,* Princeton: Princeton University Press.

Frank, J. 1995. *The Miraculous Years, 1865–1871,* Princeton: Princeton University Press.

Frank, J. 2003. *The Mantle of The Prophet, 1871–1881,* Princeton: Princeton University Press.

Gaidin, B. N. Lukov, V. A. and Zakharov, N. V. 2010. *Hamlet as an Eternal Image in Russian and World Culture* [*Gamlet kak vechnyi obraz russkoi i mirovoi kul'tury*], Moscow: Shekspirovksie shtudii IV.

Genette, G. 1997. *Palimpsests: Literature in the Second Degree,* trans. C. Newman and C. Doubinsky, NE: University of Nebraska Press.

Gillespie, M. A. 2016. 'Dostoevsky's impact on Nietzsche's understanding of nihilism', in J. Love and J. Metzger (eds), *Nietzsche and Dostoevsky: Philosophy, Morality, Tragedy,* 87–108, Evanston, IL: Northwestern University Press.

Givens, J. 2014. 'Shakespeare and Russian Literature', *Russian Studies in Literature,* 50: 3.

Givens, J. 2016. 'Shakespearean Tragedy in Russia: In Equal Scale Weighing delight and Dole', in M. Neil and D. Schalkwyk (eds), *Oxford Handbook of Shakespearean Tragedy,* 761–76, Oxford: Oxford University Press.

Grillaert N. 2016. 'Orthodox Spirituality', in D. A. Martinsen and O. Maiorova (eds), *Dostoevsky in Context. Literature in Context,* 187–93, Cambridge: Cambridge University Press.

Grob, T. 2016. '"One Cannot Act Hamlet, One Must Be Hamlet": The Acculturation of Hamlet in Russia', in Habermann, I. and Witen, M. (eds), *Shakespeare and Space: Theatrical Exploration of a Spatial Paradigm,* 191–227, London: Palgrave Shakespeare Studies.

Hamlin, H., ed. 2019. *The Cambridge Companion to Shakespeare and Religion,* Cambridge: Cambridge University Press.

Hillier, R. M. 2014. 'Hamlet the Rough-Hewer: Moral Agency and the Consolations of Reformation Thought', in P. Gray and D. Cox (eds), *Shakespeare and Renaissance Ethics*, 159–85, Cambridge: Cambridge University Press.

Hirschfeld, H. 2019. 'Introduction', in *Hamlet, Prince of Denmark*, 1–75, Third edn, The New Cambridge Shakespeare, Cambridge: Cambridge University Press.

Holland, P. 1999. 'More a Russian than a Dane. The Usefulness of Hamlet in Russia', in S. Chew and A. Stead (eds), *In Translating Life. Studies in Transpositional Aesthetics*, 315–38, Liverpool: Liverpool University Press.

Holquist, M. 1977. 'The Biography of Legion: The Possessed', in *Dostoevsky and the Novel*, Princeton: Princeton University Press.

Howe, V. K. 1973. '*Les Pensées*: Paradox and Signification', *Yale French Studies*, 49, 120–31.

Huang, A. and Rivlin, E. 2014. *Shakespeare and the Ethics of Appropriation*, London and New York: Palgrave Macmillan.

Hudspith, S. 2004. *Dostoevsky and the Idea of Russianness: A New Perspective on Unity and Brotherhood*, London and New York: Routledge.

Irish, B. J. 2019. '"Something After"?: *Hamlet* and Dread', in *Hamlet and Emotions*, 229–49, London and New York: Palgrave MacMillan.

Ivanits, L. 2008, *Dostoevsky and the Russian People*, Cambridge: Cambridge University Press.

Jackson, K. S. and Marotti, A., eds. 2011. *Shakespeare and Religion: Early Modern and Postmodern Perspectives*, Cambridge: Cambridge University Press.

Jameson, F. 1981. *The Political Unconscious: Narrative as Socially Symbolic Act.*, Ithaca: Cornell University Press.

Jenkins, H., ed. 1993. 'Introduction', in *Hamlet: William Shakespeare*, The Arden Shakespeare, Methuen.

Joubin, A. A. 2017. 'Global Shakespeare Criticism Beyond the Nation State', in J. C. Bulman (ed), *The Oxford Handbook of Shakespeare and Performance*, 423–40, Oxford: Oxford University Press.

Joubin, A. A. 2020. 'Others Within: Ethics in the Age of Global Shakespeare', in C. Desmet, S. Iyengar and M. Jacobson (eds), *Routledge Handbook of Shakespeare and Global Appropriation*, 25–36, London: Routledge.

Jones, J. 1983. *Dostoevsky*, Oxford: Oxford University Press.

Kasatkina, T. 2019. *Human yet divine: Dostoevsky [Ljudski a božji: Dostojevski]*, Belgrade: Panonske niti.

Katkov, G. 1949. 'Steerforth and Stavrogin: On the Sources of the Possessed', *The Slavonic and East European Review*, 27 (69): 469–88.

Kierkegaard, S. 1983. *Fear and Trembling*, Princeton: Princeton University Press.

Kizima, M. P. 2021. 'From Migration to Naturalization: Shakespeare in Russia', in J. Clare and D. Goy-Blanquet (eds), *Migrating Shakespeare: First European Encounters, Routes and Networks*, Global Shakespeare Inverted Series, The Arden Shakespeare, 167–88, London: Bloomsbury Publishing.

Knight, W. G. 2001. *The Wheel of Fire*, London and New York: Routledge.

Kolarov, R. 2013. 'Dostoevskii's Hermeneutic Autotextuality: *The Meek Girl* and *The Idiot*', in J. Andrew and R. Reid (eds), *Dostoevskii's Overcoat: Influence, Comparison, and Transposition*, 27–37, Amsterdam: Rodopi.

Kovalevskaya, T. 2014. 'Shakespeare and Dostoevsky: The Human Condition and the Human Ambition', *Tekst, Kniga, Knigozdanie*, 1 (5): 62–87.

Kristeva, J. 1986. 'From Symbol to Sign', trans. S. Hand, in Moi, T., ed. *The Kristeva Reader*, 63–73, New York: Columbia University Press.

Lacan, J. 2001. *Ecrits: A Selection*, London and New York: Routledge.

Lacan, J. 1979. *The Four Fundamental Concepts of Psychoanalysis,* trans. A. Sheridan, Harmondsworth: Penguin.

Lantz, K. 2004. *The Dostoevsky Encyclopaedia*, Westport: Greenwood Press.

Lathouwers, T. 2014. '"The Language of Fullness and The Language of Emptiness". Dialogue Between the Russian Orthodox Church and Buddhism? A Paradox', in K. Tolstaya (ed.), *Orthodox Paradoxes: Heterogeneities and Complexities in Contemporary Russian Orthodoxy*, 368–87, Leiden: Brill.

Leatherbarrow W. J., ed. 1995. *Dostoevskii and Britain*, Oxford, Providence: Berg.

Leatherbarrow, W. J. 1999. '*The Devils* in the Context of Dostoevsky's Life and Works', in *Dostoevsky's The Devils: A Critical Companion,* 3–59, Northwestern University Press.

Leatherbarrow, W. J. 2000. 'Misreading Myshkin and Stavrogin: The Presentation of the Hero in Dostoevsky's "Idiot" and "Besy"', *The Slavonic and East European Review*, 78 (1): 1–19.

Leatherbarrow W. J. 2002. *The Cambridge Companion to Dostoevskii*, Cambridge: Cambridge University Press.

Leatherbarrow, W. J. 2005. *A Devils Vaudeville: The Demonic in Dostoevsky's Major Fiction*, Evanston, IL: Northwestern University Press.

Leatherbarrow W. J. and Offord, D. eds. 2010. *A History of Russian Thought*, Cambridge: Cambridge University Press.

Leer, N. 1962. 'Stavrogin and Prince Hal: The Hero in Two Worlds', *The Slavic and East European Journal*, 6 (2): 99–116.

Lehnhof, K. 2014. 'Relation and Responsibility: A Levinasian Reading of King Lear', *Modern Philology*, 111 (3): 485–509.

Lermontov, M. 1951. *A Hero of Our Time*, Moscow: Foreign Languages Publishing House.

Levin, Y. D. 1975. 'Shaksperean Characters in Dostoevsky [Shekspirovskie geroi u Dostoevskogo]', in *Gruzinskaya Shekspiriana*, 4, Tbilisi.

Levin, Y. D. 1988. *Shakespeare and 19th-Century Literature* [*Shekspir i russkaja literatura XIX veka*], 149–50, Leningrad: Nauka, S.

Levin, Y. D. 1993. 'Russian Shakespeare Translations in the Romantic Era', in D. Delabastita and L. D'Hulst (eds), *European Shakespeares: Translating Shakespeare in the Romantic Age*, 75–90, Amsterdam, Philadelphia: John Benjamins Publishing Company.

Levin, Y. D. 1995. 'Dostoevskii and Shakespeare', in Leatherbarrow W. J., ed., *Dostoevskii and Britain*, 39–121, Oxford, Providence: Berg.

Levin, Y. D. 1998. 'Shakespeare and Russian Literature: Nineteenth-Century Attitudes', in *Russian Essays on Shakespeare and His Contemporaries*, Newark: University of Delaware Press.

Levitt, M. C. 2018. *Russian Literary Politics and the Pushkin Celebration of 1880*, Studies of the Harriman Institute, Ithaka: Cornell University Press.

Litvin, M. 2011. *Hamlet's Arab Journey: Shakespeare's Prince and Nasser's Ghost*, Princeton: Princeton University Press.

Love, J. and Metzger, J., eds. 2016. *Nietzsche and Dostoevsky: Philosophy, Morality, Tragedy*, Evanston, IL: Northwestern University Press.

Lowenstein, D. and Witmore, M., eds. 2015. *Shakespeare and Early Modern Religion*, Cambridge: Cambridge University Press.

Lylo, T. 2017. 'Ideologeme as a Representative of the Basic Concepts of Ideology in the Media Discourse', *Social Communication*, 1: 14–20.

Malysheva, E., G., 2019. 'Ideologeme as Lingo-Cognitive Phenomenon: Definition and Clasification', trans. Pirozhkova, I., S., *Political Linguistics*, 1 (63): 134–144.

Mann, T. 1945. 'Preface: Dostoevsky in Moderation', in *The Short Novels of Dostoevsky*, vii–xx, New York: Dial Press.

Marling, W. 1994. 'The Formal Ideologeme', *Semiotica*, 98 (3/4): 277–99.

Miola, R. S. 1998. 'Seven Types of Intertextualities', in *Shakespearean Intertextuality: Studies in Selected Sources and Plays*, Westport, Conn, London: Greenwood Press.

Mochulsky, K. 1973. *Dostoevsky: His Life and Work*, trans. Michael A. Minihan, Princeton: Princeton University Press.

Morson, G. S. 1981. *The Boundaries of Genre: Dostoevsky's Diary of a Writer and the Genre of the Literary Utopia*, Austin: University of Texas Press .

Morson, G. S. 1994. *Narrative and Freedom: The Shadows of Time*, New Haven: Yale University Press.

Morson, G. S. 1999. 'Paradoxical Dostoevsky', *The Slavic and East European Journal*, 43 (3): 471–94.

Movsesian, A. 2020. 'The Poetics of Schism: Dostoevsky Translates Hamlet', *Humanities*, 9: 111.

Murav, H. 1992. *Holy Foolishness: Dostoevsky's Novels and the Poetics of Cultural Critique*, Stanford, CA: Stanford University Press.

Murodova N. I. and Djumabayeva J. Sh. 2017. 'Translation Problems of Enantiosemy in Fiction from English to Russian', *Russian Linguistic Bulletin,* 4 (12): 12–15.

Nietzsche, F. 1999. *The Birth of Tragedy and Other Writings*, ed. R. Geuss and R. Speirs and trans. R. Speirs, Cambridge: Cambridge University Press.

Offord, D. C. 1999. '*The Devils* in the Context of Contemporary Russian Thought and Politics', in *Dostoevsky's The Devils: A Critical Companion*, Evanston, Il: Northwestern University Press.

Ollivier, S. 2001. 'Icons in Dostoevsky's Works', in *Dostoevsky and the Christian Tradition*, 51–68, Cambridge: Cambridge University Press.

Pareyson, L. 1993. *Dostoevsky: Philosophy, novel and religious experience [Dostoevskij. Filosofia, romanzo ed esperienza religosa]*, Torino: Einaudi.

Pattison, G. and Thompson D. O., eds. 2001. *Dostoevsky and the Christian Tradition,* Cambridge: Cambridge University Press.

Pevear, R. 2006. 'Foreward', in trans. P. Pevear and L. Volkhonsky, *Demons*, vii–xix, London: Vintage books.

Pope, R. and Turner, J. 1990. 'Toward Understanding Stavrogin', *Slavic Review*, 49 (4): 543–53.

Rippl, G. 2016. 'Hamlet's Mobility: The Reception of Shakespeare's Tragedy in US American and Canadian Narrative Fiction', in Habermann, I. and Witen, M. (eds), *Shakespeare and Space: Theatrical Exploration of a Spatial Paradigm,* 229–55, London and New York: Palgrave Shakespeare Studies.

Rollberg, P. 2014. 'Mastermind, Terrorist, Enigma: Dostoevsky's Nikolai Stavrogin', *Perspectives on Political Science,* 43: 143–52.

Rovda, K. I. 1965. 'Pod Znakom Realizma', Alekseev, M. P., *Shekspir i russkaja kul'tura,* Moskva-Leningrad: Nauka.

Rowe, E. 1976. *Hamlet: A Window on Russia,* New York: New York University Press.

Salmon, L. 2023. 'Paradoxality as a Specific Feature of Dostoevsky's Literary Works Techniques, Stylistics, Mechanisms of Action', in *F.M. Dostoevsky: Humor, Paradoxality, Deconstruction,* Firenze: Firenze University Press.

Seduro, V. 1966. 'The Fate of Stavrogin's Confession', *The Russian Review,* 25 (4): 397–404.

Segre, C. 1984. *Theatre and Novel* [*Teatro e romanzo*], Torino: Einaudi.

Semenenko, A. 2007. *Hamlet the Sign: Russian Translations of Hamlet and Literary Canon Formation,* Stockholm: Stockholm University Press.

Simmons, E. J. 1964. *English Literature and Culture in Russia (1553–1840),* Cambridge, MA: Harvard University Press.

Schalkwyk, D., 2019. 'Foreward', in Refskou, A. S., de Amorim, M. A. and de Carvalho, V. M. (eds) *Eating Shakespeare Cultural Anthropophagy as Global Methodology,* Global Shakespeare Inverted Series, The Arden Shakespeare, London: Bloomsbury Publishing.

Smith, A. 2013. 'Pushkin as a Cultural Myth: Dostoevskii's Pushkin Speech and Its Legacy in Russian Modernism', in J. Andrew and R. Reid (eds) *Dostoevskii's Overcoat: Influence, Comparison, and Transposition,* 122–47, Amsterdam: Rodopi.

States, B. O. 1992. *Hamlet and the Concept of Character,* Baltimore, MA: John Hopkins University Press.

Statkiewicz, M. 2018. '"Feeling of Thought": Nietzsche's and Dostoevsky's Experience with Nihilism', *Russian Literature,* 95: 1–32.

Stepanian, K. 2014. 'Dostoevsky and Shakespeare: Characters and Authors in "Great Time"', *Russian Studies in Literature,* 50 (3): 55–77.

Stepanian, K. 2016. *Shakespeare, Bakhtin and Dostoevsky: Characters and Authors in 'Great Time'* [*Shekspir, Bakhtin i Dostoevskij: geroi i avtory v bol'shom vremeni.*] M.: Global Kom: Jazyki slavjanskoj kul'tury.

Stojanović, D. 2009. *Dostoevsky's Heavenly Mind* [*Rajski Um Dostojevskog,* 2009], Belgrade: Dosije.

Thurman, C. 2018. 'Hamlet Underground: Revisiting Shakespeare and Dostoevsky', *Multicultural Shakespeare: Translation, Appropriation and Performance*, 18 (1): 79–32.

Thurman, C. 2020. 'Dostoevsky in English and Shakespearean Universality: A Cautionary Tale', *Multicultural Shakespeare: Translation, Appropriation and Performance*, 21 (36): 99–114. https://doi.org/10.18778/2083-8530.21.07

Tikhomirov, B. 2014. 'Dostoevsky's Portrait Sketches: New Identifications [Portretnye Zarisovki Dostoevskogo: iz Novyh Atribucij'] *Neizvestnyj Dostoevskij*: 82–93. https://doi.org/10.15393/j10.art.2014.7

Tolstaya K. 2013. *Kaleidoscope: F.M. Dostoevsky and Early Dialectical Theology*, trans. A. Runia and ed. F. Bestebreurtje, Brill's Series in Church History, Leiden: Brill.

Tolstaya K. ed. 2018. *Orthodox Paradoxes: Heterogeneities and Complexities in Contemporary Russian Orthodoxy*, Brill's Series in Church History, Leiden: Brill.

Tolz, V. 2010. 'Russian and the West', in W. Letherbarrow and D. Offord (eds), *A History of Russian Thought*, Cambridge: Cambridge University Press.

Turgenev, I. 1965. 'Hamlet and Don Quixote', *Chicago Review*, 17 (4): 92–109.

Turgenev, I. 1996. *Fathers and Sons*, trans. Michael R. Katz, New York: W. W. Norton & Company.

Valentino, R. S. 1997. 'The Word Made Flesh in Dostoevsky's Possessed', *Slavic Review*, 56 (1): 37–49.

Vinokurov, V. 2000. 'The End of Consciousness and the Ends of Consciousness: A Reading of Dostoevsky's *The Idiot* and *Demons* after Levinas', *The Russian Review*, 59 (1): 21–37.

Vladiv-Glover, S. 2012. '"Unreason" as a Constituent of Reason: The Structure of Modern Consciousness according to Dostoevsky's *The Double*', in Stefano Aloe (ed.), *Su Fëdor Dostoevskij Visione filosofica e sguardo di scrittore*, Napoli: La scuola di Pitagora editrice.

Walizki, A. 1979. *A History of Russian Thought: From Enlightenment to Marxism*, Stanford, CA: Stanford University Press.

Weischedel, W. 1976, 1979. *The Problem of God in Scepticism* [Il problema di Dio nel pensiero scettico], Genoa: Il Melangolo.

Wheeler, M. 1984. *The Oxford Russian-English Dictionary: Second Edition*, Oxford: Oxford University Press.

Williams, J. S. 1982. 'Stavrogin's Motivation: Love and Suicide', *Psychoanalytic Review*, 69: 249.

Williams, R. 2008. *Dostoevsky: Language, Faith, and Fiction*, London: Continuum.

Young, S. and Milne, L., eds. 2006. *Dostoevsky on the Threshold of Other Worlds: Essays in Honour of Malcolm V. Jones*, Nottingham: Bramcote Press.

Zakharov, V., (2006). 2018. 'Dostoevsky's Fantastic Pages,' trans. S. Young, in Bowers, Doak and Holland, *A Dostoevskii Companion: Texts and Contexts*, 130-137, Boston: Academic Studies Press.

Zakharov, N. V. 2015. 'Shakespearean Canon in the Russian Literature at the Turn of the 18th – 19th Centuries', *Znanie, ponimanie, umenie, ZPU Journal*: 3.

Zakharov, N. V. 2016. 'Iconic Characters: Hamlet as Iconic Image in Russian Culture', in B. Smith (ed.), *The Cambridge Guide to the Worlds of Shakespeare 1660 - Present*, Vol. 2, Cambridge: Cambridge University Press.

# Websites

Eternal Images. The World of Shakespeare: An Electronic Encyclopaedia. https://world-shake.ru/en/Encyclopaedia/3884.html

Martirosyan, Annie. 2015. 'Dostoevsky Draws Shakespeare: The Fascinating Discovery', *Huffington Post* (blog). https://www.huffingtonpost.co.uk/annie -martirosyan/dostoevsky-draws-shakespe_b_6327176.html (accesed 20 February 2019)

Rybchenko , E. S. 2006. '*Stavrogin and Prince Harry: The Question of the Level of Influence of W. Shakespeare's Chronicle Henry IV on Dostoevsky's Demons*' [Stavrogin i Princ Garri (K Voprosu o stepeni vljianija hroniki V. Shekspira "Genrih IV" na roman "Besy" F. M. Dostoevskogo] (rus-shake. ru). https://rus-shake.ru/criticism/Rybchenko/Stavrogin (acessed 13 March 2020)

Shakespearianism. The World of Shakespeare: An Electronic Encyclopaedia. http://world-shake.ru/en/Encyclopaedia/3906.html (acessed 7 December 2018)

Shakespearisation. The World of Shakespeare: An Electronic Encyclopaedia. https://world-shake.ru/en/Encyclopaedia/3905.html (acessed 7 December 2018)

The Cult of Shakespeare. The World of Shakespeare: An Electronic
    Encyclopaedia. https://world-shake.ru/en/Encyclopaedia/3908.html
    (acessed 7 December 2018)
Zaharov, N. V. 2006. Dostoevsky's Shakespearism: Introduction to the
    Problem [Shekspirizm Dostoevskogo: vvedenie v problemu]. http://www.
    w-shakespeare.ru/library/shekspirovskie-chteniya-2006-28.html (acessed 9
    December 2018)

# Index

www.ingramcontent.com/pod-product-compliance
Lightning Source LLC
LaVergne TN
LVHW021603060925
820435LV00003B/32